DEPRESSION

An Emotion not a Disease

DEPRESSION

An Emotion not a Disease

DR MICHAEL CORRY
DR ÁINE TUBRIDY

MERCIER PRESS

MERCIER PRESS
Douglas Village, Cork
Website: www.mercierpress.ie

Trade enquiries to CMD Distribution
55A Spruce Avenue, Stillorgan Industrial Park
Blackrock, County Dublin
Tel: (01) 294 2560; Fax: (01) 294 2564
E-mail: cmd@columba.ie

© Michael Corry and Áine Tubridy, 2005

ISBN 1 85635 479 2
10 9 8 7 6 5 4 3 2 1

A CIP record for this title is available
from the British Library

Special thanks to Liam Delaney for the
illustrations throughout the book

Mercier Press receives financial assistance from
the Arts Council/An Chomhairle Ealaíon

Printed and Bound by J. H. Haynes & Co. Ltd, Sparkford

CONTENTS

Dedicated to the vast numbers of human beings who are finding life difficult and who are struggling to find creative solutions

CHAPTER 1

Emotion or Disease? – Thrown off the Scent

The saying 'red herring' is used to describe something that provides a false or misleading clue. It's a hunting phrase from the 1800s which refers to the actions of hunt saboteurs who would drag a smoked herring, which is red in colour and strong smelling, along the hunt route and away from the foxes. This confused the hounds which were thrown off the scent of the fox, to follow instead the scent of the red herring.

The moment depression is classified as a disease, the medical community, and then the public, seem to lose all clarity and become as duped as the hounds, and a wrong turn is taken. Once called a disease, a cure is called for. In this way it becomes a defining straitjacket in which the depressed individual has to function. Diseases do not have meanings, therefore none are sought. Diseases should not be happening. Diseases separate the ill from the well. This classification defines the experience, limiting it to a form which society relates to in prescribed ways. By placing it solely within the realm of imbalanced chemistry we distance it from problems of living, lack of resources and our human responses, which are the primary cause. We have been misled, and the time has come to find our way back to a true understanding of depression.

In this book we take a different view from this sick-brain model. Depression is not a disease but a legitimate emotional response to life's difficulties and inseparable from individuality, race, colour, gender, creed, upbringing, belief systems, environments, relationships, socio-economic factors, life events and coping skills. We feel that to isolate a depressed human being from their thoughts, behaviours and from the workings of their world is a tragedy beyond words, as it reduces them and the rest of us to a bag of chemicals. There is no place here for uniqueness, imagination, will, acceptance, compassion, love, peace, creativity, personal freedom and the unfathomable depths of the human spirit. The sick-brain model of depression is a hideous and terrifying concept as it turns us into cogs in a machine where, if we find the going difficult and need to disengage, our distress is silenced by an emotional painkiller and we are encouraged to carry on regardless. We believe this is nothing short of chemically-induced slavery.

Illusion and Reality

While there is universal acknowledgement of the experience of depression itself, tragically there is a parting of the ways when it comes to the causes and treatment of this serious and disabling emotion. The greatest revolution in medicine came when the cause of many diseases, and the reason for their spread, was discovered to be bacterial and viral. Based on this new knowledge, more appropriate treatment approaches were pursued, which until then would never have been thought relevant. The biggest killers of all time – leprosy, tuberculosis, syphilis, the plague, typhus, cholera, malaria – were all poorly understood until the agents and the mechanism by which they spread were acknowledged.

In terms of science this medical paradigm shift was of the same monumental proportions as the consciousness change which came about in the scientific world when the flat earth view yielded to the round earth one. Another paradigm shift is urgently needed now in the area of psychological medicine.

Feelings, thoughts, beliefs, perceptions and interpretations need to be recognised as the creators of the chemical state we know as depression, as surely as thoughts of injustice stimulate the chemical state of anger, the perception of threat elicits fear, and reminders of loss invite sadness. The current dominant model in psychiatry reverses cause and effect, placing the problem within the person's brain matter, or hardware. This makes it a disease of the brain, justifying the use of medication and electro-convulsive therapy, rather than locating the problem in the sufferer's software programmes, their mind or consciousness. This is equivalent to leaving the television in for repair if the programmes cease to be to your liking.

To approach the mind like a broken machine pathologises sufferers, turning them into damaged goods or victims of flawed chemistry and defective genes. It marginalises personal consciousness, viewing the unfathomable depths of human passion, individuality, creativity, curiosity, reason, intuition, will, compassion and spiritual insight as mere secretions of the brain, akin to the way the kidney secretes urine.

The theory of a genetic basis to depression has to be relegated to where it belongs – a theory which has yet to be proven. There's a world of difference between what is transmitted in the DNA and what are familial traits. It cannot be asserted that transgenerational occupations such as farming, dentistry, teaching, law, etc., are located on a gene with no contribution from the cultural tradition within those families. Likewise, is there a gene location for a love of gardening, music, or nature?

How do geneticists explain the findings of the Health Research Board in 2003 that 'the rate of [psychiatric] admission for the unskilled group was eight times that of the employers and managers group'? (Activities of the Irish Psychiatric Services 2003) Are the geneticists suggesting the influence of a 'weaker' genetic pool? Or could it be that lack of resources and quality of life is the major factor in causing the psychological distress of the unskilled group?

The diagnosis of depression has reached epidemic proportions. Data from 2004 reveals that in Ireland (with a population of 3.9 million) between one in five and one in seven adults, were prescribed anti-depressant medication at a cost of over €100 million.

THE EMPEROR HAS NO CLOTHES!

Anti-depressants are in essence psychic energisers which have a mood-elevating and sometimes a euphoric effect. So do street drugs such as amphetamine, cocaine and heroin, all of whose effects are transient. The difference is that they don't pretend to be either medicinal or curative. The consequence of promoting emotional painkillers to be prescribed as if they were correcting some causative fault, as insulin does in diabetes, are far-reaching and serious for medicine and real science.

Most insidious of all is that depression, if seen as a disease cannot be viewed as an indicator of an individual's difficulty in dealing with the setbacks of life. Such difficulties require, not anaesthesia but corrective real-life measures, with or without the support of psychotherapy. At least drug addicts and alcoholics are not deluded that their use of substances is permanently sorting out their problems.

The diminution of the central and primary role of consciousness and emotion in mental distress is fundamentally wrong. The pharmaceutical industry, in framing depression as a disease, has set sufferers apart from their humanity and the entire spectrum of what it is to be human. Its doctrinal assertions as to the value of their product smacks of neo-fundamentalism. Having achieved cult status, it is now immune to challenge such is its wealth, power, and its stranglehold on the medical profession.

So much has the status of the pharmaceutical industry come to resemble a religion, that it is almost impossible now to name the obvious, without uproar breaking out among its disciples. If the little boy in the fairy tale, in his innocence dared to name the obvious – 'Look, the Emperor has no clothes!' in current times, he would be gagged by a court injunction.

A TRIUMPH OF MARKETING – BILLIONS IN PROFITS

No one disputes the role of chemistry in depression, in the same way that no one disputes the role of adrenaline in anxiety. The sick-brain model has singled out a deficiency of serotonin, one of the many action hormones, as the cause of the depressed state. This is the same as saying that two planes, as if acting on their own volition, were the sole cause for the 11 September Twin Towers disaster.

In depression, serotonin amongst many other neurochemical transmitters, is involved, but only in a secondary role. On this error in thinking has been created an enormous red herring, a fantastic delusion. Let us not be side-tracked from the truth of the matter. It is irrelevant whether it is a serotonin deficiency or a serum marmalade deficiency which has been identified as having a role, as the result rather than the cause of the problem.

The pharmaceutical industry has hijacked science, reversed cause and effect, and idealises the neurochemical model of illness for profit motives, a marketing triumph. It has made *bad science* its own. It parades its 'objective' findings from selectively chosen clinical trials and blatantly withholds information such as dangerous side effects which do not suit its marketing objectives. (The manipulation of scientific information by the tobacco industry bears testament to this.) And if that is not bad enough, it actively promulgates the notion that anything which cannot be measured does not exist. This is a position of enormous conceit – out the window goes consciousness and its infinite interconnectedness. Real science knows its limitations, seeing itself as a tool, using means of gathering information according to the instruments used. True scientists like Albert Einstein showed

awe and humility in the face of the unknown. Science will always be a product of consciousness and therefore cannot have
dominance over it. Rather than consciousness being seen within
science, it is only logical that science has to be seen within
consciousness. Understanding of this nature is crucial as the
pharmaceutical industry would have us believe that they know
how it all works with God-like status, and that its latest product
is the ultimate wonder drug.

In the words of the poet and psychiatrist Louis Regan:

> The sea of mind is fast beyond degree
> This science is only a looking glass to see
> Paled reflections, glimmering out inside
> Of man.

This industry feeds on the gullibility of some doctors, and the
extreme vulnerability of sufferers who, in their eagerness to
alleviate symptoms, are prepared to ignore side effects, both long-
and short-term. It also vigorously encourages the use of psychoactive medication in the young, who once started, will in all
probability continue to 'use' in different forms until adulthood.
In this way a lifetime on medication begins with the mantra
'keep taking the pills'.

TAMPERING WITH NATURE'S WISDOM
If we take a look at what goes on inside the body it can be seen
as the body electric – the city that never sleeps. Its hundred-plus
trillion cells all intercommunicate and depend on each other
according to a brilliantly orchestrated electromagnetic master
plan, certainly not one of human design. Every bodily function
such as oxygenation, food absorption, detoxification and the
generation of nerve impulses all happen at the cell wall by the
movement of positive and negative particles across it. Each cell
depends on life-supporting supplies, including oxygen, water,

glucose and protein. Waste products such as carbon dioxide and urine require disposal. Like a huge metropolis the body continues growing, replicating, defending and repairing itself. It does this whether we are in a coma, sleeping, dreaming or awake.

Consider the ingenuity of the immune system. T-cells move through the body scanning for and eliminating dangerous material. They contain the knowledge of what is 'me' and what is 'not me', then act accordingly. I am not awakened in the middle of the night by the chief T-cell seeking an executive decision as to whether or not to destroy the alien. In the same way everything from the regulation of my heart beat, to the repair of my cells in the event of damage is guided by an organising power outside of my intellectual control. This wisdom, when balance prevails, extends also to emotional healing.

Here's the conundrum. Anti-depressants work for some and without apparent serious side effects. And so people will ask 'what's so wrong with taking a pill if it can make you feel better?' Here's why:

- By ingesting anti-depressant medication you are interfering with your body's own ability to create its own. The body's natural pharmacopoeia goes out of production because the delicate interconnecting feedback loops have been tampered with.
- When you stop taking the anti-depressants, the withdrawal symptoms you experience reflect not only the falling levels of the drug in your blood, which can be short-term, but also the body's longer-term struggle to resume production of its own chemicals. In many cases, after years of use, the catch-up can never be achieved, so guaranteeing dependency on what comes over the counter, or more frighteningly what can be bought over the internet. Is this not drug addiction?
- The side effects of anti-depressant medication are *legion* rang-

ing from loss of your sex life, to loss of your life through suicide. If you have any doubts read the small print. Every cell in your body is taking a hit, because more than 95 per cent of the receptor sites for these drugs are located outside the central nervous system. Factor in altered reaction times, and you become a danger to others while driving a car. (Pilots are instantly grounded while under the influence of these drugs.)

- Falling victim to the red herring you will be less likely to seek out healing solutions, and put in place quality of life changes.
- The sick-brain model of depression reflects a frightening and insidious new phenomenon, taking hold in our society. We are being blindfolded and drowned in a sea of pills. Those who try to arrest this development are actively resisted.

W. B. Yeats in his poem 'The Second Coming' spoke of a similar spectre and the difficulties inherent in halting it:

> The blood-dimmed tide is loosed, and everywhere
> The ceremony of innocence is drowned;
> The best lack all conviction, while the worst
> Are full of passionate intensity.

CHAPTER 2

Overwhelmed by Life – Life's Soup

Depression is an emotional response, at the core of which are the feelings of helplessness, hopelessness and loss of control. Any life difficulty which we find to be insurmountable can cause depression. Being alive and human exposes us to risk and danger, placing us on a spectrum ranging from feeling effective and resourceful to powerless and paralysed. Life is fired at us point blank. From the moment we are parachuted into life's soup, emotionally, behaviourally and intellectually we are challenged to respond.

From conception to death, traumatic and stressful events come our way: intrauterine stress, insufficient nurturing, family dysfunction, abuse and bullying, betrayal and ridicule, broken hearts, dependents with special needs, marital difficulties, accidents and life-threatening situations, financial burdens, drink and drug problems, job loss, peer group exclusion, chronic pain, disability and illness, ageing and the finality of our own death.

A MEETING OF TWO MINDS

Our senses bring in raw information, forming the gateway between our inner and outer world. They give us a constantly changing inner print-out of the world around us from which we create emotions, formulate our thoughts and adopt policies about how to navigate our way. Through our senses we differentiate between pleasure and pain, and decide whether to approach or avoid. Our senses are the only means we have of experiencing a connection to the outer world.

We can think of sensations as words, feelings as sentences, and emotions as paragraphs. This sequence aptly describes our

meeting with the spectrum of circumstances in the world around us, giving it meaning.

Our emotional responses are the result of an interplay between two sources of intelligence. On the one hand is our rational mind, that part of us that uses reason or logic in thinking out a problem. On the other is our emotional mind, that part of us that is moved by strong feelings, such as survival drives, rage, fear, loss, pleasure and sexuality. This mind also influences the life-force and the regulation of the body's physiology, with respect to thirst, appetite, sleep, respiration, heart rate, blood pressure, hormone secretion and even the immune system.

The rational mind is situated in the neocortex, which means the 'new brain' and has evolved over millions of years. The emotional mind is situated in the limbic or 'primitive' brain which by contrast has evolved over hundreds of millions of years. Although these two minds talk to each other, one of the characteristics which distinguishes the emotional mind is that once it has begun expressing itself, it cannot readily be turned off at will. This is why some depressions can seem so inaccessible to appeals for reason and logic.

For example, in cases where survival responses are triggered, and the contribution from the emotional mind is 100 per cent, logic has little input and in fact must be completely sidelined in the interest of a faster response. Many trigger-hair responses, such as anger and panic, could well do with the tempering of reason, but being an instantaneous flash response driven by the emotional mind, such disinhibition does not occur. Many a bloody nose has been administered in a fit of rage following a minor insult, a reflex overreaction to the old wounds of rejection.

In other cases it is the rational mind which eclipses the emotional mind. Think of the perfectionist who is convinced that they will fail the exam in spite of plentiful evidence to the contrary, or the depressive who believes 100 per cent whatever their personal critic says.

Both minds contribute to depression. Along the spectrum with raw emotion at one end, and pure rationality at the other, the many different experiences of depression can be plotted. Those at the emotional end may have been overwhelmed by the pain of grief, wounded by heartbreak, crushed by bullying, or eclipsed by sexual abuse. While those at the rational end are tortured by self-loathing, ruminate over failures, obsess over broken dreams, and empty of meaning, logically see suicide as their release. Many sufferers of depression move from the emotional end of the spectrum in order to dampen the intensity of their feelings, frantically seeking solutions in their mind. This flight from feelings is sometimes of such intensity that elation can result.

THE TIPPING POINT

Like fingerprints, no two human beings are exactly the same. As such we do not respond to setbacks in the same way. Take a puncture for example. It's the last thing you expect to find as you approach your car in the morning. As you take in what's happened, a strategy begins to form. The meaning you ascribe to it, the action policy you decide on, and the intensity of your response is going to depend on a multitude of factors, both internal and external.

It will make a difference if you don't have a spare tyre or a second car, you can't change one by yourself, it's pouring rain, a taxi isn't an option, or you're not a member of the Automobile Association. Time-urgency tips the balance too – if you're rushing to catch a plane, hurrying to an important meeting, or rushing your child to the accident and emergency department. Cruising down to the local shop to buy the papers on a leisurely Sunday morning is a different experience.

Other factors matter too. Such as whether you're the boss or are further down the pecking order, and could lose your job because of your track record of turning up late. Your personality is in play too, you might be shy about asking a neighbour for a lift or for their help, guilty about letting others down, cringing at the idea of calling work to explain your late arrival, or still fuming from an argument with your partner over breakfast. The variables influencing our response to any setback are infinite, with resources defining whether it becomes overwhelming or manageable.

The puncture scenario is a trivial example. Many setbacks are of grave proportions, ranging from the loss of a loved one, to workplace bullying and life-threatening illness. The principle still remains however that resources are crucial, whether internal or external, and can buffer us from the slings and arrows of life or leave us exposed. (That said there are no internal resources which can buffer a child from abandonment, battery and sexual abuse, because of their tender age.)

Resources or not, the continuous everyday grind can seem overwhelming in its own right. The treadmill, be it at school, college, or on the career ladder, can dampen the spirit and take its toll. In schedules deprived of downtime, energy bankruptcy is common, with substance abuse often the most easily available relief. The ensuing collateral damage becomes another trauma to be dealt with; exams failed, jobs lost, relationship breakdown, all pushing us further off balance.

Neither can depression be isolated from the frantic juggling required to keep normal family life afloat; night feeds, school drop-offs, homework, packed lunches and child minders, side by side with long working hours, excessive deadlines, demanding bosses, all to fund mortgage repayments, school fees etc.

Depression is a valid and normal response to the uncontrollability of the poverty trap, which comes with its own inherent set of problems; living from hand to mouth, overcrowded housing, insufficient heat, food and clothing, and a wilderness of inadequate resources.

HOW A SETBACK IS PROCESSED EMOTIONALLY

It is human nature to have desires and to want to satisfy them. To wish, want and hope that our future needs will be met. Isn't every child's game-plan to become successful, contented, loved and secure? From an early age we 'look forward'; to santa coming, to being popular at school, to getting on a team, passing our exams, finding a job, falling in love, having a good lifestyle.

This roadmap keeps us motivated, giving us the willpower and eagerness to continue. If our way is blocked, there is a sense of loss as our dream evaporates, as if something concrete has been taken away. In fact it is our illusion – that our future would turn out rosy – which has been removed. A sense of loss overwhelms us, and will and action become redundant.

Now we are confronted by future scenarios which are painfully less desirable than those we'd planned on. Who anticipates rejection, sexual abuse, bullying, heartbreak, deaths, marital difficulties, failure to achieve, financial insecurity, problematic children, disability, chronic illness or lack of companionship? Unprepared and disillusioned, it can be impossible to find within us the desire or the will to remain engaged with such hardship. In shock, we wonder what happened to the game-plan. We can't go back, nor can we yet see a way forward. Confused, lost and immobilised, the drive to go on dries up: we are depressed, and in grief.

As we assess the situation, the classic stages of all grief and loss unfold within us:

- Surely this isn't happening? To me? Today? (denial and disbelief)

- It's so unfair. I should have made a better job of this! How stupid of me! (anger turned inwards, becoming self-criticism)
- Maybe all is not lost – I'll try harder, I'll turn it around. I'll do whatever it takes. (deal-making and magical thinking)
- Nothing's working. What will I do now? (fear and anxiety)
- It's hopeless, what's the point, nothing I'm doing is making any difference. (depression)
- Looks like I've got no choice but to accept that this has happened.

In setback situations our two minds, the rational and the emotional, reach a decision: if we have the resources we bite the bullet, and engage with this unpalatable future we hadn't planned for (integration and acceptance). If we're unable to, we continue abstaining from life, and defeated, spiral further into depression.

THE MOLECULES OF DEPRESSION

No degree in science is required to understand that sexual arousal and its back-up chemistry, follows a sexual fantasy or image, rather than the other way around. Likewise, the goose-bumps rising on your arms (an activated fear response) as you engage with a terrifying thriller movie have no way of knowing by themselves the difference between horror and comedy on the screen. The image in our mind is communicating the fear response to the goose-bumps. These are everyday examples of a fundamental law that mind manifests in matter – distressing images create the molecules of distress and their corresponding feelings. It is clear that these shifts in chemistry are not primary, but secondary to a context in which certain perceptions, interpretations, thoughts, beliefs and feelings occur.

If you still have any doubts about the primary source of chemical changes try this experiment. Visualise a lemon, and see yourself cutting it in half, smelling it, raising it to your mouth and sucking its juice. Now – does your mouth water at the idea, do you taste bitterness, and do you involuntarily grimace? These changes are real, and the saliva and the muscular tension measurable. Yet if a neurosurgeon were to search for the cause – the lemon – inside your brain he would be unsuccessful. One thing is sure, sexual arousal, goose-bumps or saliva do not occur unsolicited. Neither do moods or emotional states such as intense fear, rage or depression.

It is beyond dispute that images, beliefs and feelings that imply lack of control or hopelessness shape the chemistry of depression. There are hundreds of different kinds of neurotransmitter substances and hormones which affect your nervous system and play a part in making you depressed. There can be too little of them or too much. Here are some of the main players; adrenaline, noradrenaline, dopamine, GABA, serotonin, acetylcholine and melatonin.

Cortisol, the defeat hormone, is found to be raised in circumstances of low status. Among alpha-male animals and primates fighting for leadership, the internal chemistry of the one beginning to perceive imminent defeat switches from fight mode (adrenaline and testosterone) to a predominance of cortisol, facilitating his withdrawal and a life-saving conservation of his diminishing resources, which allows him to live to fight another day. A close human equivalent is the individual who is the target of bullying where defeat and helplessness are the result.

TURNING THE TIDE

If the chemistry associated with depression is seen as primary rather than secondary there is nothing sufferers can do but keep taking the pills and hand their mind, body and spirit over to a process beyond their control. If it's the opposite, and we know that changing our 'mind' can influence how we feel, then depression is ours to reverse. It can now be seen as a wake-up call, a messenger, a beacon, a soul cry to signal the urgent need to liberate ourselves from the oppression of thoughts like 'nothing I do will make any difference', feelings of desolation and hopelessness, and contexts and environments which defeat us. This book takes the stance that turning the tide in that direction is possible.

CHAPTER 3

Inside Depression – Recoil from Life

What does the modern human do when life doesn't work out as they'd anticipated? Think of the options. You face an inescapable predicament. This may be because its unexpected occurrence has shocked you, terrified you, or profoundly disillusioned you. The scenario you're confronted with may vary from sudden heartbreak, the daily anxiety of facing a workplace bully, or the dawning shock of finding that the life you've carefully constructed has come to look like a death sentence. Whatever the cause, your instinct is to recoil, disengage and have the bad dream cease.

What can your average human being do in such circumstances? There are only so many ways out. Some run away – literally, by leaving a pile of clothes at the beach or by taking the next plane out. Others change their reality by swapping it for madness, mania being the ticket out. Many become physically ill, embarking on a road which absolves them from the same level of engagement. Those who can, make efforts to inject change into the situation, bringing control by whatever measures they can. Others heal with the passage of time.

For most, although they may wish to curl up into a ball like a child, and turn their back on the problem, they can't. Modern life demands that you go on. Working lives must be continued, the care of children not shirked, relationships maintained, bills paid. You must carry on regardless. Yet this requires that you engage, and you are in recoil mode. The unconscious compromise is depression. You're still here, but really you're not.

This is a shadowy life, one where your body does one thing,

goes through the motions, but your mind screams its dissent. It withholds its enthusiasm, supplying you with not a shred of motivation, rationing your energy so you have to get by on the slimmest budget. You've torn up your contract with life. But your ship at least must still stay ostensibly afloat, albeit in an agonisingly unsatisfactory state. Privately though, the only time when you are free of this conflicted state is when you are asleep or alcohol has afforded you brief anaesthesia. Happy release, blessed oblivion. At least during the hours in bed, you are off the hook, the 'no' sign firmly placed on the door. Many increasingly find this split state unsustainable, and sign off, firing life, deciding to end the pain for good.

LAYERS OF DISCONNECTION AND SHUT DOWN

1. Survival on the Line
You wake up exhausted, there are never enough hours in bed, and your first thought is 'where will I get the energy?' Most likely you haven't slept well, either waking in the early hours or not having fallen sleep until dawn. The simple routine tasks of your daily life assume titanic proportions. The drudgery involved in going to work, caring for children, completing domestic chores and getting through the mundane nuts and bolts of life brings you close to the edge, and fills you with dread as you become increasingly aware that you 'can't go on like this'. One more demand, anything with the slightest hint of extra challenge, and you'll cave in. Although you need the energy, food holds no interest for you, and your clothes get looser and looser.

2. No Desire for Life
Withdrawing into yourself, you've lost all desire for interaction or pleasure. Numb to your needs, you may not see the point in washing, having sex, going out, getting fresh air, seeing friends

or even your children. You prefer to be left alone and those closest to you become an irritation. Why are they so demanding? Why can't they leave you alone? If you're told to pull yourself together one more time, you feel you'll box them. Unsympathetic and unmoved by the feelings of others, they nonetheless make their objections felt, and you feel ashamed of yourself, guilty about it, alienated and misunderstood.

3. Paralysis of Will

Since your interest in everything has totally evaporated, you can't muster any enthusiasm. Your motivation has dried up, and if you had your way you'd do nothing, never answer the phone, open the door, or see anyone. The spark in you has died, and with it the inclination to partake in life, to go forward, to be a player. All ambition is gone. Nothing is spontaneous, everything is a chore with a huge amount of push required. Soulless, you're marking time in a passionless way, going through the motions, inertia haunting your days.

Unable to control events, and bring an end to your misery, you're overwhelmed with a sense of powerlessness. All effort seems futile. If only you could hand over the reigns to someone else and avoid all responsibility and decision-making. Surely there's some hideaway you could disappear to, where nothing would be demanded of you? Recoiling from the grown up world of demands and roles, heaven would be living a childlike life with all your needs catered for.

4. Desolate and Hopeless

You can't care less about anything now. Cynical and detached, you see things as completely hopeless and the future bleak. You feel that the world has betrayed you, has taken advantage of your vulnerability and innocence. Feeling exploited and used, you feel you've given more than you have got back. Compassion fatigue. The words of Yeats resonate: 'Too long a sacrifice can make a stone of the heart'. Maybe you've had your heart broken by a loved one, and angry and rejected, you vent your hurt on yourself, and the world around you. 'It's not fair.' If the person you have loved all your life has died, the emptiness can't be filled. Weeping yourself to sleep, and awakening with their immediate absence, you live in a private turmoil, inaccessible to others. In the depths of desolation and despair, you welcome death by any means: 'If I was told I had cancer it would be a relief', 'If a bus ran me over I'd feel lucky'. You may have even contemplated taking your own life: 'I don't care any more, I've done my best, the world would probably be better without me'.

5. *The Lost Voice*

You've never felt more misunderstood. Nobody's getting it. Their eyes glaze over when you try to share how things are for you, so you've started keeping it to yourself now. They go on with their endless suggestions, but you just let it roll off you. What do they know? So you keep yourself hidden, and confide as little as possible. Censored from speaking your truth, and criticised for being authentic, you go silent and withdraw further into your private world: 'I'm tired of all the pretending, all the societal niceties where everybody has to play the game'.

6. *Trapped in the Puzzle Factory*

Your thoughts crash around like fish caught in a net, seeking clarity, irritable and pernickety. It's as though a rent in the curtain of life has allowed it to flutter apart, revealing to you the horrifying machinery beneath. All illusion falls away. Could it really work like this? Your mind – your traditional problem-solver – unable to take it all in, provides no solution, a shocking realisation, but yet it obsessively continues trying. Many fruitless hours are spent examining exhibits in your museum of the

past, mulling over unresolved past failures and regrets, and cataloguing your worthlessness. Old failures now piggyback onto your current setback, bogging you down even further. Misery attracts more misery, and your personal critic has free reign: 'What kind of useless person would have been so stupid and weak?' This is the territory of self-hate, self-loathing and anger turned inwards, your own mind assaulting you. Actions cease to have meaning. Your day now resembles the Greek myth of the fruitless toil of Sisyphus, whose punishment in hell was to push uphill a boulder which rolled down again as soon as he reached the top.

7. *Alone in a Senseless Wasteland*

Everything is stripped bare now, and you stand naked on a stage without props or a part to play. You're going round in circles, without any sense of direction, no framework within which to plot your way. The future seems irrelevant and the past a waste of time. The words of Dante could be yours – 'In the middle of the road of my life, I awoke in a dark wood, where the true way was wholly lost' (Dante's *Commedia*). This is the state beyond the dark night of the soul, a spiritual wasteland of unanswered pleas, and cries for help to the Divine, or some Ultimate Rescuer, which have gone unheeded. With the pain of your existence unbearable and with no let-up in sight, a final solution may begin to form – the elimination of the suffering self. You may have done your sums and decided that when the pain of the present, plus the future, outweigh the fear of dying, death by one's own hand becomes the only outcome.

> He feels as though a thousand bars existed,
> and no more world beyond them than before.
>
> Rainer Rilke

CHAPTER 4

The Empty Self
'I Owe my Soul to the Company Store'
— MERLE TRAVIS

An insidious trend which is developing at a terrifying rate is the increasing reliance on image and role as a measurement of an individual's worth and value. Celebrity magazines, along with the popularity of reality television, cosmetic make-overs, and the rise of plastic surgery are testament to this. The cult of celebrity status is generating a culture of wannabes, young and old, who feel justified to use whatever means fair and foul to join that plastic world, where wants become needs, and needs become rights, and rights become entitlements. This is not the territory of the soul. No place here for compassion, for sharing, for solidarity. Everything comes with a price tag. Money is god and greed is good. Imitation and flattery is fostered. The 'look at me' industry is flourishing. The politics of 'me' has replaced the body politic.

The parameters have been made clear. Your worth as a person is no longer guaranteed simply by the fact of being human, these days you have to demonstrate your worth in terms of achievement, money, appearance, place on the pecking order, role etc. For approval to be granted, conditions have to be met.

The first rung of the approval ladder, and the lifelong climb up it, is found in the home. For many depressed individuals it was never their good fortune to be loved by their parents for being the child they were. That love had to be earned, and was conditional on them adhering to the standards laid down. The price paid was a high one, their emerging self.

THE LOST WORLD OF FEELINGS

A child learns to define themselves through their sensations and feelings – hunger, frustration, fear, anger – all serve to 'tell' them who they are. If these are witnessed by a parent accepting of them, it is echoed back to them in a way that allows them to develop an emotional repertoire which they can feel comfortable expressing: 'You're angry at your sister, aren't you?', 'It's all right to be frightened of the big dog', or to the crying child 'Your poor knee must really hurt, let's have a look'. The cheers, singing and clapping as the child blows out the birthday candles encourage it to openly express joy, laughter and happiness.

This mirroring process is essential for the healthy development of a child's budding sense of self, and will sow the seeds that will help them to become separate and autonomous individuals. Some parents frustrate this vital process, and as the child struggles to express their legitimate feelings, they are negated: 'We'll have no crying now', 'Don't be such a nuisance', 'Stop that silly giggling'. The child's emerging feelings may be either inconvenient, contrary to the parents' rules of 'good' behaviour, or interpreted as weak or naughty, and deserving of punishment. Such a child learns very quickly not only to censor their feelings, but finally to disown them, distancing from them, no longer even conscious of being the author of them.

This invasion and colonisation of a child's feeling world ensures that the only self that is allowed acknowledgement is one that matches the parents' template of what constitutes a 'good' child. Parents achieve this through the use shame and guilt.. A pseudo-self is born. From here on the child loses contact with all internal reference points, real sensations and emotions. All awareness of an inner life is silenced. Unable any longer to report what they are feeling in any given situation, they will manufacture what they should be feeling. Schools and careers are carefully chosen to ensure the upholding of the parental ethos and to deliver the desired end product.

THE GREAT MASQUERADE

Years of emotional, intellectual and behavioural moulding ensures that in adulthood, behind the mask presented to the outside world, is a void, an empty space, without any originality – a
no-self – a clone ranger, empty of all vitality and authenticity.
Some are meek and obedient people-pleasers, some are arrogant
windbags, and some compulsive multi-taskers, scurrying around
trying to keep lids on boiling pots. Busy bodies. Everything depends on the façade remaining in place. They are connected to
it as if it were an enormous placenta, an insatiable monster, through
which their pseudo-self is fed. A lifetime of slavish effort is directed towards securing the 'must haves' – bank balances maintained, trophy partners acquired, property accumulated, cosmetic surgery undertaken, crimes and misdemeanours committed if
necessary. Should anything threaten this status quo, and cracks
begin to show, the individual has nothing to fall back on. When
last ditch frantic efforts fail, like Hitler in the bunker, there is no
plan B. Their carefully constructed bubble has burst – nothing
remains but thin air, their false consciousness revealed for what
it is.

In this state of powerlessness and emptiness, ironically depression is possibly the first original emotion such individuals
have ever felt.

They turn the guns on themselves now. A victim of their
own meaning system, having always revered those who are strong
and successful, having learned to despise the weak or needy as
losers, they must logically now begin to despise themselves. Their
contempt and loathing of this state is profound, their absence of
compassion for their plight chilling, and their inability to sanc-
tion forgiveness for what has come to pass is resolute.

They now face a fork in the road. They either take emo-

tional painkillers – anti-depressants, the quick fix – to anaesthetise the deafening silence within, or they attempt to rebuild a
new self. The tragedy is that many, having dampened down all
original feeling for a lifetime, continue to do so from this point
on under the banner of healing, ironically replicating their original emotional stunting.

THE JOURNEY TO THE SELF

The alternative choice is in-depth psychotherapy, to create the
climate where they can begin to develop a sense of an inner life,
an inner self that they can love and accept without having to
first jump through hoops. Where there has been a fearful emptiness, an unexpected wealth of vitality has the potential to be
given voice. This is not a homecoming, since no home ever
existed. It is more the creation of a home base, a place in which
to safely grow a new self. Here they will learn to create personal
boundaries – between themselves and others – a necessary platform from which to launch this self as a separate entity, empowered now to act on its own behalf. Self mastery.

This process, that of becoming internally referred, means
placing the point of reference inside oneself, not externally in
the requirements of your role as wife, mother, employee or your
particular social strata. Those who remain externally referred
are forever chasing symbols of success. All power, all value, all
approval is to be sourced from outside. Scarcity consciousness
prevails, for it must never dry up. They have an urgent need to
control outcomes, and in anxious desperation their thinking
and behaviour is always vigilant of the required response from
others. The 'right' circle of friends and membership to the 'right'
clubs – a mutual admiration society – could be seen as mirroring
the animals' life-supporting watering hole on the African plains,
from which you wander at your peril.

The process of psychotherapy becomes a place where they

learn to re-orientate their experience and consciousness towards self-definition, learning to make their own choices, boldly based on a new-found awareness of the legitimacy of their own individual needs and desires, independent of 'permission' from others. Only after they have learned to place the source of power within themselves, can they hope to begin the process of connecting with their spirit and their place in the family of things: interconnectedness.

Margot, a fifty-five-year-old solicitor was reported to the Law Society by a client for charging excessive fees and mishandling their case. The complaint was upheld and the outcome was leaked to the newspapers. Stunned by the exposure, Margot's life fell apart. Despite reassurances by her family, friends and colleagues, her feelings of shame and failure were profound. A six-month depression followed, which did not respond to medication.

Margot had grown up in a typical professional family, went to the best schools, and graduated from college without mishap. She joined a prominent legal firm, married a property investor, had two children, and ultimately found it more convenient to work from home where she set up practice. A socialite, she attended gallery showings, charity events, book launches, theatre first nights, and held and attended regular dinner parties. Fashionable clothes and the right look, the proper house décor, the newest car, moving with the 'in' crowd and making the right impression, were all of tremendous importance to her. Margot was a slave to the public gaze. She related to her children as extensions of herself, and saw to it that they were raised to the same standard as she had been. To her they were trophies hard won.

Margot could not reconcile the accusation of malpractice with her concept of herself: 'It's just not fair. Me of all people!'

She became extremely self-conscious in social settings, and had her first panic attack at a reception which she had to leave in great distress. Doing her job became fraught with difficulty as she would have to brief barristers and attend court, an atmosphere which at the best of times is self-righteous and judgemental. In such a posturing environment, her wounded pride and sense of shame were heightened, causing her eventually to cut her practice down to the minimum and to withdraw socially.

Becoming irritable and resentful towards her husband, she began blaming him for the fact that she had to work so hard in the first place, because of certain unwise property investments he had made. Like a lost soul, isolated and purposeless, her days stretched pointlessly ahead. With her business on the decline, and her social outlets off-putting, she began to spend longer and longer in bed, not answering the phone, not bothering to cook, and eventually relegating her husband to the guest room. Even her family's summer home in the west of Ireland, her traditional bolt hole, no longer held any appeal. She gratefully accepted the recommendation of her psychiatrist that a 'short stay' in hospital, and a trial of some of the newer anti-depressants would do her good.

Alan, a thirty-year-old software engineer in a multinational computer company, had been with the company for three years. From the beginning he found it difficult to accommodate to the culture and its work practices. Privately he referred to it as a 'cult', but since it paid good money and promotion was always a prospect, he tolerated it. At team meetings and reviews, he found it difficult to stay silent, airing his opinions about the robotic nature of the work, and the discouragement of any innovative ideas he had. He frequently found himself the target of line managers questioning his loyalty to the company and its policies.

Alan found himself increasingly taking on the role of spokesperson for his fellow workers, who were reluctant to make known their opinions for fear of the repercussions. He started to resent the fact that while they all quietly grumbled, they were never prepared to take action, and he would end up taking the rap. Becoming disillusioned with his colleagues, he started to feel that his efforts to improve the working environment were unappreciated, like he was merely a Don Quixote tilting at windmills.

He started to question his life's purpose and withdrew into himself searching for answers, something inside telling him that his life held more potential than he was able to live out in the company. Depression followed, as he dragged himself in and out of work and spent his days off recovering in bed. Emotionally unavailable to his girlfriend, he started to spend time moping around the house, either looking at television or staring blankly into space. In an effort to get him to talk, she brought him away on a sun holiday. With the time out, he realised that his depression was not solely linked to the job, but reflected a vague sense of guilt and despondency about the rudderless state of his life in general. He didn't know what he wanted to become, only what he did not. This insight led to his depression lifting.

Living the character of 'not' challenged him. He noticed that his feelings were all descriptive of what was lacking in his life, the absences and gaps. This guilt was not the usual – about having done something wrong and hurting someone else – but about having omitted to do the 'right thing' for himself, thereby limiting his options. He didn't know yet what exactly the right thing would involve, but found his attention drawn to the notion of hidden potential, possibilities unexplored, life as yet unlived. Intuitively he sensed that he had not yet found his destiny. He felt there was more to him than what he had experienced so far, and felt that if he didn't tap into it, that it would be a crime of squandered potential.

No longer playing the role of change agent at work, his new demeanour was viewed with suspicion. Finally, he was told by his manager that they felt his problem was that he did not 'think Intect'. The last straw for Alan was when he was admonished for not 'following the BKM's' (best-known methods) like all the others. 'If you can't add to the company then subtract yourself.' He resigned, feeling he was nothing more than a worker bee in a George Orwellian 1984 scenario.

REFLECTION

Alan in contrast to Margot had a strongly developed inner identity, and an emerging sense of what his spirit sought, which would go on to crystallise into a clearer form. He came to know his depression as the existential messenger it was. From his early days with the company the strongly individual part of his nature was the source of the problem. Yet paradoxically, Alan cared deeply about the group good, and endeavoured to raise the bar for them all. His generosity of spirit was not appreciated.

On the other hand Margot's difficulty arose from having no sense of herself as being separate from the culture she aped. The irony for her was that although merged with that very culture, when the chips were down, she did not feel supported by it, but gradually excluded. When the mask finally slipped, she had no identity to fall back on. Her depression had the potential to be constructive, as a wake-up call prompting her to embark on the process of growing a self. Instead, to her loss, that opportunity was not offered to her, and she took the road of becoming a patient. Her new reference point would now be the current status of her 'mental illness'. 'How is Margot these days?' would come to mean how bad were her symptoms. She swapped one career for another, becoming a professional patient who would spend the rest of her life ingesting cocktails of medication with regular 'breaks', in psychiatric spas.

The poem, 'Pegasus', by Patrick Kavanagh deserves serious reflection in the light of Margot and Alan's handling of their respective turning points, one going backwards and the other forwards. Kavanagh brings his deep sense of spirit to this work. We are invited on a journey where we can witness the soul's betrayal by church, state, trade and even the common man. In the end, emerging from the dark night of the soul, we see its liberation:

> My soul was an old horse
> Offered for sale in twenty fairs ...
>   'Soul,' I prayed,
> 'I have hawked you through the world
> Of Church and state and meanest trade.
> But this evening, halter off,
> Never again will it go on.
> On the south side of ditches
> There is grazing of the sun.
> No more haggling with the world ...'
> As I said these words he grew
> Wings upon his back. Now I may ride him
> Every land my imagination knew.

CHAPTER 5

Bullying – Beaten into Submission

Bullying is ubiquitous. At a micro level parents do it, so do siblings, schoolchildren, teachers, colleagues, partners, religions, organisations and institutions. Invasion and colonisation were bullying at a macro level, where entire cultures were destroyed and all forms of native expression, such as language and religious rituals, were forbidden.

In certain situations a power dynamic emerges which is fertile ground for bullying; where one human being's needs are pitted against another's, where there is a climate of total disrespect for the right of the other to have a contrary view, and where one individual sees no reason to put the brake on that primitive and unsocialised part of them which will stop at nothing to dominate. Part of the maturing process of the childhood years is to learn around the ages of three or four that others have needs too, and that contrary to our urges saying 'I must have my way!' that their wishes do in fact have to be taken into account, and a compromise reached. The family home and school are hotbeds of learning in this regard, with fisticuffs in the defence of each party's will a regular occurrence. At this age we refuse to delay gratification, we throw temper tantrums, and angrily blame others if we don't get our way, making our feelings of frustration their fault. We refuse to share our toys, and take our ball home if the rules of the game don't suit us.

When one has passed this milestone, as most of us have in the process of becoming socialised, there is a sense of shock and incomprehension when we find ourselves interfacing with someone who has not; a toddler in an adult body. Worse still, to find that this infant holds all the cards! Appealing to them adult-to-adult is a waste of breath, all you get back is an adult version of a tantrum; choice swear words, dramatic threats, below-the-belt taunts, desk thumping, door banging and file throwing – infantile adults escaped from their playpen.

The toleration of and failure to name immature behaviour perpetuates it, cultivates it, colludes with it, and makes it respectable. At the macro level, if Genghis Khan, Alexander, Caesar, Napoleon, and Hitler were properly named as bullies and tyrants, rather than tolerated as military genii, then hundreds of millions of lives could have been saved. Only in a country with the bully mentality could a 'war president' such as George Bush have been re-elected. If the so-called 'giants of industry' with their take-over bids, down-sizing and asset-stripping strategies, were named as greedy, manipulative little boys accumulating toys: there could be a more equitable distribution of wealth and resources. How different the world would be if the dynamic of sharing was a given, be it resources, knowledge or money. This can't happen of course, because in a culture ruled by artificially created market forces driven by scarcity consciousness, the bullies will always have something we need, and we will compromise our values to acquire it.

Bullying has many faces, and is used in a multiplicity of ways. A common example is to use the threat of the legal system to silence and censor another's disapproving view of you, simply because it doesn't comply with how you see yourself. Libel laws are manipulated by these so-called 'wounded', who will not tolerate criticism on any front, be that professional or personal. Their infantile pride hurt, incensed, they enlist the help of guns for hire – 'legal eagles', to shoot down and attack all opposition. Justice is not the issue, the offended child in the playground is not interested in logic, but in gratifying their pure primitive emotional knee-jerk response.

Lisa, a twenty-one-year-old arts student was admitted to accident and emergency following an overdose of assorted tablets. It emerged that she had been depressed for years following a history of bullying in school since the age of fifteen.

She had been targeted by three girls who made it their task to ridicule, humiliate and intimidate her at every opportunity. A song was made up about her, and her friends distanced themselves from her, for fear of becoming targets themselves. She ate her lunch alone, struggled with daily panic attacks, had nightmares, lost weight, and couldn't concentrate on her work. Her parents were alarmed at her distress as she would frequently come home crying, and was unable often to leave the house because of escalating panic attacks. She was taunted in shopping malls on the weekend, and could never attend any parties or concerts that the rest of her classmates went to for fear of a confrontation. Friendships outside the school were poisoned also. In spite of formal complaints to the school principal by her parents, no constructive action was taken other than to identify the bullies, and their campaign intensified as a result.

She stopped attending school, began studying at home, and was fortunate to find another school at which to sit her leaving certificate examination two years later. The new school was friendly, but she was hesitant about forming peer friendships in case of future rejection. Although a very attractive girl, she avoided boys too, and was envious of how relaxed others seemed in their company. Constantly worried that her new classmates would come to hear rumours about her from the other school, her panic attacks continued and her depression deepened.

College, to her surprise, was not the liberation she anticipated. She found it difficult to mix, still struggled with panic attacks, and was forever vigilant. Her maxim became 'if you don't get close to people, they can't hurt you'. This worked against her as she desperately wanted a boyfriend, and to be able to socialise like all her friends. Preferring her parents to think things were improving, she hid her feelings from them. As her sense of isolation deepened, and constantly expecting rejection, she became hopeless and started to stockpile medication.

Patrick, a forty-three-year-old member of the garda siochána is currently in the process of seeking retirement from the force on medical grounds.

His problems began five years ago when he sought a transfer to community policing. He was a 'people person' and enjoyed his work; involved with youth clubs, local schools, crime prevention programmes, neighbourhood watch and retirement organisations. He found it fulfilling to do courses which would help him in the job, such as conflict resolution and counselling and publishing a number of papers in garda manuals. Following a high profile article in a national newspaper on his community work, he suddenly found himself the target of abuse by a senior member in the station. This took the form of mocking, ridicule and humiliation in front of his colleagues, excessive monitoring of his work, lack of co-operation around holiday times, shift work, and allocation of time for lectures and meetings.

What hurt him the most was the ease with which his abuser seemed to enlist the support of junior and senior colleagues, and he had difficulty in activating the force's bullying policy, which he now saw as a sham. Anonymous notes were left on his desk, and a digitally manipulated poster of him wearing a priest's collar was displayed on the notice board, with the caption 'Have the Gardaí Gone Soft?' The final straw came when he found his uniform shredded in his locker, and no longer able to stick it, he went on sick leave citing work-related stress. As is the custom in the gardaí any correspondence which comes from the chief medical officer is an open letter, therefore not confidential, and hand-delivered by a third party to the home. In Patrick's case, this was done by his abuser, a further act of intimidation, and a source of shame and stigma since information of appointments with gardaí psychiatrists was now common knowledge among his peers.

When it became known that he was going to bring a bullying case against his abuser, there was a flurry of garda car activity around his home. He started to receive untraceable phone calls in the middle of the night. When driving at night his car was followed, a garda car suddenly appearing behind his, intermittently flashing its lights and sounding the siren. When he would stop, it would stop. He could never identify the driver. He felt he was being treated worse than any criminal, with the full weight of available garda resources being brought to bear on him. One night returning home with his wife and children, he was tail-gated by an unmarked car, and this incident proved a turning point for his wife who insisted he drop the case.

Sandra, a forty-five-year-old buyer in a leading family-run department store, got caught in the cross-fire following a feud between its members. Construed as being disloyal by the winning side, who now wanted her to resign and leave quietly, she became the target of their bullying. Her immediate boss turned into a conduit, passing on messages of how she was disapproved of by the top, citing examples of incompetence which had no factual basis. She was confident of her strengths and expertise, as she had worked in this area for years training and building an effective sales team. At first she ignored these criticisms, but eventually found herself in a no-win situation where she was damned if she did and damned if she didn't. When she stood her ground following an attempt to transfer her to a smaller store, involving a long commute across the city, a senior manager from head office arrived into her office unannounced.

She was on the phone at the time and indicated that she

would only be a moment. Although recognising by his demeanour that he was already pumped up, Sandra wasn't prepared for what followed. He ripped the phone line out of the wall, roared abuse at her, walked around her desk and thumped her computer with his fist. A junior colleague hearing the uproar came in to intervene, but to no avail. Pulling out all her computer connections and storming out, he slammed the door with the parting ultimatum 'Move or resign, don't make me have to come back to say it again'.

Sandra was so shocked that she was doubly incontinent, and shook uncontrollably. Cleaning herself up as best she could, she went home, taking sick leave from that day on. Her efforts in seeking justice through the courts were compromised by the unwillingness of witnesses to testify in her favour. Feeling betrayed by the company for which she had worked for over twenty-five years, but more personally by her work colleagues, and now knowing her career was destroyed and her reputation in the marketplace tarnished, she became seriously depressed, and felt suicidal. She considered pulling out of the case knowing that the company would make an example of her, but in the interest of her own integrity she persisted. Her settlement was a paltry sum, and she emigrated..

PANDORA'S BOX

Many histories of depression lead back to bullying in the past, often as far back as the young childhood years. It is impossible to underestimate the damaging effects of this on a young identity with an emerging sense of value and worth. A fundamental law of consciousness is that how you are perceived by others dictates how you will perceive yourself. This is never more true than in childhood, the stage where one is forming a tentative idea of self. If a child is repeatedly told 'you're no good, you're stupid, you're ugly', he or she will internalise that view, eventually telling themselves 'I'm no good, I'm stupid, I'm ugly'. This indelible stain is woven into the fabric of his or her personality and cellular memory.

Martin Seligman says, 'I believe that what lies at the heart of depression is that the depressed patient believes or has learned that he cannot control those elements of his life that relieve suffering, bring gratification or provide nurture – in short he believes that he is helpless'.

The essence of the experience of bullying is the over-whelming feeling of loss of control over events and situations. The belief that 'nothing I do is going to make any difference', in a heretofore highly capable person, can evolve quickly in the face of the intimidating beast which bullying is.

When we are faced with bullying, we feel affronted in a deep sense, stunned and disillusioned to find dignity and respect utterly absent in a fellow human. The very act of being forced to submit to another's will, creates in us four primary states:

- a permanent state of vigilance and fear
- an inability to trust, to the point of paranoia
- diminished self-worth and low-status consciousness
- isolation, self-loathing, exclusion and depression, often causing suicide

Bullying is an act of violence and abuse, a vicious assault on the mind, body and spirit, akin to the trauma of sexual abuse, rape and torture. It crushes the will, breaks the heart and sends the mind into turmoil. In its wake it brings shame, guilt, self-loathing, isolation and seething anger. It can destroy relationships and wreck family life. A Pandora's box of psychological phenomena opens – anxiety, poor concentration, forgetfulness, obsessive ruminations, flashbacks, insomnia, nightmares, panic attacks, social withdrawal, loss of libido, mistrust, demotivation, depression, suicidal thoughts, loss of hope and suicide.

The body takes a hammering, and the impacts can show themselves in a variety of ways – fatigue, weight loss, hypertension, chest pain, asthma, stomach ulceration, irritable bowel, nausea, diarrhoea, period problems, ligament and joint pains, psoriasis, eczema etc. The inevitable suppression of the immune system opens the way to a multiplicity of infections and the possibility of cancer cells taking root.

Hung Out To Dry

The longer the individual is exposed to the onslaught, the greater the damage, and greater still if the bully has enlisted the support of others to work as a team. Now we have a blood-hungry pack of wolves. This phenomenon is known as 'mobbing'. Because of its terrifying effectiveness, everyone not directly involved runs for cover lest they also come in for attack. Hence the victim's isolation, and the terrible feelings of rejection and abandonment. Changing the bully, or the organisation which colludes with them, may indeed be futile. 'Once a bully, always a bully' is not an inappropriate cliché, so ingrained and pathological is this sociopathic behaviour and so woven into the bully's own identity. Furthermore, dysfunctional organisations both implicitly or explicitly support the bully, as they fulfil the role of 'ass-kickers' and 'hatchet men' within it.

Some targets are change agents, unsettling those who are in favour of maintaining the status quo, and who want to protect their 'cushy number'. The dysfunctional nature of some government departments is notorious, and controlled by jobsworths and petty bureaucrats, whose primary motivation is to block and sabotage any vestige of change.

They want to avoid their performance coming up for scrutiny and the recommendation of changes in their working practices. A favourite weapon is to discredit such a change agent, by

LIAM DELANEY.

attempting to write them off as a 'troublemakers, rebels and whistle-blowers'. No label is too low in the bully's effort to undermine all possible support systems and to marginalise their target.

The emotion of depression has evolved over aeons of time stretching back to our ancient brain. We share this powerful emotional response with social animals who are bonded through relationship and attachment. Abandonment by their group can cause death. Lacking the required survival skills for life outside it, they experience overwhelming helplessness, and such animals become depressed, and surrender the will to live.

Similarly in humans the moment exclusion and abandonment is experienced, these old evolutionary pathways and doorways are opened in the ancient architecture of the brain. Now perceiving themselves to be lacking in control, they experience powerlessness, hopelessness, inner emptiness, nothing to live for, and feelings of such low status as to be of no use to anyone. They find themselves no longer able to meet the unbearable burden of living, and many welcome oblivion, their only viable option appearing to them to be absolute disengagement. Some passively wait for death, while others take a more proactive decision. The link between bullying and suicide is now well established.

Estimates show that one in every seven suicide is related solely to bullying at work. Many of the worst cases of workplace bullying are those from the garda siochána, the army, the prison services, business corporations and the teaching profession. These large, hierarchical, closed structures lend themselves to serial abuse of power, mobbing and exclusion. An individual who becomes a target, and who may previously have got along famously with his colleagues both professionally and socially, is now given the cold shoulder by them, lest they by association attract the bully's attention. For years they may have regarded these colleagues as family, and now overnight they are treated as untouchable. In these organisations bullying will only stop when it is seen as a personal injury in the workplace and the perpetrators treated as criminals.

THE CONTINUING SAGA OF THE WOUNDED HEROES

There are few survivors of bullying. If your identity as you knew it has been taken away, it's extremely difficult to build a new one, especially if it means relocation within the same organisation. Many feel so betrayed and mistrustful that the will to participate again evaporates. Those who were forced through ill-health to take long-term sick leave, find on their return that the same emotions are triggered again. Worse, to their horror, they may find that the bully is still in place or has even been promoted, so the danger continues.

Many on sick leave experience so much post-traumatic stress that total avoidance of anything vaguely representing the trauma site becomes their policy. They ignore letters and phone-calls from work, avoid socialising in the same pub as by their work colleagues, and even avoid driving past the workplace. Who wants to experience another panic attack, another flash-back, where mentally, emotionally and physically you find yourself re-experiencing the worst aspects of the bullying trauma? And then for weeks on end, to meet it in your dreams? This is the territory where day-mares and nightmares blur into each other.

Those who try to find alternative employment meet a brick wall. Many report breaking down at interviews, if they are lucky to get one, as they struggle to explain why they left their previous employment. Lack of good references don't help.

The more one comes to understand the catastrophic effects of bullying on the victim and their families, and the odds against ever getting restorative justice, the more their feelings of grief, anger, bitterness, desolation, hypersensitivity, dread, and life-threatening depression take on their own legitimacy. So deep are the wounds that professional interventions are difficult, since so many layers are involved. The therapist has to take a credulous attitude and take each individual's symptoms at face value. Any air that 'I know best' or 'I'm the expert' will instantly be interpreted as having a flavour similar to that of the bully.

Many feel re-traumatised when it's inferred that their problems are merely the result of distorted thinking, which need straightening out with a programme of cognitive-behavioural therapy. Statements from a therapist such as 'Your symptoms are not based on an accurate perception of reality, because you are over-personalising, over-generalising, mislabelling, jumping to conclusions, disqualifying the positive, etc.,' are unhelpful, judgemental and dangerous, as they inadvertently shift blame, making the victim feel counterfeit and at fault for being the way they are.

The now fashionable practice of combining anti-depressant medication with cognitive behavioural therapy with a view to keeping these highly distressed individuals at work and firmly in the line of fire of the bully, beggars belief and is another layer of trauma. Too often, members of caring professions, such as psychiatrists, psychologists, and occupational health physicians, unwittingly end up taking referrals for assessment or therapy from dysfunctional organisations who will not remove its bullies. Those same individuals would immediately report the actions of a sexual abuser. So why not report a bully to the proper authorities? Bullies thrive in a culture of silence and collusion.

Victims also report that they paradoxically find themselves traumatised by the attitude of members of the legal profession from whom they seek support. They feel they have not been listened to and are nothing more than a number. Individuals are sometimes forced into re-mortgaging their homes to meet mounting legal fees. Worse still, when push comes to shove, in an atmosphere of time-urgency, high drama, half-truths and wheeling and dealing, they find themselves pressured into making unsatisfactory settlements, adding insult to injury.

HEALING THE WOUNDS

> I am not yet born; console me.
> I fear that the human race will with tall walls wall me,
> with strong drugs dope me, with wise lies lure me,
> on black racks rack me, in blood baths roll me.
> I am not yet born; provide me
> with waters to dangle me, grass to grow for me, trees to talk
> to me, sky to sing to me, birds and a white light
> In the back of my mind to guide me.
> I am not born; O hear me,
> Let not the man who is beast or who thinks he is God come
> near me.
>
> From 'Prayer Before Birth' by Louis MacNeice

Psychotherapy is essential for healing, support, understanding, and ultimately assists in setting and reaching realistic goals. In doing psychotherapy with victims of bullying, it is often extremely difficult to shift the emphasis from 'righting the wrong' to self-preservation. Current statistics show that resolution can only come about when the bully and their target are separated (eighty per cent of cases), and that the bullying behaviour only finally stops when the bully has been effectively 'cordoned off' from interacting with any staff whatsoever or permanently removed. Victims or targets frequently hang onto the notion that they will 'show them' or 'teach them a lesson', neglecting, until it is too late, the fact that their health has run down, their family relationships are in disarray and their finances diminished.

One of the greatest challenges in helping the targets of bullying is to assist them in striking the right balance; through handing the problem over to the relevant agents to bring control over what they can, and letting go of what is beyond their influence, thereby stopping the haemorrhage of energy in that direction. Knowing 'when to hold and when to fold'. Institutions will always outlive individuals.

CHAPTER 6

Sexual Abuse – Eclipse of the Soul

I've come to realise that sexual assault is an imposed death experience for the victim. That is, the victim experiences her life as having been taken by someone else.

Evangeline Kane

The emerging self, with its inherent potential, needs to be protected, and like a seedling, nurtured in fertile ground. Sexual abuse, like no other trauma, eclipses this natural unfolding with an impact of such magnitude that is rarely appreciated. Upwards of 150,000 adult women and men in Ireland, have experienced statutory rape in childhood. Five times that figure experienced other forms of sexual abuse, ranging from inappropriate touching to the forced witnessing of exposure.

Picture an infant, whose window on the world is the rim of their cot, whose cry or smile elicits the unqualified unconditional attention of her mother and father, their watchful eyes holding her gaze completely, making her feel for those moments, the absolute centre of the world. In the infant's tiny mind an inner knowing is forming 'I am the reason this is happening'.

Now fast forward to a time when the same apparently loving father is gradually beginning to express his 'love' in a sexual manner involving her in sex games, which evolve over time into full sexual intimacy such as that shared by consenting adults. Her protestations are mollified, her co-operation validated and her secrecy rewarded. Variations of this premature sexualisation occur. Not for some fathers the process of seduction, but rather sadistic brutal intercourse instilling terror and pain, where every orifice is violated. She has no escape. Drunk or sober, day or

LIAM DELANEY.

night he has access to her. Her reason for living has been reduced to being a sexual object, a sex slave. Once again, and in both examples of fathers, the belief holds 'I am the reason this is happening'. The same interpretation will be formed if the attentions are those of a grandfather, uncle, sibling, neighbour or babysitter.

Fast forward again. She is now a teenager, perhaps at this stage no longer being actively abused, she now lives a secret life besieged by guilt, shame, depression and self-loathing. School life becomes meaningless. Recreational drugs and alcohol bring anaesthesia. Suicide – the ultimate escape – is always on the agenda.

Frequently, early sexual abuse can be of such overwhelming intensity that the immature mind buries it beyond awareness in the deepest recesses of the unconscious. However this powerful energy cannot be fully sealed off. The mental turmoil within may see her engaging in complex obsessive-compulsive thoughts and rituals – hours scrubbing her body in the shower, frequently washing and changing her clothes, engaging in checking routines and endless mental scrabble, without knowing why. The imposition of order and self-discipline quells her anxiety. She may withhold food through calorie counting and starvation rituals, and engage in self-mutilation practices for release of tension, the pain and the sight of blood reminding her that she's alive.

In adult life abuse may surface as depression. It is depressing to have intimacy problems, to fear touch, to feel confused about sexual identity, to repress and feel shame of the self as a sexual being. It is depressing to be haunted by images and sensations that she can't explain; such as feelings of stubble against her face, the pressure of body parts against hers, and the pervasive smell of alcohol and sweat. Over the years she comes to loathe and despise herself for these peculiarities, holding her personality responsible. Why wouldn't she? There doesn't seem to be any other explanation. 'It must be me, I must have a sick mind'.

GOD'S RAPISTS

Boys do not escape. Those who were incarcerated in industrial schools have borne witness to this. Many were exposed to regimes of unbridled rape and violence which lasted for years, at the hands of sadistic sexual perverts answerable to no one. Their threats of unspeakable violence ensured availability and silence. The majority of survivors – their chance of a normal life diminished from the beginning, with their lives totally derailed, and their humanity denied – learned to place no value on themselves. They drifted from one crisis to another, their past littered with criminal behaviour, prison records, substance abuse, dysfunctional relationships, mistrust of authority, and family breakdown. Powerless to bring stability to their lives, many suffered later from depression and other serious psychiatric disorders, beginning a life-long relationship with psychiatric hospitals.

The greatest tragedy of all is that these people feel robbed, not just of their innocence, but of their inner light, as if their very soul has been taken away. We have worked not just with survivors of abuse in the industrial schools but also with those who fell victim to the predatory behaviour of priests in certain boarding schools, priests who lured them in, on the basis that they were intelligent, 'special' boys with spiritual potential, needing guidance with their sexuality. The 'guidance' offered was in fact a gradual seduction process, which commenced with the exploration of things sexual, stimulating their curiosity, providing skewed answers and finally grooming them towards the acceptance of mutual touching, masturbation, and penetrative sex. To this day married or single, many are haunted by flashbacks of their abuser's body odour, the very touch of their fingers, the sound of their voice, and the image of their presence.

The experience was encoded not just in consciousness but in cellular memory, where it can be triggered into life and relived in an instant, such as, paradoxically during sexual intimacy with their partner, when the image of the first seductions by their abuser intrudes, causing avoidance and sexual dysfunction.

SOUL HEALING

The sexually abused are truly the walking wounded, living out private hells, their lives irreparably shaped by the experience. Behind the mask of many a so-called 'biological' or 'clinical' depression lies a history of sexual trauma which cannot be dissipated by a pill or a course of electro-convulsive therapy. This is the domain of psychotherapy and the painful process of peeling back the layers of trauma within a psychotherapeutic relationship, so that they can be truly seen, verbalised and integrated, is a lengthy one, sometimes without any satisfactory resolution, so all-pervasive is the damage.

To compound matters there are numerous and formidable barriers put in the path of the abused in their quest for recognition, the result of which is to protect the perpetrators, minimise the extent of the abuse, and its life-long and far-reaching effects. This denial and disbelief not only re-traumatises victims and blocks restorative justice, but also impedes their healing process. Another more subtle obstruction to this healing is the failure on the part of doctors in so many cases to link depression with trauma of this kind, diagnosing it as a 'new' illness, the treatment of which bears no witness to its root cause.

Deirdre, a 32-year-old mother of two and also a teacher, was obsessively washing her hands from the age of eleven. In addition she repeatedly machine-washed bed linen, underwear and nightdresses. If they weren't cleaned to her satisfaction she would hand scrub them. This practice of washing and re-washing consumed most of her spare time. She spent all her breaks during the school day washing her hands, often dozens of times.

Early on in her marriage there were sexual problems. She discouraged sexual touching by her husband and intermittently suffered from vaginismus, feeling such intense pain on penetration that intercourse was virtually impossible, and could only be entertained in an alcohol-induced altered state. The arrival of children put her under more time pressure, with not enough time to satisfy her compulsion to wash.

Following her promotion to school vice-principal her new duties gave her less and less time for her obsession, and her anxiety levels escalated, as she tried to catch up with the clothes washing at the weekends. The more she tried to stop her compulsion, the more panicky and out of control she felt. Beginning to lose sleep, she became irritable and depressed, sometimes having to suppress the urge to weep during class. Not knowing what to do, she sought the help of a psychotherapist. After a number of consultations the psychotherapist broached the subject of possible sexual abuse. Even though she had no clear memories of any abuse, she found the question deeply unsettled her and she began experiencing disturbing dreams from her childhood where there was a male menacing presence.

She tracked down a much older sister, who had left home, severing all connections with the family. Her sister reluctantly confirmed that she had been sexually abused by their father. This was her worst fear, and she began experiencing flashbacks of her father having sex with her. It emerged that following the death of her mother when she was five, her father started sexually abusing her and her sister and continued until he began another relationship and married when she was eleven.

The memories began to flood in; getting out of bed after her father had left her bedroom, and repeatedly scrubbing her hands and body in the hottest shower possible. When the abuse had stopped her cleansing ritual became confined to her hands only. In later consultations she realised she had been harbouring intense feelings of guilt and shame, always having felt that her body was constantly soiled and dirty. When she had actually made the link between her obsession and the sexual abuse, she was able to see that the repeated washing represented, in symbolic terms, a cleansing process.

The need to wash became less and less, and as the tension inside subsided she felt less trapped by her obsessive behaviours which had been ruling her life, and the accompanying depression slowly dissipated. Determined to leave the legacy of the abuse behind, she began to repair the havoc wreaked on her relationship. In psychosexual therapy with her husband she learned for the first time to establish a personal boundary, an experience which had been denied her by the invasiveness of the abuse, stimulating her erogenous zones prematurely. Such was her confusion following the abuse that Deirdre had always experienced difficulties sorting out the conflicting messages her body sent her, managing pleasurable influences coming in from the outside and distinguishing them from painful ones. Having felt betrayed by her body she had instead decided to ignore its signals altogether. Together they embarked on the long tortuous road towards fostering normal sexual intimacy.

David, a forty-eight-year-old accountant, and father of a thirteen-year-old girl, began being abused at boarding school at the age of twelve, by a visiting priest who conducted the school retreats. He encouraged boys to come to him to have their confession heard in the parlour. When David went, Fr Sebastian was sitting in a chair in front of a fire and David was asked to kneel on the floor beside him. The 'confession' took the form of a discussion about how David felt he was maturing as a young man, and whether or not he had experienced erections or wet dreams. Fr Sebastian used the opportunity to elaborate explicitly the facts of life, explaining penetration and ejaculation in detail. He reached over and felt David's penis, which he noted to be erect, and invited him to open his fly to allow him to feel 'more comfortable'. Then Fr Sebastian commented on his 'manliness' and suggested that he would instruct him as to its primary purpose, that of ejaculation. David, who had never ejaculated before, did so when Fr Sebastian started masturbating him. Fr Sebastian then lifted up his robes revealing his own genitalia, inviting David to masturbate him, in order to check whether he had learned how to do it effectively. He told him before he left that he would be regularly visiting the school and would take a personal interest in his development, because he was a very mature and spiritual boy.

Each time Fr Sebastian visited the school David was called to have his confession heard and his 'spiritual progress' monitored. On every occasion detailed conversations about sexual matters preceded mutual masturbation. On one occasion to his surprise there was one other boy already present in the parlour. Fr Sebastian showed them photographs of a group of boys of a similar age engaging in oral sex, and told them that the time had come for the next stage of their 'sexual education' to begin. He assuaged any feelings of awkwardness or embarrassment the boys had, with reassurances that what they were engaging in was the fostering of an attitude of openness between them, as 'dropping inhibitions' was a healthy development in young boys. He then asked them to perform oral sex on him also. He bound them to secrecy on the basis that there were certain private details which were 'sacred' and were best kept within the confines of the sacrament of confession.

The abuse continued for two years, and the visits to the parlour stopped when Fr Sebastian no longer sought him out for 'spiritual direction'.

LIAM DELANEY.

On leaving school, David went to college and was plagued by doubts as to his sexual orientation. He drank heavily, and experimented with bisexuality. In later years, on falling in love with a female colleague, he got married. Initially their intimate life was mutually pleasurable and fulfilling, but with time he found himself having to draw on the sexual imagery of his encounters with Fr Sebastian in order to become aroused. He gradually began to avoid intimacy and used the excuse of his wife's pregnancy to justify this. After years of avoidance, by which stage they were virtually celibate, his wife became distressed enough to seek out psychosexual counselling. During one consultation he broke down, revealing the torment of the last number of years and his sexual history with Fr Sebastian. He explained that he had been having such vivid and real flashbacks that he was finding himself swept along in a sensual and kinaesthetic experience. These could occur at any time, usually when he was under stress, and he often had to resort to alcohol to lessen his anxiety. Nonetheless they continued to break through. During the flashbacks he could literally smell Fr Sebastian's body odour, taste his sperm, and feel the touch of his hands on his genitalia. Terrified, he thought he was going mad, and considered suicide on a number of occasions.

David somehow managed to keep his life afloat and his marriage and job intact. He feels Fr Sebastian robbed him of his innocence, his sexuality and his fundamental human right to fulfil his potential. He continues in psychotherapy and will need such support for the foreseeable future.

Peggy, at age eight, was taken from the playground by a local man, brought to a derelict building and brutally raped in the toilets there. Since he used a broken bottle she sustained severe vaginal injuries and spent several months in hospital. With the passing years Peggy became a nervous timid child who never went out except occasionally in the company of her sisters. She had many nervous habits, among them always needing the front door to be open at night, wanting to sleep downstairs, spending much of the day standing outside in the front garden of the house, and sometimes inexplicably rushing outside in the middle of meals. She would go to the local pub only if she could get a lift or a taxi, but would never go by foot.

Her husband was her first and only boyfriend ('I could trust him'), and she had four children. During sex she said she would 'space out' until it was over, and gave it up once they had completed their family. All the family thought Peggy was odd and somewhat stupid, with all her strange habits that she refused to discuss. The relationship with her husband was not tranquil, as he would lose his patience with her frequently and shout at her with a raised voice. After these episodes she would be nervous for days, and experienced frequent bouts of depression for which she had been prescribed anti-depressants over the years.

At the age of fifty-two, following a minor car accident in which the other driver got out of his car and began shouting loudly at her, she became hysterical and had a severe panic attack which resulted in her being brought to the local casualty department. Following this she was referred to a psychotherapist to whom she confided her fear that the other driver, who was drunk and abusive, was actually about to assault her. Although the accident had shaken her it was fairly minor, and it was obvious even to Peggy that her terror was an overreaction. When she subsequently developed disturbing nightmares, and when her psychotherapist became aware that she had in fact been having panic attacks for years, Peggy was instructed in how to control them with abdominal breathing and relaxation techniques.

It was during one such deep relaxation that Peggy got her first insight into the source of her problem. Although she hadn't

forgotten the fact that she had been raped, she could not remember many of the details of the experience, and had not made
any connection between that and her subsequent panic attacks.
She thought that all her odd behaviours were due to the fact
that she was stupid. Her mother had blamed her for going off
with the man and not having 'more sense'. It was swept under
the carpet and never mentioned by the family. When she turned
into such a nervous child they reasoned that her mental dullness
was the cause, which was reinforced by the illogical nature of
her behaviours.

On one occasion, while practising her relaxation exercise
she could clearly hear (for the first time) her rapist's voice saying
to her. 'Your father sent me to bring you home'. This meant that
he must not have been a stranger to her. Other memories which
re-emerged included noting that he had worn spats on his shoes,
that as he had taken off his shirt she had seen a tattoo on his arm,
and that he had smelled strongly of sweat. Remembering that he
shouted loudly all the time he was with her, and threatened to
kill her if she ever told, she recalled again the terror she felt as
he blocked the door to the toilets so that he would not be disturbed. The thought 'if that door is closed I'm dead' flashed into
her mind. Retrieving the images helped piece together many
loose ends for Peggy.

The driver of the car which had crashed into her, had unwittingly brought back several of the elements which had been
present during the rape but lost to her memory. Like her original
assailant the driver was drunk and abusive, and she was once
again feeling shaken, hurt and in danger. Although unable to
process an experience of such traumatic magnitude as a child, as
an adult she found these parts of her history were now unfolding
and seeking integration.

Her terror of being in a room with a closed door now made
sense, as did her need to sleep downstairs – for a quick get-away.

Her certainty that her breathing would stop whenever she got frightened, resonated with being held by the throat. Since the derelict building in which she'd been raped was on the way to the local pub, she now knew why she refused to pass it on foot, and why she was terrified of any aggression whatsoever on the part of her husband. Most startling for her was the moment she recognised who he was, by the shoes he wore. She knew a man locally who wore spats. He was married to a friend of her mother. All the family knew she feared him, because she would run to her room if he had occasion to come to their house. When his wife died, fifteen-year-old Peggy had adamantly refused to go to the funeral, causing a row at home. Nobody, even Peggy, knew why before now.

Peggy's opinion of herself changed dramatically. From being obese she lost a lot of weight, became interested in clothes for the first time, and began to venture out to the shops alone. She could stay inside the house now with the doors shut, and would sleep upstairs in the bedroom sometimes. Knowing where her fears came from allowed her to see that she was no longer in any danger as he was now an old man. Most importantly she knew now that none of her reactions were 'stupid' but of a survival nature and as such highly intelligible, warnings to keep away from certain situations and from him.

Once she was able to see that what had once been a useful survival response had now turned into a life-restricting habit, she had more motivation to uncouple the two. She learned to feel the unpleasant sensations and know that, unlike during the rape, they wouldn't kill her, and that this time she could do something about them.

John, a fifty-four-year-old father of two young children from a second relationship, was detained in St Conleth's, Daingean, Co. Offaly in June 1965, at age fourteen, where he remained for two years. Its reputation as a place of unspeakable violence and sexual abuse has been well established. In John's words 'Such was the unbridled violence that we were treated as sub-humans. We were regarded as little more than animals. It was a brutal, mindless system. Everyone was ground down to their level. It was an existence beyond redemption. They were totally shameless. All the brothers knew what was going on. They were living their version of a religious heaven while we were struggling in hell.'

He was sexually abused and beaten on a number of occasions, one of which he describes vividly and which haunts him to this day. That night he and another boy were accused of trying to run away.

'Suddenly Br Fitzpatrick appeared and took me out of bed. He brought me down the marble stairs. At the end of the stairs I could see Br Cummins, a huge man, of over twenty-six stone. Then I was hit at the back of the head by Br Fitzpatrick, and Cummins started to kick and beat me, both rained down blows on top of me. Then I was told to kneel down on the first step and Fitzpatrick told me to lean forward and place my hands on the step above. When Cummins stood on my fingers, I started to scream with pain. Br Fitzpatrick pulled the night-gown over my head, leaving me completely naked. I started to plead and beg "we were only talking about it, we had never planned to escape, we had never planned to escape".

'Suddenly I felt this shock going right up to my head. Br Fitzpatrick had hit my backside with a leather strap. I thought I was going to pass out, and kept trying to look over my shoulder to see what was happening next. Fitzpatrick was running towards me and I can still see that face, that look. It was all happening in slow motion. When he hit me I thought I was going to die. Then I saw four brothers standing in the background, and recognised two of them as Sheehy and Gallagher. They were just standing there leering. I knew they were getting off on it. I felt

I was worthless, with no bargaining chips left, an object, a thing. I started to pray to God. After the third belt of the strap I passed out. I just wanted death to come. By the time the fourth blow came I was in some kind of a dream. I was numb. I was gone. I was empty.

'I have no memory of how I got back to bed, I don't know if I was carried up or walked up. I remember none of the other boys came to my assistance. Everybody was hiding under the sheets, no one was talking, everybody was terrified, no one could sleep. Up until that night I felt I was useful, that I had some role useful to them as as either a slave or a sex toy. But during the beating I realised I had no say in anything. I felt abandoned by God. He did not rescue me because I was nothing. I realised then that I didn't have a present, a future or an afterlife. I had nothing after that.'

Whenever John, in all the years in psychotherapy, refers to this particular beating he starts to sweat, gets to his feet and paces up and down the room. He describes in detail the vivid memories of that night, literally starting to relive the experience, becoming animated and profoundly distressed. After he has gone through the process step by step he sits down exhausted. He usually emphasises 'It was the night everything was taken away from me, everything. Nothing has given me meaning since that flogging – no job, no children, nothing. They have just helped to fill in the time until I die. I have nothing inside me, no purpose'.

THE UN-INTEGRATED EXPERIENCE
Some depressed individuals, such as Deirdre (who also suffered from obsessive-compulsive disorder) who had no conscious memory, and those suffering from post-traumatic stress disorder, such as Peggy who had only a fragment of a memory of a traumatic event happening to them, find the cause of their symptoms a mystery.

Frequently, early childhood traumas of a physical or sexual nature remain unhealed. The trauma was never recognised and never treated. At the time of the abuse these children were not developmentally equipped to handle the intensity of such experiences, or to put it into words. Their inability to process the trauma at the time meant that it became sealed off in their unconscious mind, and as such obscured from their awareness. It was nonetheless experienced, stored within their energy field and cellular memory, and years later is often expressed as a physical, emotional or mental symptom.

In childhood these symptoms may include acting-out behaviours, learning disabilities, bed-wetting, truancy, delinquency and other maladjusted behaviours. In adult life they may find expression as depression, psychosomatic disorders, sexual dysfunction, eating disorders, substance abuse, obsessive-compulsive disorders, psychosis, self-mutilation, suicidal behaviours, personality disorders, acts of violence and other serious crimes.

A child's mind explains the reason for events in different ways to an adult's. As to why painful experiences keep on happening to them they will rationalise 'it must be me. I have to be doing something wrong. I'm bad. That's the only reason something like this could keep happening'. The true reasons cannot be integrated by a child's psyche, as the implications would be too contradictory and disturbing to take in. A loving father abusing his innocent child in such a way could not possibly make sense in a child's mind, which might shatter under such realisations. In order to maintain the father as loving, the child has to interpret him or herself as bad. Wiser to air-spray out such details and keep the illusion that the adults who run your world are trustworthy.

Over the years, traumatised individuals come to loathe and despise themselves for their deficits, holding themselves responsible. Why wouldn't they? There doesn't seem to be anybody else to blame. An intuitive psychotherapist is invaluable in these cases, one who gets a sense of the charge or unseen dynamics underlying the more obvious surface symptom, such as depression or obsessive-compulsive disorder. The wise physician would hold off from prescribing medication in order to facilitate such unconscious material in finding expression. This will never happen if it is sealed off under the influence of the medication, which works on the level of energising behaviour and mood rather than insight. A valuable opportunity lost. Those who work with young children who have been sexually abused know the power of art therapy, psychodrama and role-play to assist them in expressing the unspeakable. In order to process unconscious memories they have to first be brought into awareness. This is what is meant by integration of such experiences. How could you make sense of disturbing noises coming from under your floorboards, if no one had ever told you your house had a cellar?

HONOURING THEMIS – JUSTICE FOR ALL?
Pre-Hellenic Greeks personified the natural way, order, or balance of all things as the Goddess Dike, also known as Themis, whose scales representing balance are familiar to all as the symbol of right and justice. The Greeks understood that whenever the natural order of Themis was violated the powers of righteous anger, Nemesis, and shame, Aidos, would be invoked, so that wrongs might be righted and the single strand of wrong-doing rewoven back into the web of life making it whole again.

Aidos represented the sense of reverence for life that holds us back from wrong-doing, and the sense of shame we feel whenever the bonds of trust are broken and personhood is violated. Shame carried a sense of respect for the sacred, and served to remind us, that as human beings we can make mistakes, allowing us to acknowledge them, and finally prompting us to remedy them to the best of our abilities.

Formal apologies and efforts to compensate for damage done were essential for the restitution of balance. If efforts to redress the injustice were not forthcoming, or worse if it was denied outright, Nemesis came into play in the form of righteous anger and punishment. Once again balance was restored and the victim was satisfied that justice has been done, presided over by Themis.

The way the legal system is being manipulated at present, particularly in the case of sexual abuse, the scales of Themis are rarely balanced. Shame now rarely lands, as it is designed to, on the shoulders of those who commit the transgressions. Rejected by the perpetrators, it passes instead on to those treated shamelessly, the victims who already harbour Nemesis, satisfying Themis' need for balance. Psychotherapists working with victims towards healing the wounds of sexual abuse will attest to the profound depth of their sense of self-loathing, shame and disgust. Although intellectually understanding that as a child, with no control or choice in the situation, fault should not be placed at their door, they do it nonetheless. It's as if by having been a participant in the act at all, they must pass judgement on themselves, for what individual with any decency would not? Deirdre cannot make herself clean enough. Even Peggy holds it against herself for it occurring at all. 'What made me go with him?' she would repeat over and over, unable to understand how she was not in some way at fault.

The experience of profound shame is excruciating, so unbearable that we usually develop ways to compensate and defend ourselves. We disown parts of ourselves – our needs, emotions, or perceptions that were painfully exposed in shaming incidences – and cultivate false selves to protect ourselves and please others. In so doing we lose the ability to validate our own experience and to relate compassionately to ourselves, and we come to rely on external standards of performance to guide our actions in order to gauge whether we are a good person or not.

The present judicial system, believing itself to be an agent of justice, is not fulfilling many of the requirements of Themis for balance. If hearings such as occur in the Residential Institutions Redress Board are not held in public, but in secrecy, this negates another basic need of the victim, that of their own vindication, only possible by the wrongdoers demonstrable acceptance of responsibility in the eyes of the whole community. Victims like John are horrified at the thought that their stories will be left untold, their sufferings forgotten and trivialised. With their abusers shielded, the political system having washed their hands of them, and the legal system going for the most expedient route, their distress is never given validity.

COLLUSION – SECRETS AND LIES

In a society such as ours, we stridently refuse to face the hideous imperfections and failings of our judicial system with respect to the sexually abused. They feel abandoned by the political process and unprotected by the legal system. They will never feel exonerated and they will bring their sense of injustice, pain and suffering to the grave, feeling punished so that the rest of us feel exonerated and the communal mores can be maintained, justified and reinforced. Shamelessness, arrogance, deceit and moralising thrives at the highest level and the ultimate authority is power, money, reputation and respectability.

In spite of the uncovering of the miasma of sexual abuse in Irish society – with its unwholesome and foreboding stench polluting and affecting us all – attempts are still being made to cover it up again, and deny the extent of its existence and the depth of the trauma caused. Every possible legal mechanism is brought into play to prevent the constitutional right of every individual to have their case heard in the courts, in front of their community, where society can bear witness to it. This primitive instinctual need is a universal archetype recognised in all societies.

Religious orders with their huge financial resources, will stop at nothing to protect their members who have abused. Their strategies are endless – delaying tactics, legal loopholes, mountains of paperwork, judicial reviews appeals to the Supreme Court, anything to put off the day they take responsibility for their shameful acts. Many victims are left dumbfounded and re-traumatised when their case is overturned by the highest court in the land. The religious legal machine, with their highly paid solicitors and barristers, are well versed in manoeuvring through plans A, B and C, to protect its members from ever appearing in court. They happily sit down with the victim's legal team, as they did with David's, and through back-door settlements negotiate a satisfactory outcome, one which is to their own advantage, and which ultimately buys silence. For the victim the atmosphere of such negotiations is one of fear, intimidation, bullying, time-urgency and a tissue of half-truths. The victim's own legal team will tell them, as his did, 'You don't have a case, there's no guarantee you'll win, your name will appear in the papers, the costs are going to be prohibitive, the judges are not sympathetic, this could take years to get heard, if you win they'll appeal to the Supreme Court' – anything to discourage them from proceeding.

Many victims of abuse feel that their 'own side' has betrayed and abused them. Justice is no longer a principle within such interactions, only a means of professionals earning their living, their clients pawns in their daily game-playing of one-up-man-ship and out-manoeuvring. The only game in town where win, lose or draw, all the players except the victim, go home with their pockets filled. Tragically they are supported in this effort by 'expert' psychiatrists who will ruthlessly minimise the trauma suffered by the abused individual, some even going so far as to state that the abuse 'never happened at all' by calling it a false memory – a fiction – presumably contrived by unscrupulous individuals to extort money.

The office of the director of public prosecutions is virtually a black hole where sexual abuse cases seem to disappear, some taking years to be processed. This ineptitude in acting swiftly causes unnecessary suffering for victims, and strengthens the hands of those protecting abusers. These time delays themselves are being used to justify cases being overturned due to the 'age' or 'infirmity' of the abuser.

One of the greatest abuses perpetrated against the victims of sexual abuse in religious-run residential institutions was the setting up of the Redress Board in 2002, the result of an agreement between the church and the state. Not being a court, it is held in secret, away from the eyes of the community, and no perpetrator of a crime is ever sentenced to a punishment. Justice for the victim is not the purpose, only financial compensation, which is capped to a maximum of €300,000. (To date the average award paid out to 2,555 victims has been €78,000) The award is commensurate on them signing a secrecy agreement. If the victims disclose the amount they were awarded, they can be fined up to €3,000 and can face a summary jail sentence of six months. After a second disclosure, they face a fine not exceeding €25,000 and a two year jail sentence. One victim used this analogy:

> An adult – man or woman – abuses a child. It is their 'secret'. To make sure the 'secret' is kept, the adult will give the child money or sweets. They buy silence. By making secrecy a condition upon payment, the board is doing exactly what an abuser does to a child.

The Redress Board is a virtual gold mine for solicitors who have to date been paid over ten million in legal costs for representing victims. Since there are thousands more waiting to have their cases heard, their fees may finally be greater than the original estimate of total compensation costs agreed by the government when it signed its €127 million indemnity deal on 5 July 2002 with the eighteen religious orders involved in the scandal. The state's potential liability for legal costs was grossly miscalculated, and are now projected at 800,000 million.

The original abuse perpetrated against the victims goes on and on, in a continued atmosphere of fear, secrecy, lack of control, bullying and betrayal. These victims who were incarcerated in Dickensian environments through the children's courts, for the most trivial of reasons, such as truancy and petty theft, were the most under-privileged and vulnerable of our society. The Lyons brothers, James and Gerard, were sentenced in 1963 aged twelve and fourteen for trespassing in a deserted building while catching wild pigeons to keep in their loft at home. They were each detained until the age of sixteen in two industrial schools; Upton and Letterfrack. They were used and abused, and like so many of their peers remain to this day in emotional turmoil.

Others committed no crime at all except to find themselves orphans or the offspring of parents designated unfit on the word of the local parish priest. Paddy Doyle, the author of *The God Squad* was sentenced in a district court to be detained in an industrial school for eleven years. He was four years old. His crime – his mother died from cancer in 1955, and his father committed suicide shortly afterwards. He was sexually abused and viciously assaulted, all of which culminated in questionable brain surgery, contributing to serious permanent disability. His book gives an inner voice account of his horrifying experience, and will stand as testament to the lack of protection, interest and compassion shown not just by his carers, but by Irish society as a whole.

The sexually and physically abused are still being treated as having no value, and the blind eye approach to their pain and

LIAM DELANEY.

suffering continues. This hideous legal circus – The Redress Board – that they have been channelled towards, is a crime against humanity. Inevitably one can only hope that its unconstitutional nature will be revealed, leading to its abolition and replacement by an open forum where the victim is not only properly compensated, but where their perpetrators are named and the scales of justice balanced.

> Our lives begin to end the day we become silent about things that matter.
>
> Martin Luther King

CHAPTER 7

*Fear, Panic, Post-Traumatic Stress Disorder,
Obsessive-Compulsive Disorder – Battle Fatigue*

Wave a wand, take away fear and helplessness and depression would virtually disappear. The fight or flight response is the most primitive and ancient of all survival responses, dealing as it does with the matter of life and death. The degree to which this is aroused is dictated by the threats we face, and their severity places us along a spectrum between fear at one extreme, and safety at the other. To spend extended periods of time at the fear end, teetering on the edge of panic, with no possibility of controlling it or disengaging from it, has to be one of the most disempowering and excruciating states a human being can experience.

Fear is the demon of peace, compassion, acceptance, spontaneity, love, happiness, health – life itself. Bertrand Russell, the philosopher and mathematician, described those who live in fear as 'already three parts dead'. Living in fear is lonely, energy-draining and depressing. It's a tortuous juggling act running parallel universes: trying to engage with the world of work, family and friends while at the same time grappling with frightening images and feelings. This adrenaline-driven state of arousal is recognisable to all of us in its milder forms as butterflies in the tummy, sweaty palms, trembling and worrying thoughts of things going wrong.

Many are living with the more extreme versions of fear, on

constant red alert, where the body and mind can at any moment be swept away by the adrenaline cascade which creates the symptoms of high anxiety or a panic attack; shortness of breath, pounding heart, dizziness, wobbly knees, nausea, feeling spaced out, and the catastrophic thoughts that predict death, madness and loss of control. The aftershock of such an experience leaves one feeling wrecked, mentally and physically beaten up, terrified of, and feeling helpless to prevent, the next attack. More extreme again is post-traumatic stress disorder, a cluster of symptoms, the underlying one being fear. Those suffering from obsessive-compulsive disorder keep constant fear at bay by preventive rituals and complex, repetitive mind-games.

An added burden with all of these anxiety disorders is the constant struggle to find the energy to keep on fighting the fight. For many, this is a secret battle sealed by fear of ridicule and stigma. There is a profound sense of desperation and helplessness when our life feels taken over, and we feel powerless to stop it spinning out of control, with perceived disastrous consequences. Trying to live a life in this helpless, hopeless state, preoccupied and hyper-vigilant, mistrustful and paranoid, battling with poor concentration, memory lapses and burnt-out resources, renders the simplest of demands a Mount Everest to deal with. Unable to help ourselves and disapproved of by others, feeling trapped, demotivated, and weighed down by life, we withdraw into our shell becoming defensive, emotionally unavailable, irritable, impatient with ourselves and others. Misunderstandings flourish, fuelling further alienation. The formulation of the belief that 'nothing I do makes any difference' ushers in the emotional state of depression.

A PORTRAIT OF PANIC
Picture this fictional scenario. Your home has been broken into and the intruder has assaulted you repeatedly over the last

month, leaving you battered, bruised and exhausted. None of your familiar surroundings appear the same any more, the home you used to so enjoy is ruined. In spite of all your efforts, there seems to be nothing you can do to either predict or prevent the attacks. You think of nothing else now, vigilant all the time, waiting, expecting the worst. Sometimes the attack is during the night, taking you off guard, when you're at your most alone. Of those you seek help from, some wonder whether you're imagining it, since they see no intruder or signs of a struggle, suggest that your distress is an overreaction, tell you to 'pull yourself together', and then leave you to handle the attacks on your own.

If this were really happening to you, do you suppose you might feel your zest for life ebbing away, since it would now all be sapped by having to be constantly watchful for the next onslaught, or recovering from the last one? Each morning on waking, might you not be likely to begin thinking 'oh God, another day, maybe I'll just stay in here under the covers'? It's hard to believe you wouldn't begin to lose faith in yourself, becoming ruthlessly self-critical over your inability to get your life back on track.

Would you still be as keen to socialise, when that would mean hearing about the trouble-free lives others were living, when all that was on your mind was your hopeless situation? Might you lose interest in sex, in keeping the garden, in reading, while it seemed more urgent to keep checking the windows and doors, a permanent ear out for any sign of impending danger? Surely the future would begin to look bleak if all it held was more terror? Would anaesthesia, in the form of a couple of glasses of wine, even during the day, look like a reasonable solution to blot out the constant paranoia in your head?

And if your doctor offered you a pill as the solution to your distress, would you not be unbelievably relieved that it could be sorted so easily, even though deep down you would wonder how that could make the continual assaults cease? And if the side effects of that medication involved gaining weight, becoming impotent or nauseous, might you not think it was a reasonable trade-off?

The experience of panic attacks has some parallels with this scenario, but in many ways is so much worse because your assailant is inside your own body, and when the assault happens, there is literally nowhere to hide, and often no one to turn to. There are few experiences so terrifying, and the fact that there's no rational explanation of why its happening causes most people to fear the worst – that it's life-threatening, that it'll cause a heart attack or stroke, that it's the first sign of a terrible psychiatric illness. Instinctively you want to hide it from others, lest you be labelled mad, stupid or weak. The isolation is profound.

Panic attacks are very common and becoming ever more so, given the increasing stress modern living brings. They are caused by a sudden surge of the hormone adrenaline in the bloodstream, so you can be feeling perfectly normal one moment, doing some routine activity, and in the next begin to experience a cascade of symptoms which you never had before and which most people find alarming and highly unpleasant.

The word 'panic' derives from Greek mythology. Pan was the god of shepherds and flocks. He was depicted as half-man, half-animal, with a reed pipe, a shepherd's crook and a crown of pine leaves. He had horns, a wrinkled face and a very prominent chin. His body was hairy, the lower part of which was that of a male goat with cloven hoofs. He was adept at hiding, loving nothing better than his afternoon nap. He avenged himself on those who disturbed him with a sudden blood-curdling screech, causing them to run for their lives.

The experience of a *panic* attack has parallels with this myth. Suddenly your body is in a state of emergency. You feel totally out of control, terrorised and in the grip of an irrational state of mind, with an overwhelming urge to flee to safety.

What distinguishes panic from chronic fear (anxiety), which is caused by a constant 'drip' of adrenaline, is that in panic the chemical is released in a sudden dam-burst which floods the body. Since adrenaline receptors are found in every cell in the body, the experience is widespread and affects every system: the cardiovascular, the respiratory, the gastrointestinal, the neurological, even the skin:

- You feel light-headed, dizzy, disoriented and on the point of fainting. You doubt if your jelly legs can support you as far as the nearest exit.
- You may notice fleeting sensations of pins and needles in your hands, and numbness around your lips. Blurring or double vision makes it difficult to focus normally.
- Trembling in your hands can be so bad that you can't hold a cup or write a cheque.
- There never seems to be enough air. 'Where's the window?' thoughts fill your mind. You take short panting breaths, or feel yourself choking or smothering. Every breath feels like it might be your last. 'Getting outside' is a question of survival.
- Waves of heat and cold chills pass through you. You want to take off layers and undo buttons. How you wish you could splash your face with cold water or plunge your hands into a bucket of ice-cubes! Your hands are clammy and sweat rolls off you. At night the sheets get saturated and need changing.
- You're sure you're about to vomit. Waves of nausea convince you that you're going to make a social spectacle of yourself. Crampy pains in your gut tell you to get to the bathroom now and allow the bout of diarrhoea to run its course.
- A fast thumping heartbeat terrifies you, and you may believe that you're having a heart attack. Chest tightness and shoot-

ing pains down your arms confirm your worst fears. By this stage you may want to get the doctor or call the ambulance.

- The pressure in your head convinces you that you're about to burst a blood vessel in your brain. If this is not the first time it's happened, you might think you have a brain tumour.

In summary, these terrifying symptoms are:

- Difficulty breathing
- Fast, forceful heartbeat
- Dizziness, unsteadiness or feeling faint
- Excessive sweating
- Lump in the throat, difficulty swallowing
- Trembling or shaking
- Nausea, churning stomach or urge to use the toilet
- Perceptual changes, feelings of unreality
- Numbness or tingling in the face, hands or feet
- Intense fears – of dying, losing control, going mad
- Urgency to get to safety, to have someone near, to leave

The attack feels like a wave passing over you, coming out of nowhere, rising to a crescendo and lasting for a varied amount of time, averaging from less than a minute to an hour. But many people hover all day on the verge of having one, in a state of heightened anxiety. When it's over you feel exhausted and drained.

After your first few attacks, you're overwhelmed with questions, absolutely convinced that something has to be seriously wrong. Visits to the doctor or hospital may follow, but invariably nothing is found to explain it, and many become increasingly anxious if more attacks follow and no cause is found. At this point medication is usually tried, a combination of anti-depressants and tranquillisers, but most people find that it has a hit-

and-miss result and don't feel comfortable becoming reliant on it. In some cases their panic attacks intensify, since these 'uppers' actually raise adrenaline levels. Bad news for an already over-aroused system.

As the attacks continue, occurring often in more and more different situations, apprehension and vigilance set in, and a permanent state of watchfulness becomes the norm. When is the next one going to happen? This begins to dictate where you can go and what you can and can't do, because your overriding goal now is to avoid triggering another attack. Ordinary everyday activities can become excessively challenging, such as supermarket shopping, using public transport, even driving the car, attending meetings, going to the cinema, your sense of safety always measured by the distance to the nearest exit.

A policy of avoiding the terrifying sensations at all costs can lead on phobias of anywhere from which it is difficult to escape, such as meetings, planes, lifts, trains. Or anything which brings on intense fear, which for you could be dogs, birds, or spiders.

Life begins to shrink and you can find it a strain hiding your anxiety from others, fearing their judgement. Indeed, you loathe yourself for your inability to control things, feeling constantly fed up at letting yourself down. Although you might only get one attack a week or a month, you're living with a consistently high level of anxiety, thinking of little else.

You begin to be drained and defeated by the whole thing, just wanting your old life back, and unsure how to plan your future any more, with your new travelling companion now having to be factored in. How can you accept a promotion if it's going to involve giving presentations to clients and there's a danger you might have an attack in front of them? How can you go abroad if you might get one far away from home, or if the flight was a couple of hours long? How could you go ahead with a pregnancy before the panic had ceased?

The collateral damage at this point can be profound. Sufferers begin to withdraw, feeling overwhelmed by the daily onslaught of fear. Many will cut out socialising, since hot pubs and crowded restaurants can trigger attacks, and they feel more vulnerable to having attacks the day after a night out. Leisure pursuits can become a thing of the past, since exercise can bring on attacks for some. Relationships go downhill as too many restrictions now have to be placed on a couple's activities, and you may even avoid sex as it can act as a trigger. Work standards may deteriorate, as your concentration wanes, and sick days become more frequent, causing many to worry for the future. Substance abuse is common, which brings its own set of problems. You're living life with the flag only at half-mast.

The right psychotherapist can teach you the appropriate skills to control attacks while you look at the reasons behind the attacks, and your mind's reaction to them, for example:

- Physical threats such as accidents, assaults, operations, out-of body experiences, burn-out.
- Emotional threats such as bereavement, betrayal, bullying, rejection, a broken heart.
- Mental threats such as drug-induced changes in perception, or the terrifying experience of the flashbacks, memory lapses, and hallucinations which can accompany post-traumatic stress syndrome.
- Social changes of status, such as those following unemployment, redundancy, financial ruin, divorce or public humiliation.

PORTRAIT OF POST-TRAUMATIC STRESS DISORDER – TAKEN OVER BY THE REPTILIAN RESPONSE

This disorder has many faces. Classically it may develop in the aftermath of experiencing (or witnessing) a traumatic, life-threatening event to which your response was intense fear, helplessness or horror. Road traffic accidents, plane crashes, violent assaults, rape, natural disasters, war, etc. are all common triggers. Such life threatening events can leave a death imprint.

It can also result from feelings of helplessness and utter lack of control in the face of wilful traumas such as torture and sexual abuse, which relate to a death of another kind — soul death. The growing phenomenon of bullying and harassment in the school and workplace, with its associated prolonged duress, is also a frequent cause.

Fear of death is instinctive. Every living organism has an inbuilt avoidance reflex which is triggered by life-threatening situations. It is a protective survival response whose function is to keep us alive and safe from harm, a carry-over from our reptilian ancestry.

In the core of the human brain is the ancient limbic or 'reptilian' nervous tissue. It's millions of years old but is still a major player. When it needs to, it has the power to override the programmes of the newer parts of the brain, principally the neocortex, the seat of rational, logical thought and self-awareness.

When we're confronted with a life-threatening situation this reptile part instantaneously propels us, using the innate emotions of rage and fear, into the fight-flight response, as happens in panic. This emergency response is automatic and involuntary; a reflex. It's independent of will, and once instinctively turned on it cannot be turned off by will alone.

Once the trauma is over, this part of the brain shifts its focus to the future, to make you more aware of danger, to sharpen your survival reactions and in so doing prevent a possible recurrence. It does this by repeatedly rerunning the traumatic event in your waking mind and in our dreamworld, like a security video, in an effort to scan every detail. It's looking for any possible slip-up in your attention which may have initially exposed you to the trauma. The 'video' will continue running in your mind night and day, also reminding you of the feelings you experienced at the time. These emotionally charged images won't stop until your reptile brain is satisfied that the 'higher levels' have got the message and that safety measures have been put in place:

- Hypervigilant, your adrenaline running high, you're on guard and wary all the time. Suspicious and paranoid you blow things out of proportion. Panic is never far away. You often feel your heart racing and your breathing laboured, and you sweat profusely. Your muscles can go into tension spasms. Tremors are common.

- You startle easily, jumping in alarm to a sudden sound such as a door banging or the phone ringing.One of the first casualties is sleep, which is also one of the last things to return to normal. This causes extreme fatigue and allows no let-up from the constant barrage of mental imagery. Your mind is in 'on mode' all the time.

- Intrusive vivid images of the event haunt you, replaying the trauma over and over without mercy. Such is their intensity that you feel as if you've been catapulted back into the initial trauma and are experiencing it for the first time. These flashbacks can occur when least expected. Jim, who survived a road traffic accident, would find himself at his desk or at the dinner table clinging to an imaginary steering wheel, urgently honking the horn and shouting 'Get back on your own side, get back on your own side!' His mind was literally reliving the head-on collision in which his girlfriend was killed.

- This persistent rerunning of traumatic events on your screen of perception is comparable to a Vietnam veteran, newly returned from the front, being repeatedly compelled to watch the horrific opening scenes of the war movie *Saving Private*

Ryan. Every rerun re-opens the original trauma, and what is so frightening and despairing is that they can't be voluntarily stopped. You get frustrated trying to explain to others how something in the past could still be so real in the present. Months later smells, sounds and tactile sensations may remain vivid and disturbing. Three years on Steve, a policeman serving with a rapid response unit, could still smell the gunpowder of a Kalashnikov rifle which was discharged at him at close range.

- Nightmares destroy your sleep and can be so terrifying that you eventually dread the moment when you close your eyes. You regularly wake soaked in sweat and in the middle of a panic attack. Bizarre sleep patterns become the norm, and sleep deprivation is common.

- Avoidance strategies. In a desperate effort to control your escalating anxiety levels you avoid everything associated with the event. You try not to talk about it, and you avoid the scene of the trauma or any reminders of it, such as television programmes. If you've survived a car crash you'll postpone driving. If you've been raped, having sex can trigger a flashback.

- Emotionally you're on a roller coaster. You experience the full spectrum – panic, anger and rage, episodes of crying and sadness. Feelings of hopelessness and despair become the norm. As a result, being in the company of others becomes an extra stress because of the unpredictable and trigger-hair nature of your emotional outbursts. Ordinary life is merely a memory. Suicide passes through your mind – 'I don't want to be here'.

- Paranormal experiences that occurred at the time of the traumatic event are difficult to make sense of, and therefore your mind is drawn to them. Such experiences include time standing still (where the traumatic events happen in slow motion), apparitions and visions of dead loved ones, 'out of body' and 'near death' experiences. From a viewpoint outside your body you may have felt that you were looking down on yourself while trapped in a car, on the operating table, or in the process of being attacked. It's as though you were watching a drama unfolding in which you were the main player. While being raped at knifepoint in the back of a car, Jean remembers looking down on herself and at the same time being comforted by her dead grandmother, who held her in her arms, whispering over and over, 'You'll be OK, you'll be OK'.

- The near-death experience has the added distinction of the sensation of moving up a tunnel, at the end of which is a white light, perceived as being the next life. There, you may have met dead relatives or heard a voice from the earth plane calling you back. While being wheeled into an operating theatre with multiple injuries, David felt that he was dying. He experienced himself travelling up a tunnel and emerging into a light-filled area. It was like a 'football stadium full of spirits' with his dead relatives standing at the entrance. He was deeply upset that his mother, to whom he had been so close, instead of welcoming him said, 'Go back, your time hasn't come'.

- Shutdown and shock. It can seem as though you're looking at life from behind a glass pane. A state of emergency reigns. You may feel totally dislodged or fractured from your usual ways of thinking, feeling and behaving. Normality has disappeared. You feel alienated, split-off, de-skilled, dazed and anxious. You wonder if you're mad. Your work, leisure and family life are turned upside down.

- You live in parallel universes — your ordinary life and your extraordinary inner world. Because you're in emergency mode, you can focus on nothing else but the trauma and what will become of you. As a result of not being fully present, you have trouble with your short-term memory, your attention span is limited and poor concentration is the norm. Inevitably you make mistakes and lose confidence in your ability to carry out simple tasks. You start to feel stupid as names are forgotten, car keys are lost, conversations become difficult to follow and routine tasks require more focus than you're capable of. Your inner movie constantly distracts you.

- Emotional numbing. You may find that after six months or more, in an effort to dampen down your emotional distress, you unconsciously anaesthetise your feelings. You 'numb out'. Feeling as if you're in limbo, like the walking dead, you merely go through the motions of living. You neither express emotion nor register the feelings of others. This state of suspended animation can be extremely distressing for those around you, making them angry and concerned as you become ever more unreachable. 'He's in his own world and has tuned out what's going on around him. A train could pass through the house and he wouldn't notice!'

- Collateral damage. Another way of numbing your pain and inducing sleep is to use alcohol and other substances. As you increasingly withdraw into your own world, your relationships suffer, deadlines cease to exist and problems at work arise. Now chronically awash with adrenaline, suspicion and paranoia increasingly alienate you from others. In order to distract yourself, you keep frantically busy and on the run from the feelings and images which flood in as soon as you stop. Out of character behaviour such as gambling and promiscuity can begin. Feeling you've nothing to lose, you might engage in reckless behaviours and expose yourself to unnecessary risks. Jeff Bridges' character, who survived an air disaster in the film *Fearless* is a good example of a PTSD sufferer. He balanced on the ledge of a tall building, jay-walked through fast-flowing traffic, drove his car into a wall and ate food he knew he was dangerously allergic to.

- You feel misunderstood by others. Much to your surprise, sympathy and support for your difficulties is time-limited and starts to wane. A recognised ritual exists in traumas such as bereavement, whereby support is given immediately and recognition of the impact acknowledged. Flowers, cards, phone calls and practical help follow. There are no similar rituals in place for the post-traumatised individual, who can feel ignored and rejected. After a number of weeks questions may be asked of you, like 'When will things settle back to normal?' and 'Shouldn't you be back in the saddle by now?' Subtle innuendoes are made which have a judgemental air about them. 'He looks fine and he's able to mow the lawn, why isn't he back at work?' It may be inferred that you're 'playing it up', 'malingering' or 'milking the system'.

- Socially you withdraw, fearing the judgement of others. Now it's easier to avoid situations where you might have to explain yourself. Doors aren't answered, phone calls aren't taken and you start living like a recluse. Bitterness and cynicism may set in. If you had your way you would hide away in some isolated sanctuary. There you would be free to eat and sleep when you wanted, act out your distress without concerning others and have no responsibilities.

- Past the heal-by date. As the months and years roll by, you're shocked that normality hasn't returned yet. 'How can it take so long.' You become increasingly frustrated and impatient with the healing time-frame. A beautiful insight into this was unfolded in the book and film *The Horse Whisperer*, the story of a post-traumatically-stressed horse named Pilgrim, who was brought to a horse whisperer for healing. The owners of the horse, on pressing the horse whisperer for a definitive heal-by date were always greeted with his knowing reply:

'that depends on Pilgrim'. He acknowledged the unique nature of the horse and its healing time-frame, which could only be assisted but not hurried. Impatience had no place here.

- Grief eclipsed. Your anxiety can be so much in the foreground, and your mind in such turmoil, that there's often no room for grieving for what has been lost. This could be the loss of a physical function through disability, of loved ones who died in the same trauma, or of your career and financial earning power. You may sense a dam-burst of grief awaiting when the mental spin-cycle stops.

- The problem of the 'extra piece'. You know you'll never be the same again. You're like Humpty Dumpty falling off the wall, breaking into hundreds of pieces. On attempting to rebuild yourself you find extra pieces, which means that your life can not be rebuilt in exactly the same way again. The pieces of the traumatic experience are just too different to be incorporated. Where before you may have fitted hand in glove into a relationship or a working life, now you may feel at odds, sensing that there's a mismatch.

- Fear of stigma. You may be the kind of person who has always been wary of psychoactive medication, and the last place you ever imagined ending up in was a psychiatric hospital. Suggestions that you need one or the other can be terrifying, confirming your worst fears that you're going mad.

PORTRAIT OF OBSESSIVE-COMPULSIVE DISORDER

You feel permanently caught in a web of dread. You fear that you may, for instance, contaminate others with the germs you carry on your hands, in your nose, in your saliva and even on your clothes. You imagine that you've picked up these germs from toilet seats, door handles, money, handshakes, etc., and can subsequently pass them on, causing serious illness. With such thoughts in place cleansing rituals evolve. You become obsessed with washing. Avoidance rituals are a compulsion, such as using a hand-kerchief on a doorknob, turning taps on with your elbows, and taking care to avoid body contact at all costs.

Elaborate, inconvenient and time-consuming behaviours fill your days. You might go so far as to believe that, while you yourself may not have AIDS, you are a carrier. Therefore you will take elaborate steps not to contaminate others through sneez-ing, hand-shaking, etc. These convictions are to your mind ab-solute and not open to contradiction.

Other forms of safety-conscious thoughts are common. You may have doubts that electrical and gas appliances have been left on, windows and doors left unlocked and taps running. The list is endless, and your checking behaviours always need to be repeated. The simple routine of leaving your house for work, or to do a school run, can consume hours of time and become hell for yourself and those around you. The execution of a morning ritual means you have to get up at the crack of dawn. This is in-comprehensible to others who cannot appreciate that these rituals must be performed to your satisfaction before you can leave the house. Anyone who lives with an OCD sufferer is a worthy nominee for the Nobel prize for patience!

Sometimes superstitious thoughts predominate. If things aren't done in a particular sequence, such as getting out of bed, dressing and walking downstairs in a specified way, you are con-vinced that there will be disastrous consequences, most com-monly for the well-being of others. This exaggerated sense of duty and responsibility towards the safety of others can even extend to the notion that you've knocked someone down in your car. This means that you have to drive back over the route any number of times, or frantically phone the local accident and emergency department hoping and praying that an ambulance hasn't attended an accident on your particular stretch of road.

The sinking of the Titanic involved many variables, no one

of which was entirely responsible, but all played a part. Similarly, the mindset behind OCD is multicausal and incredibly complex.

Any of us in the grip of fear, doubt and mental turmoil can find comfort and appeasement in behaviours such as de-cluttering the garage, cleaning out cupboards, washing floors and generally engaging in tidying and cleansing activities, sometimes for days at a time. The Japanese would call this a Feng Shui of the mind. Order in the midst of chaos can give someone a psychological foothold from which to operate.

The present-day mindset for some OCD sufferers may have evolved from sexual or physical abuse in childhood, as the child's only way of 'rationalising' the traumatic event. The carrying-out of compulsive behaviours helps move them away from fear and chaos, in the direction of control and safety. Anorexia is unquestionably a variant of OCD with its mental addiction to calorie counting and weight monitoring, and its behavioural equivalents, vomiting and purging with laxatives. Underlying many cases is a history of sexual abuse in childhood and an avoidance of sexuality in adult life.

One distinct form of OCD, whose rituals are played out entirely at the mental level, involves no external behaviour. Even so, these obsessions can be even more depressing, energy-draining and time-consuming than other forms. Nonetheless, they still illicit feelings of shame, disgust, anxiety and the same sense of wrongdoing. Suddenly sufferers see horrific, depraved and shocking images in their mind's eye, which can take the form of mutilated bodies, decaying corpses, bestial sexual acts and bloody acts of violence. They see themselves as active players in inappropriate behaviours like blasphemous acts in public places, or gang rape.

Such is the life-like and overwhelming nature of these images and the anxiety they provoke that sufferers urgently need to neutralise them somehow. These emergencies demand complex, often mind-boggling, distracting manoeuvres. Running alternative mental images of a soothing nature, engaging in complicated mathematical calculations and playing mental scrabble afford relief.

THE OCD MINDSET – WRITTEN IN STONE

• There is a focus on wrong-doing, which reflects a black-and-white moralistic view of themselves and the world, usually learned within the family home. No shades of grey are tolerated, and everything is divided into good and bad, right and wrong.

• A punishment orientation emerges from such moralistic beginnings. Badness must be punished and the label 'good' is only earned following designated acts. It is not uncommon for sufferers to have experienced inquisitions held by parents, with the child being treated as a virtual criminal over some minor misdemeanour which another family would ignore. These children's lives became ruled by clauses – shoulds, musts, have-tos – and conditions before they could feel intrinsically good or deserving. Thoughts from an early age might include, 'Have I done the right thing? Am I going to be blamed for something? Will I be punished?' It's difficult for them not to grow into fastidious, rigid, perfectionist, self-critical, over-responsible, guilt-ridden and shameful people. Their life is full of trip wires.

• A trigger hair arousal of guilt and shame exists – as does a distorted relationship with pleasure, spontaneity and often sex. Pleasure has to be deserved, earned and is certainly not allowed spontaneously. Every pleasurable experience goes through the filter of good/bad, right/wrong, and a detailed internal analysis made of it. Sex is number one on the hit list. Normal exploratory sex acts like masturbation may be interpreted by such a child as being perverted, shameful, sinful and a further example of their flawed make-up.

- A vigilance exists relative to the well-being of others and a heightened sense of responsibility and duty towards them. This others-first focus is ever present and OCD sufferers are always concerned whether they're injuring or harming others. This anxiety spreads into their work; for example an electrician may believe that he has wired a house incorrectly. Still others believe they will cause harm by stabbing someone dear to them with a sharp implement, strangling a child in their care or punching someone standing beside them in a bar.

- Being accustomed to punishment, following a 'bad act', as a form of atonement, a child now becomes conditioned to penalising themselves. They will automatically devise their own appropriate penance so that the scales are balanced. Some children will say extra prayers, deliberately avoid food they like, try to be extra helpful around the house and promise themselves that they will never ever repeat the behaviour. In this way the guilt subsides and they begin to feel like a 'good child' again.

- Self-blame. Where there is any doubt as to the wrongs of a situation, they will automatically assume that they are at fault. This comes from a basic sense of badness or unworthiness within them. This is such a core habit that it seems to cancel out sources of merit that they could draw from, such as achievements in their work and family life.

- Mistrust of their own perceptions. 'No, no, that's not what you saw; no, you don't feel angry; no, your sister didn't mean it; no, that's not what happened; no, you have made that up; no, you must be dreaming; no, your father would never do that ...' If this is the feedback that a child gets, they begin to mistrust themselves, presuming others, and in particular adults, are always right. When they themselves are adults and there is no monitoring parent present, they devise checking rituals to decide if their perceptions are right or wrong, such is their implicit doubt. They need to know if a wrong-doing has occurred and therefore needs to be atoned for. This tragic cycle squeezes out freewill, joy, spontaneity and pleasure.

- An intolerable rise in tension levels occurs if there is a question of having done wrong. OCD behaviours can be seen as an addiction. Like all addictions they go through a recognisable cycle of feeling the tension rising, doing a certain behaviour that provides the 'fix' and experiencing a temporary relief until the cycle begins again.

- Secrecy. Given their sensitivity to guilt and shame and their belief that others are always right, as children these individuals are unlikely to report an abusive event, and as adults are unlikely to share their inner turmoil with anyone. This fosters a sense of isolation and alienation.

- Depression. The unforgiving unrelenting treadmill of OCD guarantees an appalling quality of life, with burnout, despair and hopelessness a reflection of the sheer inability to sustain the required energy levels.

TREATMENT AND MANAGEMENT

All these serious disorders are treatable in the context of a psychotherapeutic approach. Working with a psychotherapist specifically trained in these areas is crucial, one who has a firm grasp of the physiological mechanisms underpinning fear. Specific adrenaline-lowering techniques can be learned, and provide the platform for examining those issues which created the turbulence within you in the first place, be they current or a carry-over from times past.

The treatment of PTSD and OCD are outlined in specific detail in our other book *Going Mad?*

It is beyond the scope of this book to address fully the treatment and management of panic. This is done in detail in Áine Tubridy's book *When Panic Attacks*.

CHAPTER 8

Manic Depression – What Goes Up Must Come Down

There is a line drawn in the sand between those who experience manic depression and the more usual forms of depression. Much mystique surrounds the experience of elation, and this is understandable. How is it possible that an individual in the prime of their life, with all the external trappings of normality in place, suddenly finds themselves experiencing superhuman amounts of energy, which drive them relentlessly, without sleep? Like a person on a mission, they become insatiable for social contact and avenues for their escalating ideas, contrive fantastical 'big picture' projects which they feel convinced will jettison them to fame and fortune, or at the very least will present to the world the 'grand solution' to many of its problems.

Within weeks, such a person finds themselves in a psychiatric hospital, their life in shreds, and with family and friends feeling bewildered and confused. The future has taken an entirely different depressing flavour; gone are the confidence, the powerful energy, the grandiosity, the great plans of the preceding weeks. And most depressing is the fact that there is huge collateral damage to repair – the swathe of destruction wreaked during their manic episode. In addition they have to make sense of their diagnosis, the news that they are suffering from a mental illness, a disease of the brain, which will require a lifetime on medication, with no guarantee that it can prevent further episodes occurring.

How can they engage with such an uncertain future, where overnight their entire identity, how they and others see them,

has evaporated, only to be replaced by some alien 'patient' identity? This rock-bottom state is the stuff of a serious emotional
crisis or depression. This depression should be called post-elation depression, a normal emotional response to the situation
they are in, and not the 'tail end' of the disease known as manic
depression or bipolar illness.

Because this end-state depression, and the mania which
preceded it, are seen as inseparable processes which are the ultimate result of a disease of the brain, no attention need be given
to any other possible initiating causes. Diverted by the sick-
brain model, few pay attention to the primary cause, the emotional triggers preceding the mania, which are a reflection of a
stress or predicament placing a strain on the personality one has
in place. Instead the focus is on biochemical shifts, defective
genes and medication regimes, all secondary phenomena. Would
it make sense to repair a series of crashed cars, driven by the
same driver, over and over, without ever asking why he keeps
crashing them? Relevant questions must be asked such as: Has
the driver been drinking? Has he passed his driving test? Is he
driving too fast? Trying to kill himself? Does it always occur on
exactly the same spot in the road? One point is clear. The car is
not the source of the problem. The problem is the consciousness
behind the wheel.

This broken machine model clearly cannot work since it
marginalises the unique contribution of each person's mindset,
value system, life experiences, vulnerabilities, special gifts and
talents, socio-economic status, level of responsibility, support
systems, relationships, and the place in which they find themselves along their life plan as mind-body-spirit organisms. In
short, while there is some commonality with respect to symptoms, no two manic depressives are the same as far as causality
goes, which is always personal to each.

MANIC RESPONSES
Certain stressful contexts contain the ingredients to provoke the manic response in some individuals.

DEFENCE AGAINST FAILURE
For some, mania can be seen as an unconscious defence against an imminent failure, a manoeuvre to essentially avoid, deny and escape from acknowledging an imminent set-back, disappointment or failure – events which are so much a part of everyday life for the rest of us. Feeling ordinary, vulnerable and out of control are not part of this person's everyday mindset. Their leaning is towards being extraordinary, invulnerable and on top. Uncomfortable with the down position, as the elation gathers momentum they will distort any evidence that a problem is on the horizon, instead overcompensating in the opposite direction. With the elation in full flight, their last-ditch efforts to pull it off in the face of all objective evidence to the contrary are legendary. These denial behaviours are akin to rearranging the deckchairs on the sinking *Titanic*, encouraging the band to play their hearts out while they keep the champagne flowing!

Richard, a thirty-eight-year-old, highly successful property developer, with a reputation for arrogance and risk-taking, lived a high-flying palatial life. He owned homes in many fashionable parts of the world, and lived in a magnificent mansion with stables in Kildare. He was part of the hunting and polo set, and moved with the rich and famous. The golden boy in a family of girls, he went to the best schools, achieving some acclaim as a sportsman and debater, then made his entrepreneurial debut at a young age, taking up the mantle from his father. Lacking his father's tack and political savvy, he threw his weight around and refused to compromise and play the political game. In this way he made enemies in high places.

He did not see his Waterloo coming when he overextended himself on a huge property deal and the banks threatened to foreclose. In a state of elation, refusing to take any advice, and make the obvious financial steps, he instead took off to the Epson Derby with a party of friends where he backed a number of winners. Convinced now that his luck had turned he hit the town. Fielding frantic calls from his wife and business associates, he took up residence in the Ritz. He started entertaining round the clock, set up business meetings and planned a merger with one of the biggest property developers in London, believing that if he pulled this deal off his troubles at home would be sorted. The way forward was now clear – he would move his offices to London, and relocate his family. Newly-inspired, he partied on, full of energy, and getting no sleep. Reaching for the moon, he felt nothing could stop him now.

He became a caricature of himself, pompous, loud and aggressive, and filled with an air of triumphalism. Following a series of complaints from other guests about the noise in his suite, he had an ugly show-down with the hotel manager, insisting that his consortium was in the process of buying the hotel and that the manager would be fired when that happened. When the police arrived he was standing on the reception desk inviting other guests to the bar where, as the new owner, the drinks were on him. He was eventually taken to the Maudsley hospital where he was involuntarily detained.

THE EUREKA EXPERIENCE

Some individuals, consumed by an intensely intellectual project or piece of research, working marathon hours, their brain turbo-charged and exhilarated by the implications of their findings, without the brake that downtime provides, enter into a phase of sleep deprivation which opens the door to an altered state – mania. They now become mind-blown by the immense impor-

tance of their work, seeing its interconnectedness to the wider world, and how it could influence the future of mankind for the better. Obsessed now by the implications of their 'discovery', they are high and think of nothing else, talking to anyone who will listen, and soliciting support from the influential and powerful. Criticism is brushed off and condescendingly interpreted as ignorance. Seeing themselves now as a messenger of great good, they feel divinity and righteousness to be on their side.

Sylvia, a twenty-five-year-old PhD student in sociology, was completing her thesis on an aspect of group dynamics. She was behind schedule and it was now absorbing her totally, day and night. Particularly exciting to her was the notion that in any group, certain members had a predisposition to feel and express the thoughts and feelings unconsciously held by other members. This, she felt, had huge implications on the world political stage, for those in leadership roles and in the area of conflict resolution. She formed a theory that if leaders could be made conscious of this fact their power to influence people would be unlimited. This insight directed her towards a study of famous political and religious leaders. Day after day, holed up in her flat, unable to sleep with excitement, eating little, and not communicating with anybody, she read voraciously, spent hours on the internet and made copious notes.

Her first outing in months was to be bridesmaid at her sister's wedding. She arrived bursting with energy, engaging people vivaciously, but her over-the-top excitement was passed off as wedding-related. Finally, unable to contain herself any longer, she used her bridesmaid's speech as an opportunity to launch on the stunned but receptive guests her theory of mass influence. She was reluctant to stop speaking, in spite of interventions by her family. When the best man instructed the band to begin playing, she grabbed the microphone from the singer and continued on, passionately insisting on her message reaching as many people as possible as it had implications for world peace. Arguing, screaming and wrestling with anyone who tried to stop her, she was bundled into a side room and a doctor called, who had her admitted to a psychiatric hospital.

THE SPIRITUAL OPENING

The spiritual experiences had in the past by ascetics, monks, prophets and other religious devotees, followed a consciously sought 'communing with God' breakthrough. This was facilitated by long periods of fasting, meditation, isolation and sleep deprivation. The state they reached was in essence a psychotic experience, an altered state of consciousness of a transcendental nature. The cultural context at the time was accepting of their revelations, genuinely seeing them as divine messengers, if not divinity itself. Let's not forget that Buddha, Jesus and Mohammed experienced visions and insights into their life purpose, in such deliberately created settings.

In modern times some individuals suffering from mania, experience spiritual openings in environments where the focus is on their inner journey, such as during meditation retreats and intensive personal development workshops. It is not uncommon for ordinary people to return from places like Medjugorje, Machu Picchu, Lourdes and other vortices of such concentrated spiritual energy with an expanded sense of their place in the grand scheme of things, and in a state of manic elation.

David, a forty-one-year-old managing director of a public relations company, joined his wife in Medjugorje, where she had gone with their only child Sarah, aged twelve, who was suffering from muscular dystrophy and had been in a wheelchair for a year. Being a non-practising Catholic for many years, and really only there in solidarity with his wife, he was surprised to find

LIAM DELANEY.

that the energy of the place inspired him. He embraced every ritual with great enthusiasm – from night-time candlelit vigils, to prayer meetings, to the outdoor celebration of masses, to hours spent in silent prayer.

In the church where the Blessed Virgin is believed to appear on a regular basis, during a mass, he became aware of a golden light filling the church and auras like halos of different colours around members of the congregation. Waiting in line to receive holy communion, with his daughter in her wheelchair, he suddenly felt drawn to place both his hands on the crown of her head. As if like a bolt of lightning, he felt a huge force coming through his head, down his arms, and into his hands. He began to shake uncontrollably and could not remove them. Although frightened, he was relieved to find that his daughter was enraptured by the experience, and had a beatified smile on her face. The entire event lasted a minute, and afterwards he asked his wife to take over and left the church feeling very confused and disorientated. Reluctant to risk a repeat of the experience, he did not attend any more ceremonies and unable to sleep, wandered the town at night.

On his return to Ireland, still not sleeping, and finding it hard to re-engage with work, he took a few weeks off, and began to spend more time with his daughter, who he felt had benefited by the entire experience in Medjugorje. One morning he decided to bring her to mass in their local church where, once again, as he was waiting in line, the experience of a bolt of energy running through him occurred. Later at home, in an excited state he informed his wife and daughter that these high energy experiences meant that he was a spiritual healer, with the power of Jesus Christ acting through him. He told them that he would be leaving his job to pursue this important mission.

For the next couple of weeks he was rarely seen at home. Living rough and walking in his bare feet through the streets of

Dublin, he was eventually found, penniless, having given away his money and credit cards to the homeless. This precipitated his first admission to hospital.

DRUG-INDUCED MANIA

Over thirty per cent of individuals diagnosed with manic depression follow from the use of street drugs such as amphetamine, cocaine, crack and some hallucinogenic substances. (Antidepressant medication also, because of its stimulant effect, is capable of triggering an episode of mania in some individuals.)

Sophie, a twenty-two-year-old aspiring model, hung around the edges of the 'It' crowd, partied every weekend, and started to use cocaine regularly. She found that it gave her energy, suppressed her appetite, enhanced her libido, and made her extrovert and confident. She became the darling of the designers and fashionist as and her career took off. Enjoying her newly found celebrity status, she appeared at every premier, attended all their parties, and became the trophy every man wanted to be seen with. In such circles she found the supply of cocaine unlimited, but started to stockpile her own in case her source ever dried up. Day and night blurred, and weekend party bashes began to spill over into the working week. Now she was consuming up to six grams of cocaine a day which she needed in order to function. Because she was such a successful model verging on the supermodel status, allowances were made for her petulant cantankerousness, frequent late starts, and her flippant approach to her work.

At a weekend country house birthday party hosted by a rock musician, cocaine was falling like snow and she snorted more than usual. Suddenly she experienced a rush of unprecedented energy and power and became imbued with the sense that she was the diva of all divas, the re-incarnation of the sex goddess Marilyn Monroe herself. Monopolising the dance-floor, she openly

began a seductive titillation of the male company, seeking particularly to impress her host with her 'Happy Birthday Mr Rock
Star' song. On finding that he has already been solicited away
by a young wannabe model, she stormed off the floor in search
of him, burst into his bedroom, and attacked the girl viciously,
striking her with her stiletto heel. Having been pulled away, she
ranted around the house breaking windows with anything that
she could find. Bundled into a car, she rapidly found herself being
delivered home to her flat in the early hours of the morning.
She immediately called every newspaper and media contact that
she had, informing them that she would hold a press conference
later that day at which she would tell the world that she was in
fact Marilyn Monroe. Her agent arranged her hospitalisation.

REFLECTION

The sick-brain model of mania focuses on the effect (the symptoms) rather than the causal context, particularly in the first
three of these types. It can be no other way, once the cause is
understood as a disease process, a defect in the hardware of the
brain. Within such a model the treatment would be the same for
all four; psychotherapy would not be thought relevant, nor personality a factor to be addressed, notwithstanding all the other
existential issues in a person's life.

A PORTRAIT OF MANIA

For the purposes of understanding the natural timeline of a
manic episode, we have decided to focus on the classic type, which
forms the largest group, namely the defence against failure.

THE PREDICAMENT ON THE HORIZON

The pre-manic years are relatively trouble free. No shrinking
violets, mania-sufferers are more often high achievers, socially
skilled, confident, proactive, competitive and familiar with suc-

cess. They are good all-rounders and some may well be voted by their class as being the 'most likely to succeed'. Because of this apparent head start they enter the world of work full of promise. The first sign of a psychological hiccup can come therefore as a total shock to patient and family alike. Their game plan for the future was one of continued success! To return to the analogy of the *Titanic*, their predicted life seemed unsinkable and lifeboats were never dreamed of.

How they appear to others is important to them: the public gaze, material things, getting ahead, and the need for power and approval is crucial to their identity. They are often larger than life, the life and soul of the party and are well liked. Their bonhomie and extroverted nature attracts people to them. When it comes to having their own needs met, they expect doors to be opened for them and see no reason why they should not be facilitated.

They expect others to give their all and share enthusiastically in their dreams and visions. If challenged on practicalities they become annoyed, impatient and frustrated. Familiar with the 'high horse' position, they can if obstructed ride rough-shod over colleagues, family and friends. A setback is not on their agenda. At all costs they are survivors.

When a setback occurs, the predicament it throws up will illicit an exaggerated response in this pre-manic group. While others may sympathise with them, few appreciate the depth and intensity of their newly-felt vulnerable feelings as their ego is challenged for the first time. Typical setbacks might include missing a promotion, a failed business investment or any perceived experience where losing face in public is an ingredient. What would be experienced as a minor obstacle to others becomes an earthquake to them in psychological terms. It's as though they have put everything, even their very personhood, on the line. The reverberations are huge, and the setback proves too much for their system to integrate.

Rather than experience feelings of failure, the incoming evidence is rejected and distorted by the mania mindset, and the blame for setbacks is located elsewhere. They contrive explanations which free them from any personal responsibility. They bend the truth. Reasons and rationalisations are dragged up to offload the responsibility for failure. This has the unfortunate consequence that the core problem is never addressed and the slide downwards continues. A point is inevitably reached where denial can no longer hide the reality of the situation, and they are forced to acknowledge that a failure is imminent. When the dam burst occurs and the truth of the situation is no longer avoidable, the personal lie starts to break down.

There are recognisable phases to the manic process akin to the launching of a rocket into space, its orbiting and its return, re-entry, crash landing and fall out.

THE LAUNCH PAD
Staring failure in the face, mania-sufferers move rapidly in the opposite direction, back to the success end of the success–failure spectrum. In this way they impress upon themselves and try to impress upon others that they are still in control, proving this by overcompensating.

There is a noticeable speeding up of thoughts and behaviours. Subjectively they feel a surge of energy, power and invincibility. It's as if they have become the Greek character, Sisyphus, who has suddenly found the extra strength to push the boulder over the ridge of the mountain and down the other side, finally freeing himself from repeated failures. There is an air of triumphalism: anything is possible!

This is the stage where a psychotic break has not yet occurred but is about to. It is an exaggerated and magnified version of themselves in top form, a caricature. As they move closer to the launch pad, the possibility of aborting the mission rapidly fades.

LAUNCH-PAD SYMPTOMS

- Unstoppable rapid-fire speech, full of inflated high-sounding rhetoric. They are incapable of listening.
- 'Eureka' ideas. They get light-bulb insights, which they are convinced would provide a blanket solution for past misjudgements and mistakes. They set up meetings, make phone calls, and send faxes and e-mails towards this end. An example might be attempting to recruit the support of Bill Gates in person to invest in and to save their company from liquidation.
- The Holy Grail and other quests. They may become passionate adventurers, heading off for example to the pyramids of Egypt, to white-water raft in New Zealand or to find a guru in India.
- Sleeplessness. Their mind is never still, racing thoughts and flights of ideas is the order of the day and night. This, coupled with enhanced energy, interferes with their sleep pattern, reducing it to one or two hours a night. 'I have too much to do to waste my time sleeping'. This can reach the stage where they literally don't shut an eye for days at a time, in some cases for weeks.
- Time urgency. They get impatient at the pace at which things move and want everything to be done yesterday.
- Short fuse. There is an anger and irritability when challenged and criticised about their behaviours. They don't suffer fools easily, are impossible to reason with, and strenuously resist the restraints of normal life.
- On the town. There is a sense that 'I deserve the best'. Money is spent on clothes, presents, nights on the town, champagne, a new car, a foreign trip.
- God's gift to women and men. Both sexes who are on the launch pad can become sexually uninhibited and engage in amorous one-night stands.

- Political incorrectness. This can range from telling the wrong jokes to the wrong people, making sexual passes at people they would never in their wildest dreams have any interest in, such as their neighbour, an in-law or the boss' wife. This form of promiscuity has no gender difference.

LIFTING OFF INTO ORBIT

The die is cast. The dice is rolling. An unstoppable energetic and chemical shift is underway. Their metabolism is turbo-charged and their consciousness is so single-minded, passionate and goal-orientated that it will not be deflected. They feel fantastic and 'on top of the moon', hence the association with the term elation (which comes from the Latin *efferre* meaning to lift up, inspire with pride, lift the spirits of, or to feel exalted and lofty).

Lift-off is recognised by a total loss of contact with consensus reality, as they assume an alternative persona. This role usually has a grandiose quality to it, giving sufferers a sense of power, success, confidence, and a feeling that everything is going really well and that they are in full control. They become super-fixers with God-like powers, and believe that they are the custodians of the solutions that humanity has been waiting for, such as Third World economic programmes, global conflict resolutions, scientific discoveries, and breakthroughs in medical science.

Others believe that they have extraordinary talents in the area of music, acting, film, as yet undiscovered by the entertainment world. Like a good method actor they take on the persona that best fits the furthest-out dimensions of their prior personality and live this role around the clock. They have entered the megalomaniac stage (from the Greek word *megas*, meaning great or very large).

LIFT-OFF SYMPTOMS

• Increasing distance. The gap widens between their reality and that held by those around them. This gives rise to reciprocal frustration, irritability, angry outbursts and a total breakdown of normal communication and relationships.

• The loss of a personal censor. Anything goes: 'I will not be stopped, and no one is going to stand in my way.' There is a refusal to be censored by the outside. Threats such as loss of job, collapse of relationship, suspension of credit and legal interventions all fall on deaf ears.

• Hostile behaviours. With the combination of time urgency, grandiosity and their conviction that the end justifies the means, support is extorted to validate their views which are patently obvious to others as ludicrous.

• Conspiracy theories abound. This provides a logical explanation to them as to why they are not being facilitated with urgent meetings, financial support and public acclaim: 'Those that are not with me are against me.'

• Hitting the wall. As in the old proverb, they have given themselves enough rope to hang themselves and the noose begins to tighten. Spouses, children and friends withdraw. Financial resources dry up and all credibility collapses. Lack of sleep, excessive substance abuse, inadequate diet, erratic routines, emotional turmoil from ongoing conflict, begin to take their toll on their energy reserves.

• Hospitalisation. Inevitably there comes a time when long-suffering relatives reach their limit, and decide that in the individual's own interest the best thing that could happen to them is something akin to a shot from a tranquillising gun. There is general agreement among onlookers that the cycle has to stop. This may mean that they are coerced or involuntarily committed into a psychiatric institution.

RE-ENTRY AND CRASH LANDING – POST-ELATION DEPRESSION

- Energy bankruptcy. Metabolically there are insufficient reserves to deal with the overwhelming demands at this time. The batteries are now flat and biochemically they are in a state of metabolic burn-out. Sleep deprivation, lack of food, substance abuse and the relentless chaotic activity has created a toxic state from which the individual now needs to recuperate.

- Psychoactive medication. This is used to bring the manic phase to a close. It does so by slowing the metabolism, reducing the manic thoughts and the hyperactivity. Essentially the initial phases of medication act as sleep therapy. The restoration of sleep reduces the hypersensitivity of the nervous system to the amine family of mind-brain chemicals (i.e., adrenaline and serotonin, the struggle-striving hormones). This allows the choline family (i.e., acetylcholine, the hormone of balance and maintenance) to catch up and restore normality. In the words of Shakespeare, 'Sleep is nature's balm'. While medication is essential to end the destructive manic flight, functioning like a pharmacological straitjacket, it creates a state of suspension or twilight zone, where normal psychological and emotional responses are slow to return. This phase can be extremely distressing for relatives, particularly children, who find parents zombie-like and unresponsive.

- Wounded pride. Pride comes before a fall. A free-falling manic topples from a great height, and the impact reflects that. As they return to everyday consciousness and their previous identity, they are faced with a scene equivalent to the post-battle scenario, much like a defeated general reflecting on the number of lives needlessly lost, and the futility of the cause fought for with such blinkered single-mindedness.

- Disillusionment. As the medication is gradually decreased and awareness starts to percolate through, many become deeply depressed by the outlook, making problem-solving an additional overwhelming burden. One of the primary disillusionments is that in spite of their 'great escape', on their return they are still facing the predicament of impending failure from which they took flight, now seriously compounded by the visible debris resulting from the manic episode itself. This can include severed relationships, financial ruin, loss of others' confidence and trust, the jeopardising of a good work record and promotional possibilities. In some cases there are even more serious consequences, such as legal proceedings pending as a result of car accidents, broken contracts, violent behaviour, barring orders, protection orders, paternity suits, all of which demand urgent attention at a time when sufferers are at their lowest.

- Suicidal thinking. For some this seems like the only reasonable solution, so great is their shame. 'There is no way out. Their flight into mania, which was an unconscious effort at a solution, has inevitably created more problems than it has solved. So deep is the feeling of despair, desolation and hopelessness that the pain of it dictates an action which will end it. In this sense it is a form of self administered euthanasia.

- The medication see-saw. Manic patients, having been brought back to consensus reality by high doses of sedative medication may now find themselves, particularly if they are deeply depressed and suicidal, being prescribed psychic energisers (antidepressant medication) to provide a mood elevation. Often as a result, the mood will elevate to such a point that another manic episode is feared, and corrective sedative medication is prescribed to dampen it. This relapse can be a further blow to patient and family, so soon after the manic episode. Alternating mood swings of this kind, highs and lows, can give rise to the diagnosis of a bipolar disorder (manic depression) and the goal becomes one of balance – balancing out the sufferer's mood.

- The career patient. Having left hospital, many sufferers become professionally-trained mood watchers. They may lose their sense of perspective as to what are acceptable normal levels of joy and excitement, or their opposite, grumpy bad form. Juggling doses of medication can become the sole focus of out-patient consultations, reinforcing the notion that relapses are caused purely by chemical shifts and unrelated to any other factors in the person's life. In this way medication is seen as corrective. Unfortunately this balancing act can become a life-long process. To break this disempowering cycle, psychotherapy is vital to make sense of the beginning, middle and end of the manic experience, and the multitude of factors, both external and internal which influence that.

PSYCHOTHERAPY

Strictly speaking, the question is not how to get cured, but how to live.

Joseph Conrad

If ever there was a critical component in the understanding and resolution of a psychological distress it has to be the use of psychotherapy in manic depression.

What arrives in the door of the psychiatric hospital is an exploding bomb which requires emergency measures to extinguish it. The climax of mania – the psychotic phase – is a medical emergency, and can only be reversed through the use of sedative medication, which in most cases is only possible within a hospital environment. Any effort at logical conversation has no place at this stage, the furious firestorm in their mind needs to be urgently dealt with and has to be done so with high doses of tranquillisers. It can take days and weeks for the madness to clear and normality to return. During this phase the individual not only requires sedation, but a nursing input with full medical back-up, bordering on intensive care protocols, to restore health to a body depleted of its nutritional resources, and often so compromised in its immune system that infections have taken root. A matter of additional urgency is the process of detoxification where substance abuse has led to addiction.

This medication phase should be transitory, like the need for morphine in a case of a broken leg. Once consensus awareness has returned, it should be phased out and replaced with a psychotherapeutic approach which has as its primary aim a search for the unconscious triggers, and conscious preventive measures should be put in place. This process, once started, should continue following discharge until the causal factors have been deconstructed and medication terminated.

We feel that the depression phase, the opposite pole, should be interpreted as a normal emotional response to the shockingly out-of-the-ordinary experience which an elation is. The catastrophic fall-out resulting from the chaos left in its wake is depressing stuff to have to deal with at such a vulnerable time, and as such depression is a perfectly natural reaction. This phase is best integrated and healed through the process of psychotherapy which provides a de-briefing opportunity in which the entire experience can be understood. In a sense, those who experience mania have travelled to another world and back, such is the extraordinarily unique nature of their experience.

In its own right, depression is the appropriate natural emotional response to feeling sapped of all energy, and realising you have been the cause of so much chaos, hurt and ruin to yourself and others, and newly aware of the awesome task pressing down on top of you of rebuilding your life. If this perspective is not taken, this depression is in danger of being made into a purely chemical disease process, as all depressions within the current dominant biomedical model are. In such a framework, in addition to the cocktail of major tranquillisers (anti-psychotics), lithium, and anti-epileptic medication, anti-depressants are added. The individual on discharge is related to as a ticking time-bomb, with all those around them anxiously awaiting the next explosion.

FAILURE? I DON'T DO FAILURE!

Richard's case is the stereotypical manic story where its exponent takes the elevator approach – on beginning to become aware of a scenario which is not to his liking, nor in his emotional repertoire to handle, he metaphorically presses the button to remove himself to a more pleasing and manageable scenario on another floor, at another level of consciousness. When this in turn begins to contain ingredients which offend, he repeats the manoeuvre again until he runs out of floors and ends up stark raving mad on the rooftop. One manic, having gained insight during psychotherapy, described the dilemma in these words: 'It was as if I was running from a war party of Apaches who were rapidly gaining ground. I felt I had to keep running because if I stopped and turned to look at them, I would get a hundred arrows in the face'.

The goal of psychotherapy in Richard's case is directed towards helping him acquire the emotional maturity and skills to deal with setbacks. Ordinary people experience setbacks, they see them coming, and have accumulated along the way a repertoire of strategies to use in such situations. A person who can only be extraordinary as a way of being, cannot readily do this, and this is what Richard needed to learn. He has always spoken the language of success and now has to get his tongue and his mind around the dialect of the common man, and ultimately live a 'smaller' life with equanimity.

If on the other hand he is treated within the sick-brain model – 'you have a chemical imbalance and must keep taking the pills' – this conversation will never be had, no learning will ever take place and a window of opportunity will be missed. Evidence painfully shows that if personal responsibility is not taken, i.e., learning how to manage one's life in a psychotherapeutic (soul-attending) way, then no amount of medication will prevent a further episode and future admissions become a way of life. A career patient has been created.

EINSTEIN, HAWKING MOVE OVER!
Sylvia has one vulnerability. She so enjoys the world of her intellect that she has a tendency to indulge it, as if it were her entire life. She has willingly forfeited meaningful relationships, sporting activities, pleasurable pursuits and contact with nature. She had a brilliant academic record and has been known since her early schooldays as a 'brain-box'. Her recent immersion in her PhD project was the most exciting period of her life. It allowed her to lock herself away, disconnect from social contacts and live like a hermit. In such a climate no reality testing was occurring and as we saw her inner world took over.

The psychotherapeutic work here is to help her gain awareness of her tendency towards imbalance, excessively favouring her inner world to the negation of healthy connections outside. Her task is obviously simpler than Richard's, and is merely one of maintaining the right lifestyle balance.

MAY THE FORCE BE WITH YOU
David's case reflects a rare ability or gift to experience phenomena in the non-physical realms, of a spiritual and energetic nature. The problem arose for him because he had never had such transcendental experiences before, and was at a loss as to how to interpret or contain them. He would therefore require a

very particular kind of therapist, one familiar with transpersonal and energetic phenomena. Dr Stanislaus Grof, a psychiatrist and leading pioneer of transpersonal psychology would regard David's case as a spiritual emergency. As countless clairvoyants and healers will testify, their initiation into the non-physical or energetic world was far from smooth. David ultimately has to learn to manage his energy, appreciate its limits and stay grounded.

LINING UP FOR STARDOM

Sophie's is a straightforward case of addiction, with the added dimension that some addicts have an energetic tendency to experience altered states more easily than others. Her drug of choice, which she was abusing for years, is an upper, designed to lift the mood, and create an over-expansive sense of self. Sophie, like all addicts, needs to develop her own inner strengths, finding the buzz in a balanced lifestyle and attending regular NA meetings.

REFLECTION

Helping an individual to reframe their anger is a particular difficulty with manics. Since they were to all intents and purposes 'not there' when their outlandish behaviours required curtailment, either by the law or through medical intervention, they feel a miscarriage of justice has occurred. Seeing themselves as innocent victims of a system not taking their rights into account, many harbour angry feelings against family members and doctors for years. Many refuse to recognise the difficulty others have in condoning this altered state and the chaos it wreaks, stubbornly seeing it as merely a turbo version of their extraordinary gifted nature. To them hospitalisations are human rights violations. Those family members attempting to curtail their activities are viewed as spoilsports who 'just don't get it', and their doctors as corrupt. They share with the recidivist revolving-door criminal a lacuna in consciousness, having no insight whatsoever into their pattern of behaviour, its origins and its effect.

Their lack of insight resonates with the following story. A judge, before sentencing a serial jump-over thief who robs cash registers for a living, asked him 'why do you keep doing it despite serving a jail sentence every time you get caught?' The reply was 'with all due respects your honour, that's where the money is'. The serial manic, who carries on regardless of the consequences which greet him at the end of each episode, should not be surprised that his behaviour is interpreted as a disease. Only someone who either has a diseased brain would be so incapable of learning from the experience; tracking its beginnings, identifying the context which repeatedly triggers it, and taking preventive measures to make absolutely sure it never recurs again. How many times does your house have to burn down before you start looking for clues to help you piece together the train of events which led to each fire? If you yourself can't or won't, the fire department should at least do you that favour, instead of rushing in with the hoses each time, no questions asked.

While this may seem like a harsh interpretation of an existential difficulty, there is some justification, as some manics wilfully create the launch-pad context, feeling that the ride which the elation provides is worth repeating. Like a drug, the best fix in town and certainly the most long-lasting, they become addicted to it, and to the exhilaration and total abandonment of all curtailments and restrictions of the mundane self. We don't call it 'the great escape' for nothing. Everything about it is great. The eminent psychiatrist, Dr Edward. M. Podvoll wrote an entire book about this phenomenon, called *The Seduction of Madness*.

Like an addict stalking their dealer, they will travel a well-worn path; staying up around the clock, playing particular evocative music, drinking to excess, smoking cannabis, snorting coke, frequenting high-energy haunts, reviving old 'dial-a-party' contacts, being promiscuous, seeking out changing-the-world conversations, and taking a vacation from routine life. And like the pop of a champagne cork; they're gone into orbit. Should anyone be surprised? Not if it's labelled a relapse. There is a lot to be said for calling a spade a spade, and there is no doubt about it, certain types of elation have addictive qualities in them which need to be challenged, just like those who abuse alcohol and drugs, in whom insight and responsibility are just as slow in coming.

We believe that psychiatry has lost its way and its reliance on excessive use of medication, its revolving door hospitalisation practices, and its ultimate fall-back, electro-shock therapy, urgently needs to be questioned. Could this have anything to do with the fact that most of the psychiatrists practising in this country do not have a registered university qualification in psychotherapy?

If your only tool is a hammer, everything looks like a nail.

Ludwig Wittgenstein

CHAPTER 9

Love and Loss – The Broken Heart

No one ever told me that grief felt so much like fear. I am not afraid, but the sensation is like being afraid. The same fluttering in the stomach, the same restlessness, the yawning. I keep on swallowing. At other times it feels like being mildly drunk, or concussed. There is a sort of invisible blanket between the world and me. I find it hard to take in what anyone says. Or perhaps hard to want to take it in. It is so uninteresting. Yet I want the others to be about. I dread the moments when the house is empty. If only they would talk to each other and not to me.

C. S. Lewis

Writer and academic, C. S. Lewis, a confirmed bachelor, was swept off his feet by the only love of his life, who died of cancer within a year of their marriage. His desolation and depression were fathomless, and he gives us a flavour of this in the quote above.

While those who grieve have in common numerous physical symptoms, such as broken sleep, loss of appetite, lack of energy and restlessness, the similarity ends there. The meanings, feelings, fears, images, evocations, memories, intensity, behaviours, and attempts to cope with it are exquisitely unique and at times inexplicable to others. The experience is made all the worse because there is no frame of reference within which to make sense of what's happened. You are lost for words. You don't know how or what to think about it. You look to your mind, your traditional source of answers, and you find a blank. An internal Tsunami. How do you begin to integrate such a catastrophe?

The stunned disillusionment, which grinds your entire system to a halt, is the essence of the depression which follows grief and loss. The future has suddenly vanished, and with it your map. In a rudderless demotivated state, you seem to go round in circles.

Grief as an experience says more about us than the lost loved one. The sense of loss is in proportion to our connection to them, the role they played in our lives, what function they provided, and what they protected us from. Loved ones support us in a range of ways which we may not be fully conscious of until they are gone. We lose a reference point through which we knew and valued ourselves. Grief therefore has as much to do with the sudden change in our own identity, which we still depend on for the future, as it has to do with the absence of the loved one.

In our faster moving society there is less and less time now for grief. Our treadmill routine is suspended for shorter and shorter periods. Children are expected back at school, and parents expected to resume work within an ever-shrinking time-frame. There is little time for reflection or the integration of the experience. These days 'unresolved grief' can mean 'it's taking too long', and 'not coping' can mean you're not back to 'normal' quickly enough.

In modern society grief is sanitised, packaged, and slotted into a prescribed acceptable form. The listening space provided is limited in terms of what can be said, and to whom. How many bereaved spouses feel free to discuss their residual sexual longings with their friends? How many children have the freedom to express their unhappiness at the replacement of their dead parent within a year or two? How many of those grieving would admit to others that they drive in the middle of the night to the graveyard, and lie on the grave weeping for hours? How many share the fact that they take comfort in continuing a relationship with their dead loved one through feeling their presence, speaking to them, and setting a place for them at the table? There is a veil of secrecy around some of the phenomena of grief. The pressures of the public gaze dictate political correctness even in such a private and personal experience.

THE PHANTOM LOVER

Agnes was seventy-four when her husband of forty-five years died suddenly of a heart attack on the morning they were leaving for a sun holiday. They were the parents of six children, and were sweethearts all their lives, with a close and demonstrative relationship. Since John's retirement ten years previously, and with all the children off their payroll, they enjoyed the empty nest. While they adored their grandchildren they were careful not to become swamped by them, in order to finally have time together as a couple.

For Agnes, John's death was a personal earthquake on many levels. Although a capable homemaker, she had never become versed in paying bills, making bank lodgements, servicing the car, and house maintenance. There were many things Agnes now felt unable to do on her own such as drive, entertain people and attend family functions. She even began to find the grandchildren too much to cope with. He had been the rock on which she relied, they had made every decision together, and her insecurity was intense and not fully appreciated by her family. She needed time to gather her wits and adjust to the new challenges before her. Although profoundly lonely, she sought out time alone more and more, and preferred to avoid social engagements, which were now a source of so much pain and anxiety.

John was like a phantom limb which had been there all her life and was now gone, but which she still experienced as real. Every morning began with a panic attack as she rolled over in bed and was suddenly faced with his absence. She panicked in social situations also, where she would turn to share something with him, only to remember that she was alone. This would precipitate tears and she would often have to be brought home. No longer having any reference point for many of her thoughts, feelings and behaviours, her future life seemed unliveable on her own, and filled her with dread and despair.

She confided in one of her daughters that she wished for death in order to join him. A visit to her family doctor was hastily arranged and he recommended a short stay in a nursing home, and a course of anti-depressant medication and sedation. Reluctantly Agnes co-operated, but felt bullied, and withdrew into herself, lacking the will to resist their good intentions. When they began making suggestions as to how she should structure her future, such as moving to a smaller house or sharing with one of the family, she became suspicious of their motives, feeling that she was losing control over what remained of her life.

The only person she trusted was John's brother Frank, with whom she could talk freely, and who seemed to fully understand her distress. Frank also realised something which her family didn't – that Agnes and John's relationship had been a fused one in which they relied on each other totally, but which he always knew would be a double-edged sword for the one left behind. He knew that what Agnes needed was help to acquire practical skills which would make her feel more secure and independent, and that moving her from her own home would increase rather than reduce her anxiety.

He encouraged her discharge from the nursing home, and noticing her confusion as a result of the medication, consulted her doctor about a phasing out regime. Frank went about helping her rebuild her life in practical ways; he helped her simplify her finances, put her legal affairs in order, encouraged her to drive herself alone and reconnected her to bridge, an old pastime. His unconditional support gave her the confidence to start re-engaging with her life on her chosen time-frame. At this point Agnes sought bereavement counselling, which helped her to speak about her feelings and master her panic attacks. Feeling more in control of her life her depression began to improve.

THE COMFORT OF LINGERING SPIRITS

Such is the intensity of some people's experience of loss, ripped as they are from their psychological moorings, that the energy of their emotion can connect them to the spirit of the deceased.

Seán, a fifty-two-year-old financier, could not accept the death of his eldest son who was knocked down by a car. Two years later he was suffering from irritable bowel, high blood pressure and chronic fatigue syndrome. His doctor, sensing an unresolved grief and depression, referred him to a psychiatrist who specialised in psychotherapy. Seán was a reluctant participant: 'I don't see how talking is going to help my physical problems'. After a number of consultations, with intermittent cancellations, he finally began to talk about his son's death and the impact it was having on his everyday life.

He revealed that he had made a deal with his son that if he repeated his final year in school to get the necessary university points, he would help him to build a sound-proof music studio in the attic of their home, where he could develop his percussion skills and mix music. His son worked diligently at his studies and the studio was built. He practised most evenings on arrival home from school, and this was humorously referred to as 'Steven letting off steam'. One month before he was due to sit his exams he was killed. It emerged that Seán had never visited his son's grave, had preserved his room unchanged, and had even left the laundered clothes he had worn on the morning he was killed neatly folded on the bed.

Although Seán worked in the city centre, he used a circuitous route to get to work in order to avoid the site of his son's death and the graveyard in which he was buried. His son was never talked about in the house, and life on the surface went on as if he had never existed. Since Steven had been the apple of his father's eye, Seán now found it increasingly difficult to relate to his two younger sons. He told his psychiatrist that he continually felt his presence in the house. With reluctance he admitted that every evening the following sequence of events happened. He would hear his son come in, use the bathroom, go upstairs to the attic, begin his drumming practice, come down for the evening meal, return to finish his study and finally enter their bedroom and Seán would clearly feel himself being kissed on his right cheek. Although aware of the unusual nature of this experience, he related that he found it comforting, as he was maintaining some connection with the boy.

His wife was aware that he hadn't moved on, that he was depressed, but had no idea that he was experiencing these paranormal phenomena. His children felt him to be withdrawn, distant, grumpy and irritable. His psychiatrist put it to him that in some way he was still holding on to his son, albeit metaphysically. He also explained that this was using up vast amounts of energy and probably accounted for his physical illnesses. Seán agreed, but still felt that to initiate a process which would let go of Steven was too high a price to pay.

He dropped out of therapy and only reappeared some nine months later, after he had been discharged from hospital following the successful removal of a potentially fatal cancer from his right cheek. When he connected that the site of the cancer was on the area he was 'kissed' on a nightly basis, he took it as a coded message to let go, both for the sake of his own health and to let his son move on.

Over the next six months, he embarked on a series of letting go rituals. These included visiting the grave and reading a letter to his son documenting his feelings – what had happened to the family since his death – and then symbolically burning it at the graveside. He started driving by both the site of the accident and the graveyard, redecorated Steven's room, gave his clothes to charity and as a final act disposed of his drum kit. Six months afterwards he related to his psychiatrist how his youngest son, aged twelve, told him in a quiet moment that he looked 'happy' and added that it felt 'as if a ghost had left the house'.

THROUGH THE EYES OF LOVE

> Dance me to your beauty
> With a burning violin
> Dance me through the panic
> Till I'm gathered safely in
> Lift me like an olive branch
> And be my homeward dove
> Dance me to the end of love

Leonard Cohen

Romantic love, typified in Leonard Cohen's song is a state which, once experienced, is never forgotten. When in love, our identity immediately changes. We let down the barriers of separateness, allowing ourselves to merge totally with the other. Perceived from the inside there is the experience of oneness, harmony, trust, unconditional love, acceptance, perfection, innocence, expansiveness and bliss.

The experience of love overrides other considerations such as duty, power, money, status and threat. No risk is too great. Nothing else matters but being together. Belief in the other is absolute. The fused energy and chemistry creates a world of its own. We positively glow with health, on a physical, emotional and mental level. This expansion of energy allows us to express ourselves creatively, to enthusiastically embrace the world, and relate to others compassionately: 'All the world loves a lover'.

Falling in love offers us the experience of having a believing mirror held up to us by the loved one. As we look into this mirror, our features are pointed out and admired, which we previously may not have recognised. We come to believe we are attractive, loveable, worthwhile and desirable. This feedback gives us confidence, self-esteem, a future and a sense of belonging. With our lover we co-create a new personal identity.

Between lovers there are two parallel relationships. Lover to lover (interpersonal), and each lover to themselves (intrapersonal). When romance dies, there are therefore two deaths. One public, and one private. The private death, the loss of the believing mirror, is little understood, difficult to articulate and can drive us into the depths of desolation, depression and even suicide.

THE LOSS OF THE BELIEVING MIRROR

> From rejection, or from a real or imagined loss, the lover suffers the crushing disappointment of an intense conviction. His 'conviction' might be of his destined place in another's life, or of his sexual irresistibility, or of having found an ultimate mate, or of living only the shadow of a life when not with the other. And so on in countless variety. He has reconstructed a 'self' that can only exist in the presence of the 'other'.
>
> Dr Edward M. Podvoll

Holly, a twenty-six-year-old aspiring actor, was swept off her feet by Marty, a talented theatre director. A passionate love affair ensued in which for the first time ever she felt valued and loveable. He called her a goddess and she revelled in her new found sexuality. A stunningly beautiful man, heads would turn when he entered a room. Holly, who regarded herself as plain-looking, began to look equally beautiful. She dressed extrovertly, and received compliments that they made a striking couple. They worked together on a number of theatrical projects. It was the first time she felt that she had real talent as an actor. An outsider all her life, who had always found it hard to make friends, she suddenly found herself the centre of a huge social circle.

A year into the relationship, Holly got a leading role in a play. The rehearsals took her over and their time together was limited. She went on tour with the company. On her return, he told her that he had fallen in love with her best friend. He rationalised his behaviour by accusing her of being wrapped up in herself and emotionally unavailable. This came like a bolt from the blue as he always seemed supportive and because he was in the business seemed to understand her commitments.

Decimated, Holly dropped everything and returned in panic to her home town and the safety of her parents' house. Inconsolable in her grief she took to the bed. Any attempt by her parents to talk about it would reduce her to tears. Such was her mental turmoil that her parents had her referred her to a psychiatrist. After trials of different medication she slid deeper and deeper into depression.

After six months she found sympathy towards her diminishing. Pressure was put on her to 'snap out of it'. The usual clichés were trotted out – get a life, forget about him, he's not worth it, there's plenty of fish in the sea. She hid the way she was feeling as she realised that they were all tired of it. Feeling isolated and lonely, Holly began to anaesthetise her feelings with alcohol and medication.

Holly's experience is like a bereavement, and is typical of a broken heart. Unlike in death, however, the elements of rejection and betrayal are forefront. The issue of 'not being good enough' does not have to be dealt with when a loved one dies. The object of her love is still alive, continuing his work, socialising in the same places, and happily living with her best friend. To avoid the pain of ever meeting them she uprooted herself and fled to the last place she expected she'd ever end up, home, living with unsympathetic parents. Her loss is far greater than it would seem on the surface. Without his believing mirror, she no longer feels like a goddess, beautiful, sexually desirable, intelligent, witty, etc. Her identity has died, having being rejected absolutely. Resurrecting a new one seems to her an impossible and depressing task.

WRETCHEDNESS AND DESPAIR – THE DOWNWARD SPIRAL

The loss of such love, and our new way of defining ourselves, can have an earthquake-like impact. Having tasted bliss, in its absence we are worse off than we could ever have imagined. We're now living our worse nightmare. What is often not understood is that it is more than just our lover's presence that we miss, but the way we had come to feel about ourselves as part of that unit. The self that we had constructed in the presence of the other no longer exists. It has collapsed. The self that had found an ultimate partner, the self whose future was secure and taken as a given, the self who was sexually irresistible, is no more. Our identity has died. It's the end. There is no future for it.

Core issues instantly surface such as abandonment, rejection, betrayal of trust and loss of control. Groundless, like a kite no longer held, we are cut adrift. Fear, anxiety and panic prevail and we enter the depressed state of hopelessness and defeat when our attempts to re-attach prove futile.

Like one possessed, as grieving lovers we feel the constant presence of our absent lover in our mind. We can think of nothing else. We become obsessed. We ruminate over and over about how it ended, the reasons that put it beyond repair, and what we could have done to prevent it. Imprisoned and haunted by all-pervading images, and overwhelmed by our feelings, it becomes impossible to engage the outside world. Unable to concentrate, retain information, carry out simple tasks, maintain appearances, we become detached and indifferent. The world literally passes us by.

Our main relationship now is with a memory, rather than the real flesh and blood person. The energy connections or cords, the 'heartstrings' which were established during the relationship, have now been severed. Agonisingly, however, like phantom limbs we still feel their presence. Broken cords translate into last-ditch desperate behaviours. Demented, like addicts in the height of withdrawal, we crave our loved one's smell, their touch, their presence, everything about them. To make matters worse, we idealise them and adore the ground they walked on. We would do anything to reconnect and get the 'fix'. We cannot accept it's over.

The relationship is lived out through any activity that keeps it alive to us – visiting familiar haunts, rereading letters, looking at photographs, and compulsively talking about the loved one to who ever will listen. Anything to keep our old identity in place.

Like the bereaved, our grief goes through stages. We deny. We run through possible strategies to get them back, plotting and planning, recruiting the support of accomplices, seeking miracles, selling our soul. We vent our anger at ourselves, our ex-lover, their new lover, God or whoever. Unable to control our thoughts we find our mind parasitised. No let-up. We experience flashbacks during the day and our sleep is broken by nightmares.

Obsessed by our mental turmoil, panic-stricken we ride an emotional roller coaster. Behaving out of character we are nothing short of mad. We may lose weight, socially withdraw, rant and rave, weep, break things, drive dangerously, disappear for days, binge on drink and drugs, neglect responsibilities, and have thoughts of killing ourselves. We resemble the obsessed and the post-traumatically stressed.

We slide into the black hole of despair as we lose the grip on our previous identity. Finally we realise that the believing mirror is broken. More pathological expressions of these stages can take the form of delusions, blackmail, stalking, crimes of passion, psychosis and suicide.

LOVE'S EXECUTIONER

Paul, a twenty-five-year-old tradesman, unexpectedly committed suicide. His family were stunned as he had been prescribed anti-depressant medication by his general practitioner and was also attending a counsellor. Always a sensitive boy, he'd been the target of bullying in secondary school. Because of this, he left before his leaving certificate and served his apprenticeship in carpentry. He was an excellent worker and was employed by a small family-run construction company.

Six months before his suicide he began drinking more heavily, missing days of work, and did so without seeming to care about the consequences. His family, friendly with his boss, did their best to cover up for him with sick notes and various excuses. He became argumentative when confronted about his demotivation, drinking and lack of commitment to his work. His boss initially did everything to facilitate him, but he too finally had to challenge him about his absenteeism.

To break this cycle, his family encouraged him to live with his godmother, with whom he had a close bond, a nurse who worked in the nearby town and lived alone. The idea was for him to get a fresh start, and begin a healthy regime of early bed and early rising, exercise, and phasing out the heavy drinking. His boss agreed to hold open his job. Contrary to everyone's expectations the new arrangement made little or no impact. All concerned felt that he was 'sitting on something' – was he gay, had he been abused, was he an alcoholic, did he have a drug problem? His counsellor could make no headway, feeling his resistance. She later disclosed to his family that she felt like the surgeon who was unable to operate because the patient was holding the scalpel.

All was revealed when a friend of his told the family after the funeral that he had in fact had a girlfriend, his first and only one, who had ended the relationship after six months because of his possessiveness. He had kept this relationship secret from his family because his siblings were all very extrovert and he knew he would come in for a slagging. In the open and vulnerable state the lovesick know well, her rejection was a catastrophe, made

Intensified by the sense of shame he felt before his friends. The loss fed into his old history of bullying and the self-loathing that resulted from it. He withdrew from them and began drinking heavily, on his own. After one such night, he hanged himself.

CHAPTER 10

The Lost Tribe – Disenchanted Youth

'I just want my children to be happy', goes the parental mantra. So why are so many of our children unhappy, depressed and lost? And this at a time when parents on the whole are working harder than ever before at being child-focused, and meeting children's needs to a high standard.

There is a crisis of unprecedented proportions occurring among our young people. Daily we are bombarded by the statistics on drinking, drugs, school dropout rates, illiteracy, unwanted pregnancy, violent and homicidal behaviour, depression, self-mutilation, obsessive dieting, and suicide. Many feel empty, disenchanted with the world around them and disconnected from themselves. These are a lost tribe and their numbers are increasing.

Given that every child starts life with a sense of wonder, curiosity, awe, spontaneity, vitality and the joy of being human, it's obvious that in many cases, such creative seedlings have failed to land on fertile ground. How does this inherent potential become stifled by the time they become teenagers? Traumas aside, are the qualities of playfulness, creativity and wonder being dampened along the way?

Well-meaning parents, with only the children's good at heart, entrust them for an average of fourteen years to our school system, an educational process which is failing many. The blame for its failure, when they buckle under the stress, when they turn to drugs, or when they become depressed, is being put on the child.

Lucy, an eighteen-year-old in her final year of secondary school, was already struggling by the end of October and was wondering how she would cope with the increasing workload. Not sleeping well, she would wake early in a tearful state, dreading the day ahead. Each class seemed endless, and she found the teachers all single-mindedly pushing their own subjects. A conscientious girl, she was keen to make the best of the year, and get the necessary points for art college. She couldn't identify with many of the subjects she was doing, in particular Irish, maths and history, and her lack of enthusiasm for them made it difficult to concentrate, which brought admonishment from her teachers.

Everyone around her was finding it hard but they felt they could do nothing about it, and like her, they were just putting their heads down to study but little else. She would get home exhausted, and after dinner would still have to study for three hours or more just to get the homework done. 'What's the point of all these irrelevant f***ing subjects? I'm not going to need Irish, maths and history for art college' she would complain to her parents. They were supportive, but felt as trapped as she did, knowing she had to get the necessary points. Her only solace was her art work and listening to music on the weekends, which she did alone, not having the energy to go out.

As November came she was finding it increasingly difficult to get out of bed, and started to suffer from severe headaches. With no appetite she lost weight, which alarmed her parents enough to bring her to the family doctor, who started her on Seroxat, an anti-depressant. Within a few days she started to feel nauseous, dizzy, sweaty, more anxious, found her dreams disturbing and noticed that she had constant tremors in her hands. Her doctor advised her to persist, telling her that the symptoms would decrease in three or four weeks. She became confused and found it hard to retain information. Withdrawing further from her friends Lucy started spending more time alone, brooding.

Her teacher phoned her parents, concerned that she was not herself, and told them that this had been noticed by other teachers, who felt that she was unusually tense, fidgety and non-communicative. Her mother, worried now, searched Lucy's room thinking there might be a drug problem. Instead she found a stockpile of Paracetamol. Alarmed, she challenged Lucy, who admitted that she had been feeling suicidal for the last two weeks. Her parents stopped her medication, which they felt had obviously made her worse, and since school was the source of Lucy's problems, called a meeting with the principal. They made it clear that her health was the priority and not the points, negotiated a scaling down of her subjects, an exemption from homework and the end-of-term tests, and a substitution of an evening yoga class in lieu of sports which she had never liked. A package holiday was booked for a week in the sun with her mother. Buoyed up by the support of her parents and the flexibility of the school, she returned to her old self, now that the pressure was off. She sat her exams, got the minimum required points, and undertook a portfolio course for a year to prepare her for art college.

Jack, aged sixteen, finds school boring, gets bad reports, daydreams during class, for which he gets detentions, and has ongoing rows with his parents about his lack of application and refusal to study. He goes for weekly guitar lessons at which he excels, as he does in all areas of sport, as well as socially. The only subjects he enjoys are English, Spanish and classical studies, and the rest he has no interest in. His fantasy is to play for Manchester United, to which end he spends all his spare time training with and playing for his local team, and doing summer soccer camps.

When his parents found out that he and his friends were missing classes and spending the time in the nearby park kicking ball and smoking, they grounded him and took away all his privileges including television and his MP3 player on weekdays.

Private grinds were arranged in his weak subjects, and a tight roster of homework put in place. He started to see home as no different from school, a prison, and became aloof and non-participatory, spending more and more time in his friends' houses. In school he became rebellious, and as his form of protest he dropped out of all involvement in sport, letting go of his place on the school teams. The coach of the local soccer team contacted his father informing him that Jack was not turning up for training, citing that he had missed a number of club games.

Jack began sleeping later and later on the weekends, often not rising until mid-afternoon. Rows continued, this time over staying out too late, and his general 'don't care' attitude at home. Matters reached a head when his parents were called to the local garda station at one in the morning, to be informed that Jack and his friends had been found drinking and smoking hash in the local park. When they searched him they found some ecstasy tablets. He was allowed home into the custody of his parents with a warning.

Simultaneously, a stalemate had been reached with the school who felt that they had exercised maximum tolerance and flexibility already. They felt he no longer fitted into the school's ethos, and that expulsion was their prerogative in view of his history of truancy and the latest drugs episode. In short he was now a bad example. His parents realised that events had reached a critical turning point, and that they risked losing the confidence of their son and had inadvertently accelerated him into the drink and drug culture as yet one more misunderstood teenager.

Family brainstorming sessions followed. Some things were obvious – unlike his older sisters, and some of his friends who liked school, it wasn't meeting Jack's needs, his strengths not being reflected in the school curriculum: 'Grind' schools would mean more of the same. All agreed that a possible solution would be to begin an apprenticeship in sound technology under the supervision of his godfather, who was a director of a successful music production company.

Alice, a twenty-five-year-old business studies graduate, had been working for two years in a large accountancy practice. Miserable, unfulfilled and depressed, she took extended sick leave. Rather than take medication she decided to go to the west of Ireland, rest, read books and try to get some perspective on her situation.

Alice had always enjoyed school, finding learning a stimulating process. While the academic side was satisfying, she found the social aspects of school less smooth – the pressure to be extrovert, popular, one of the 'in' crowd, to have a boyfriend, to have sex, to drink and smoke, and to go to concerts, music festivals and raves. Alice was not this kind of girl, being quiet by nature, her preference being to play music with her few friends at home in her room, and to read and go to the movies in her spare time. Unsure what to do after school, she took the advice of her father that 'you can't go wrong with a business degree' and went to Trinity College.

The same scenario played itself out there, except that this time Alice made an effort to be more adventurous. She had a number of boyfriends, with whom she was sexually active, participated in many of the frequent weekend parties, and tried cannabis although the 'spaced out' feeling didn't appeal to her. At a couple of concerts she took ecstasy and although she enjoyed the heightened response to the music and the open heart feeling it gave her, she felt the buzz was somehow 'artificial'. Unlike at school, she now found her new studies unstimulating and too 'left-brained', but continued with them nonetheless.

When she started working she was disillusioned to find that looking at figures all day was harder to do than she thought. Additionally she found that she was surrounded by people very unlike her, who worked and played hard. Each weekend her colleagues went on 'blow outs', meeting up in a pub, where they drank until closing time, and then going on to a club until the early hours, consuming a cocktail of different drugs and sleeping all the next day. Sex when it happened was casual. The partying was repeated on Saturday night, with Sunday spent in bed and Monday and Tuesday spent in a haze, only coming round fully on Wednesday. The binge cycle was picked up again each Friday as typified in the movie *Human Traffic*. Having tried a few such weekends, Alice decided it wasn't for her, but was at a loss to know what to replace it with. 'How come it suits everyone else? What the hell is the matter with me?'

Alice knew something wasn't clicking – she wasn't fitting into the work-hard-play-hard stereotype of the young Celtic Tigers, yet had no urge to join many of her school friends who were marrying, settling down and having babies, a lifestyle she found equally unappealing.

For the first time in her life, she felt completely alone, with many of her school and college friends gone abroad. To distract herself she bought an apartment and tried to focus on decorating and furnishing it, but it was short-lived. Her days became a hum-drum cycle of work-home-work-home *ad infinitum*, and she spent most of her weekends alone, analysing why she couldn't fit in and get on with things like other people. As her sense of alienation increased, she began to scrutinise every aspect of her personal life. All she could see was negativity, and she started to loathe herself, her inner voice berating her day and night: 'Perhaps the reason I'm not happy is my weird personality, after all something must have made me so out of step even back in secondary school? Do I not like my work because I don't have the staying power that the others all seem to have in bucketfuls? It's just as well I don't want to have children. A child deserves an outgoing sociable mother, not an introvert like me.' Her sense of desperation overwhelmed her, and she wondered when was the last time she had ever felt happy and contented. It hit her immediately. Summers spent in her grandparents house in the Burren in Clare. That night she rang her granny and headed for the west.

It was May, and she spent her days walking the hills, recognising alpine flowers pointed out to her as a child. She swam daily, enjoyed the sunsets over the Aran Islands and slowly began to feel reconnected to something she'd lost, as the emptiness inside dissolved. Still on sick leave, she booked in to the Burren yoga centre for a week-long course run by a visiting yoga master. As the week went on, she felt alive and connected to her body as she never had since she was a child. Her mind stopped buzzing, and with it came a growing sense of calm.

On her return to work, she continued her yoga classes, and signed up for a two-year part-time teacher training course in yoga. Although she could not afford to leave her job just yet, having her plan to teach yoga in place gave her enough of a sense of life purpose to continue until then.

DOING TIME – UNTAPPED POTENTIAL

Schools don't always embody the true meaning of education, which comes from the Latin *educare*, to lead forth potential. Parents frequently find themselves in the impossible position of having to send their children to schools into which they have little input; schools that teach subjects which their children find irrelevant, impose too much homework at the end of long days and that emphasise competition. Much teaching is done in an atmosphere of fear, pressure and intimidation

Our children are interfacing with an expanded world which requires new skills. They find the presentation of school material outmoded and often meaningless. Unlike in their parents' day, the information of this technological age is delivered to them in high speed sound-bites, in contrast to the slower delivery through the written page and the blackboard. The youth now are adept at mobile phones, texting, satellite television, computers, internet facilities, MP3 players, digital cameras, games consoles, and so forth. In addition the orientation of this generation is towards the present and the future, not the past. Some of our ways of looking at life, to their young eyes, have long passed their sell-by date. Who killed who in 1916 holds no interest for them. (Although paradoxically they would be impressed to hear that Pádraig Pearse, a revolutionary leader at that time, referred to school as the 'murder machine'.) Nor does it matter to them if this country was occupied by an alien power for 800 years: 'Doh! They've gone now, so can you stop going on about it?'

Educators as a whole are not embracing this new reality, and have little understanding as to the enormous novelty today's children are experiencing. And so, in our ignorance, we thrust on them the familiar well-worn structures which were imposed on us in the past; methods such as rote learning, the over-reliance on textbooks, poetry beyond their life experience, and meaninglessness hours devoted to the compulsory learning of a language that most will never speak. Subjects such as geometry and algebra, are likewise irrelevant to as many as ninety-nine per cent of the class as far as daily living goes, yet the whole class must struggle with it.

This tribe of young people are feeling confused and alienated. Many have lost faith in the education system and have withdrawn their energy from it, impatiently enduring it as a prison sentence. Merely marking time until it's over, they duck and dive, their only escape being 'getting out of their heads' on the weekend. With their imagination on hold, their spirit deadened, they drag themselves from classroom to classroom wishing they were somewhere else. They feel that their vision of the world, even though it is only in the embryonic stages and not fully formed, is being invalidated, and their pain ignored.

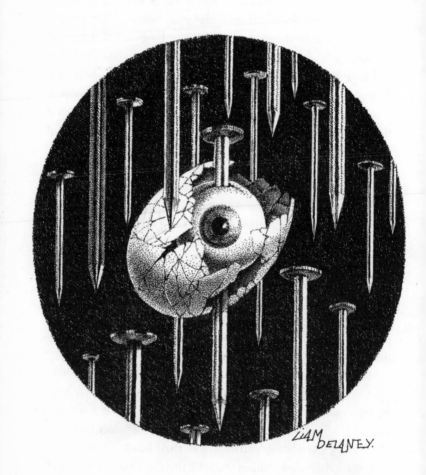

LIAM DELANEY.

It takes an enormous investment of energy to keep engaging with a process which has no relevance to you, but they suffer it, and for the most part do so in silence, convinced that their parents don't understand and won't support them. Numerous angry flash-points in the home centre on school issues – lack of motivation, truancy, homework not done, as in Jack's case. Parents are as concerned as their children about the stress which the points' system generates, particularly if they are right-brained and mismatched with our left-brained school system, as in Lucy's case. Finally, at the end of their schooling, standing on the launch pad preparing for their impending rite of passage into adulthood, many find themselves out of step with their chosen career as Alice did, and more lost than ever. The ever increasing drop-out rates at university level bear testimony to this.

DOMESTICATION OR FREEDOM?

The education experience is not neutral. It can dampen the spirit, will and creativity of a child through testing, labelling and regimented curricula, in an atmosphere of relentless judgement and comparison. Or it can open the doors to the discovery of talents, strengths, resources and a sense of purpose and direction. Under the present system this latter is happening only for a few. For the many, potential goes untapped and, tragically, zest for life also. Helpless to change their situation, and overwhelmed by the demands on them, their lot is fear, panic, disillusionment and a deadness inside. Diagnoses of depression, attention deficit disorder and social anxiety follow. It stretches credibility and logic to prescribe anti-depressants and amphetamines (such as Ritalin) for children, rather than identify shortfalls in the school system.

The theory of multiple intelligence was developed in 1983 by Dr Howard Gardner, professor of education at Harvard University. He suggested that intelligence did not reside in the head alone, but was distributed throughout the person. He identified nine separate forms of intellectual abilities which if fostered could be the basis for a multiplicity of careers and lifestyles:

- Bodily-Kinaesthetic Intelligence: the ability to control one's bodily movements, to handle objects skilfully and prioritise personal health care – careers in sports, manual labour, dance, acting, yoga, cookery, dietetics, massage, acupuncture, physiotherapy.
- Interpersonal/Emotional Intelligence: can empathise with the moods and feelings of others, negotiate to have their needs met and deal effectively with conflict – careers in the health care professions, child care, service industries, human resources, politics, business.
- Verbal-Linguistic Intelligence: the skills of listening, speaking, writing, foreign languages – careers in journalism, writing, teaching, languages, law, politics.
- Musical Intelligence: appreciating rhythm and pitch, singing, playing instruments, composing music – careers as a musician, disc jockey, sound engineer, singer.
- Visual-Spatial Intelligence: thinking in images, pictures and form – careers in design, art, engineering, architecture, photography, mechanics.
- Intrapersonal Intelligence: capacity for self-awareness, intuition and flexibility of thoughts and beliefs – careers in research, psychology, literature.
- Naturalist Intelligence: a connection to plants, animals, and nature – careers in horticulture, agriculture, landscape architecture, farming, animal care, environmental science, sustainability.
- Existential Intelligence: a sensitivity and capacity to tackle deep questions about the meaning of human existence and the purpose of life – careers in philosophy, poetry, theology,

science, psychotherapy.

• Mathematical-Logical Intelligence: the skills of number-reasoning, abstract thinking, and problem-solving – careers in science, engineering, accountancy, maths.

An educational renaissance is long overdue. It would ensure that if young people had been made aware that they had a range of rewarding talents, in a combination unique and different from their peers, they would have ways and means in which to engage with life. As things stand if they don't speak the language of the left brain, the last on our list above – interpretation, analysis, number-crunching, rote-memory – they are set for a rocky ride through a competition-orientated system intent on measuring only these qualities without relating to their many others. There is something fundamentally wrong when children are forced to engage in the compulsory learning of subjects they hate. Irish is the classic example, the force-feeding of thousands of hours of the subject over thirteen years becomes more about will-breaking than true learning.

By contrast, in a curriculum based on the knowledge that multiple intelligences exist, every child would have their potential awakened, developed and seen as a platform for life in terms of earning capacity, personal fulfilment and a satisfying role in society. What child wouldn't thrive if they proved to be good at something? What young person wouldn't like to feel equipped to work, travel and live anywhere they want? To know that they'll never be out of their depth, to have a confidence in their linguistic, personal and life skills which will open up the world to them. And in a world of increasing stress to have a strong emotional intelligence and the skills to engage with and successfully negotiate the wide range of situations thrown up as part of living in life's soup, with all its many complex ingredients.

BLIND SPOTS

If the skills to maintain one's personal health were taught in the pre-adult years, then much physical and mental breakdown could be prevented later on. A knowledge of how their own body works is a blind spot in some of the youth of today. They are unaware of the optimum conditions it requires to become healthy, factors which cause disease and useful practices to prevent them – proper diet, yoga, meditation and exercise. Mental and emotional distress and the symptoms it generates are misread. They are being seen as diseases requiring psychiatric medication, and not as the confusion and disarray of those out of their depth, many of them interfacing with an unfriendly fossilised school system. If the principles of emotional health maintenance were taught in school, an understanding of states such as depression, anxiety, and panic would be in their repertoire, ending the culture of secrecy, stigma and isolation. Surely suicide rates would drop in such a climate.

The hideous state of our health services, whether it's treating physical, mental or emotional suffering, is testament that it has failed. Its present obsessive orientation towards symptom eradication, is at the cost of immeasurable human suffering and billions of euro. Where has preventative medicine gone? A melt-down is imminent unless radical and rational thinking is engaged in by those ultimately responsible, namely the ministers for health and education.

> You can't see clearly if your imagination is out of focus.
>
> Mark Twain

LIGHT AT THE END OF THE TUNNEL

It is an extremely healthy sign that Irish secondary school children are finally insisting on having their voice heard through the setting up of the website www.ratemyteachers.ie. Despite criticisms, it has to be seen as an attempt to redress the imbalance of power where the teachers are holding all the cards. Although they may be blamed, the teachers are mere puppets in a Punch and Judy show, the strings manipulated by the misguided supporters of the outmoded 'flat earth' theory of education.

Those listening to the winds of change, the round earthers, realise that for successful daily living, remembering the dates of battles lost by kings and generals, knowing Pythagoras' theory, the exact location of the source of the Nile, or what W. B. Yeats was trying to convey in his poem 'Sailing to Byzantium', are not the most essential wisdom chips.

This dinosaur of an education system operates on the concept of 'banking' – where data is deposited into a child's mind for the sole purpose of it being withdrawn later, on the day of an exam, to reap the interest in points. But on what account are they taught to draw when faced with an emotional dilemma such as a broken heart, a sexual disorientation, bullying, an unwanted pregnancy, or the break-up of their parent's marriage?

PATHFINDERS

The phenomenon of the mid-life crisis is well-known. By then decades have been spent striving to better oneself, to move upward, as if climbing a ladder, arriving on each rung only to find one more beckoning upwards. And then, one day – oh joy! – to reach the top, only to look around and realise that all along your ladder has been leaning against the wrong wall. Wretched, you are flooded with feelings of despair, entrapment and cynicism. What now for the future? Most, like beached whales, will never be able to return to the ocean of possibilities, and can only look forward to a future of frantic distraction, backed up by antidepressants such as Prozac or Seroxat.

The youth of today are different. The more creative among them, the pathfinders, don't need to spend decades finding out which ladders or walls suit them. Intuitively many take a read-

LIAM DELANEY.

ing early on, and recognise incompatibility instantly, refusing to engage with even the bottom rung. They prefer quality of life over the treadmill of their parents and older siblings, a path strewn with casualties which wisely they avoid. These evolved young people are to be found travelling, exploring and working their way around the globe, acquiring new skills on a need-to-know basis, be it a new language or a new qualification. Within them burns a clear sense of their ultimate destination, not a particular place or career, but an inner connection with their purpose in life – their manifesto celebrating creativity, financial independence, integrity, happiness, an inner contentment and a sense of being part of a bigger picture.

Jack and Lucy initially unaware of what was troubling them, had nonetheless a sense of what was toxic for them, but within the limited manoeuvrability available to young people, attempted to deal with it in their own way. In both cases, their talents were not being drawn forth by school, in the true spirit of *educare*. Jack decided early to take the only action open to him, to withdraw his energy from something he did not believe in, and took on the role of rebel to survive. Lucy's response was to try to kill herself, egged on by the uninhibiting 'green' of her anti-depressant, Seroxat, rather than go on suffering. Alice, suffering what could be called a quarter-life crisis, came to the realisation that deep down there was a mismatch between her way of being and the life she had drifted into. She ultimately found her path in yoga which connected her to something deeper in herself besides the social hypnosis of her conditioning. It made her feel alive and aware of an aspect of herself which had not found a voice before – a sense of spirit and her place in 'the family of things' echoed in Mary Oliver's poem 'The Wild Geese':

> Whoever you are, no matter how lonely,
> the world offers itself to your imagination,
> calls to you like the wild geese, harsh and exciting –

over and over announcing your place
in the family of things.

CHAPTER 11

Post-natal Depression – New Frontiers

It takes a village to raise a child.

African Proverb

The journey from the positive pregnancy test to the labour ward and beyond, is akin to stepping onto a spaceship headed for Venus. First time voyagers agree that nothing could have prepared them for the experience. Whether it proves to be a smooth uneventful trip or the roller coaster ride to hell and back, is influenced by variables too numerous to mention. It's fair to say that the medical community has had no success at clearly identifying has had limited success at clearly identifying why postnatal depression occurs for some. Independent of hormone levels, prenatal states, labour conditions, socio-economic factors: nothing serves to identify the mother who will become post-natally depressed from those who will not.

This is one area where the exceptions to the rule stand out, where even in the face of extraordinary trauma or prenatal history, a mother's emotional reaction against all the odds, is not one of depression. Contrast this with the mother who was totally prepared and supported, who had an uneventful healthy pregnancy, with the ideal context in place. It can be the greatest shock, out of the blue, to find herself in the grip of the last state she expected to feel, eclipsing and spoiling the joyous arrival of her much wanted child.

THE ONE-WAY TICKET
Motherhood is irreversible. Although you could decide to give

the baby away and to abandon your post, you can never erase the fact that you've experienced the birth process, an extraordinary event in its own right. Yet how many such monumental events are given so little time and space to be integrated, to be understood and processed? For many mothers it is the most terrifying experience of their lives. Never is your body so out of control and taken over by a process which is supposedly natural, yet feels anything but that, and from which there is now no escape. Far from being in the driving seat, you can find yourself a panicky passenger on a bus heading over a cliff. Catastrophic scenarios run through your mind as the intensity of the pain exponentially builds, stretching endlessly ahead. Many visualise their abdomen or pelvis bursting wide open, and 'getting the baby out' by whatever means the only sure release from their pain. For some the entire process is one interminable panic attack and a life-threatening event for both mother and child.

Physiologically your body has major readjustments to make in the hours and days after birth. Blood loss, blood pressure changes, hormonal shifts, tissue repair, notwithstanding breast milk coming in, are all being dealt with simultaneously. You may be still reeling from the shock, the overwhelming pain, or the exhaustion following a traumatic protracted delivery, caesarean section, vaginal tears, or problems with urinating. Many feel betrayed, conned and deliberately kept in the dark about what to expect. The experience of feeling bullied by the labour ward staff, and man-handled by their doctor, leaves many bitter and resentful. Home deliveries, with the best midwifery expertise, can be equally as turbulent: 'Nobody ever told me it could be this bad'.

From the delivery onwards, the baby takes centre stage and it becomes a juggling act. In between receiving adoring visitors and medical checks, you struggle to initiate breast feeding, bath both of you, and attend to your own recovery. If sore nipples are a problem, it colours your view of the hungry little mouth approaching them, which you can't refuse. In the event of mastitis or being unable to produce enough milk, your sense of failure grows, your confidence plummets, and with your best laid plans in shreds, you try to resist bottle feeding, but give in in the end.

The moment of arrival of the baby, the birth, will have been coloured by the previous nine months. Factors such as a threatened miscarriage or blood pressure problems requiring bed rest, persistent vomiting, the pregnancy being an unwanted one and possibly even resulting from a rape or incest, or being a sole parent unsupported by the father or their own family. Even a normal pregnancy is a state of dislodgement from a woman's former self and previous ways of thinking, feeling and behaving. Everything has changed; your body image, your confidence, your sex life, your sleep pattern, your posture, your pain threshold, the predictability of your emotions, your relationship to your partner, to your work life and to life in general.

In addition to these normal post-natal adjustments, many mothers have the added burden of grave concerns over a sick or premature baby, where life hangs in the balance, or of surgery or a disability appearing on the horizon. Visits to the neonatal intensive care unit, fraught with anticipation of further bad news, are tension-ridden experiences, and utterly contrary to the happy scenario you had imagined. Helpless and out of control; fear, sadness, weeping and disillusionment is the norm. Partners too are equally shattered.

THE ECLIPSE OF YOUR ORIGINAL SELF – FOR LIFE?
Life is sexually transmitted, and the role of mother is the means through which this is achieved: an awesome archetype to inhabit. Every issue within your make-up which relates to nurturing begins to surface. Unresolved issues around your own parenting and nurturing experience inevitably emerge. Your own parents

are the only models you have experienced at close quarters, and your expectations of yourself and your partner rest on that. 'Good' mothers are able to meet their child's every need, put a smile on their face and never complain, have no needs of their own, and are adept at juggling the needs of the entire household in spite of the profound exhaustion resulting from sleepless nights.

'Bad' mothers are those who fail to be so perfect, who sometimes feel like screaming at the baby if it won't settle, who may want to throw it down into its cot, who at times wish it would disappear in a puff of smoke, who think they'll crack up at the invasiveness of having someone hanging out of them constantly even during their sleep, and who lust for time on their own. The incessant proximity of your baby and its insatiable all-consuming appetite for your energy is a fact which, when it dawns that it is inescapable, can be an overwhelmingly depressing realisation.

All normal mothers occasionally feel such inclinations, and since verbal expression of these feelings is often taboo, a mother can find herself in the isolated position of not having an avenue by which to ventilate them and be offered reassurance. As a result, guilt and feelings of inadequacy erode their self-esteem and can sow the seeds of depression.

The grieving for the old you who has permanently disappeared can be profound; the you who was in control of her energy, body, sleep, time, social life, work identity and had a rewarding sexual and emotional relationship with the child's father. Since the baby's arrival, the future will have to be made up as you go along, nothing taken for granted any more, no assumptions and no guarantees. For some this is a joyous process and happy to set aside their own lives, they embrace the adventure eagerly. For others, the time away from their own calling can seem to stretch into the future like a life sentence, depressing them.

Why do some mothers take to the role so naturally? Even yearning to repeat the process later in life, eagerly awaiting the arrival of grandchildren to partake in the process all over again. Others in extenuating circumstances somehow seem to transcend the difficulties and turn the whole experience into a joyful one, as if it was second nature to them, as if they'd done it thousands of times before. Against all expectations some mothers, having had no role modelling and after a busy career, find that the baby is the 'making of them' and effortless. Some men likewise, if they had breasts, would make better mothers to their baby than their wives, so natural and familiar does the role seem to them, almost second nature.

Many believe that past life experience accounts for this, for having lived many female and mothering lifetimes, the task this time must feel less awesome. Conversely it is thought that lack of prior mothering experience and 'know how' accounts for some mothers being more prone to becoming overwhelmed and ultimately depressed. The animating principle in males, the animus, and that in females, the anima, are entirely different in their *modus operandi*, their way of being in the world. Tackling tasks male-style means identifying what is to be done, bringing your energy to bear on the job, and completing it, packaging it away. Tasks are discrete things with beginnings and endings. In the female psyche tasks can be interwoven, one flowing into the next without punctuations in between. 'A women's work is never done' never more truly applies than to housework, feeding babies, shopping, cooking, etc. In short nurturing is never over as long as those dependant on your energy have needs. This dynamic can hugely frustrate a woman whose prior life-times have mostly been male ones, and who struggles to comprehend the never-ending tidal wave of demands, each one of which when seemingly under control and completed is instantly replaced by another demand! Depressing to the male-oriented psyche, unused to such chaos and mayhem, for those experienced in female lore, this is just 'the way it is', and is celebrated as part of the great flow of life.

Your partner meanwhile has taken on the mantle of fatherhood. You look at him through a lens tinted with your own past conditioning combined with your very real present day needs, and the reality of whether or not he is meeting them. This period of time has the potential to generate conflict between the father you want him to be, and the one he is portraying. Like the female of all species, you unconsciously assess him on his ability to be a 'good provider', a protector who backs up the main act, you and your baby, with an extra pair of hands, compassion and tolerance. Unsuspecting, he is sitting an exam he doesn't even know he's taking, and you don't know you're setting. Without any prior experience he now finds himself facing the challenge of sharing the responsibility for two extremely vulnerable people.

The mother's overriding drive now is to do very little, trimming all her activities down to the minimum, needing to rest and be fed, so that she can build the reserves necessary to meet the constant demands of the baby, and possibly other children who may become clingy at this time. If the father is unable or unwilling to provide the hands-on support she needs, then this task becomes inescapably hers, and she is dependant on the often unreliable and patchy substitute support of family. Some fathers recoil from the responsibility, perhaps having been bachelor husbands, and now predictably progress on to be bachelor fathers, their life going on undisturbed. They find the trade-off worth it – arguments wash over them as does having to move out of the bedroom. The status quo is maintained at all costs.

BINDING CONTRACTS

It's part of the human condition to have contracts with yourself
and others with whom you are conducting a relationship. The
terms of some of these are implicit such as the agreements and
promises you have unconsciously made to yourself; to fulfil your
potential, to express your creativity, to honour and respect your
needs, to care for your health, to make your life meaningful, and
to endeavour to find happiness. Should you ignore or fail to fulfil these, there is a gnawing discontent, a sense of guilt, a feeling
that you have somehow betrayed a higher purpose, that you've
let your soul down. In some, this existential disquiet expresses
itself as depression. One of the difficulties in articulating this
feeling stems from the fact that the contract is non-verbal, has
never been clearly stated and may even be unconscious.

On the other hand the explicit contracts, those with others,
are conscious and binding. The mother-child relationship may
start even before the pregnancy, if the conception was planned.
In essence the mother is inviting in an unborn spirit, and pro-
mising to nurture it. When the child comes in, this contract
deepens, and her relationship to her partner changes, as he becomes the father. Three contracts are now happening concur-
rently for the mother; the one with herself, the one with her
child and the one with her partner. Ideally, they're confluent,
and don't conflict with each other. However this is often not
the case, and much confusion and turmoil results.

Caroline, a thirty-one-year-old journalist, had felt driven to write
all her life. A vivacious lively storyteller, her short stories were
acclaimed for their unique colourful style and she worked in a
weekly newspaper. When she became pregnant, she fully embraced it; watching her diet, going to yoga, and planned with her
partner to have the baby at home. The delivery went normally,
but she found it a nightmarish experience. Terrified by the in-

LIAM DELANEY.

tensity of the pain, and the panicky out-of-control feelings she thought it would never be over. It took her some days to recover from the exhaustion of the experience, and in spite of plenty of hands-on support, she found it hard to rally. As her energy plummeted and she became increasingly anxious, she began to dread having to handle things on her own when her partner went back to work, and progressively became disheartened and disillusioned.

Her depression changed in nature over the weeks and months. Initially she felt hopeless and trapped by the endless feeding and caring schedule, and the sleep deprivation. Sometimes she re-ferred to the baby as her 'Buddha' so much had it taken over their lives.

Living life as a mother was difficult, even when doing the most basic things. Everything seemed insurmountable, from cook-ing to cleaning. And a worrying shift was occurring between her partner and herself; she felt so wrapped up with the baby that it was often a strain for her to relate to him, as if she could only make room for one intimate relationship at a time. It concerned her that sex no longer interested her and that doing couple things had become another chore, and she felt guilty about ne-glecting him. The months dragged on, and she became plagued by a growing irritability about never having time to write, al-though her mind was always feverish with ideas. She called this frustration the 'pressure of the uncreated creation' and she hated it.

Almost a year later, continuing to breastfeed, she persisted in trying to be the best mother she could be, which she felt was the baby's due. Now working freelance from home, she found that her writing was frustrated by her inability to 'get a good run at it', so constricted was she by the baby's schedule. Her partner, a patient and supportive man, hated to see her like this, and encouraged her to return to her job. She resisted, but he insisted that this wasn't benefiting anyone, and even the baby was picking up her distress. She decided to find a psychotherapist, and gradually over the following months was able to put words on her confusion, and learn to balance the conflicting demands.

Joseph, a forty-year-old laboratory technician, was married for ten years to Janet, a successful businesswoman. Having tried for years they had given up on the idea of ever having children. The marriage had cooled, and Janet had become absorbed in her work. When they had met, she had been a French teacher, and at that stage they had both shared a yearning to work in the third world, to 'give something back'. However as her new career took off, she lost interest in their initial plan. Opportunities overseas came and went, a fact which frustrated Joseph, and since the marriage no longer seemed worth salvaging, he privately considered leaving and pursuing his dream. When the next temporary contract came up, one in Uganda with the WHO which involved setting up a laboratory there, he considered it seriously.

Although sex was now a rare event between them, it happened spontaneously on the night of an after-party following a highly successful concert she had handled, and they were both shocked to find that she had become pregnant. Although Janet was delighted, this news threw Joseph into a tailspin. He no longer loved her, but now felt a growing sense of responsibility towards the child. At the same time he was painfully aware that he was facing a dilemma. It would be wrong for him to jump ship now and renege on his duty as a father, but at the same time it would be inauthentic to go on with the pretence of their life as a married couple, and depressing for him to remain trapped in the life they had.

He decided to see Janet through the pregnancy and gauge how he felt after the baby was born, hiding his confusion and ambivalence from her. Following the birth, which went smoothly, Joseph was moved to find himself deeply attached to the child. Intense inner turmoil followed. He was now more trapped than ever, but couldn't tear himself away, however strong his calling was to leave the dead marriage and start a new life. Stuck and hopeless, he grieved for the future he would have to let go of, and feeling numb inside, found it increasingly difficult to motivate himself for work. His only solace was his time with his son. When Janet stopped breastfeeding and returned to work, more of the primary care fell to him, dropping and picking the baby up from the crèche, doing the night-feeds and minding him on the weekends. For a brief time the novelty of this new role as house husband and 'mother' sustained him, but as the months wore on he found himself doubting whether the price was too high. Often too tired even to enjoy his time with the baby, he started to feel depressed.

Joseph had reached a crunch point where nothing seemed to be working; his job was now meaningless to him, his relationship was empty and unrewarding, and the future held only more of the same. He went on Prozac in the hope it would give him a boost. When it didn't, he negotiated with Janet that in the interest of the baby and due to his disenchantment with his job, that he'd take temporary leave of absence. He resigned six months later. His depression continued, although he went to great lengths to hide it from his growing son.

Wendy, a thirty-one-year-old mother of a two-year-old boy and a ten-week-old girl, began to experience mounting anxiety and panic attacks soon after the second birth. Her husband held a junior diplomatic job which meant weekly travel to Brussels, and very soon after the birth, she found herself having to manage alone for several days at a time. Each day began with palpitations, difficulty breathing, dizziness, and a knot in her stomach, even before she left the bedroom. Being a paediatric nurse, specialising in the neonatal area, she was mortified at the thought of admitting to him that she felt such fear, and hid the panic from him. On the days when he was home, the anxiety was much less.

It was her thoughts which concerned her the most. They predicted every possible catastrophe. She worried that through some oversight of hers the children would come to harm, that she might not have paid enough attention to whether the fire was on or off, whether they were wearing enough clothes, or if she was spending enough time with her son. The responsibilities, and her probable shortcomings as their mother, constantly plagued her. This also confused her, for as a neonatal nurse, she very capably cared for as many as twenty babies in the nursery without the slightest hint of hesitation. She had experienced overwhelming insecurity after the first birth also, but put it down to first-time motherhood, and the fact that they were living in the UK for many months. Whenever her mother came to visit, since the responsibility was shared, she had felt less anxious. Although the nervousness lingered for at least a year, it had eventually passed.

While she found the waves of anxiety troubling, it was the mental symptoms which really undermined her confidence in her mental stability. Losing control was her worst fear. Sometimes, as the panic swept over her, she would get images flashing in, where she would see herself hurting the baby, flinging her against the wall, or suddenly getting the urge to push her head under the bath water. Secretly she feared admitting these thoughts to anyone in case a mental illness would be diagnosed, and the social services called, resulting in her children being removed from her care.

However hard she battled the thoughts, they persisted, and increasingly by the end of each day, she found herself tearful and depressed. Putting on a brave face in front of her husband, she would feign tiredness and go to bed before him, often crying herself to sleep. Eventually she consulted her family doctor, telling him that she felt drained of energy and motivation, and he recommended she try an anti-depressant. This cemented in place her conviction of being mentally ill, and her anxiety escalated. She tried them for a week, but too frightened to continue, stopped them. Instead she sought out a psychotherapist, saying she was taking a parenting class.

Wendy's father had died when she was twelve, leaving her mother to raise five young children. In telling her psychotherapist about that time, she remembered her mother trembling with anxiety, and holding her forehead in despair many times, muttering 'what'll I do? What'll I do?' Small upsets easily became unmanageable for her distraught mother, and she remembered always leaving for school in a state of disarray, often without a lunchbox or her homework done. Being able to cope with her own children had always been a priority for Wendy and she dreaded letting them down, like she felt her mother had with her. Her depression gradually lifted as she learned how to handle the anxiety attacks, and to realise that the thoughts of harming her baby were common expressions of feeling out of control, not of a mental illness.

RE-WRITING THE CONTRACT

Joseph's dilemma is more complicated than Caroline's. He is caught between honouring the contract to himself, and upholding the one to his son. His was a no-win situation. The cost of such a predicament was a continued sense of entrapment, expressing itself as depression. He arrived at an uneasy truce, to some degree having to accept that there was no solution. Although traditionally regarded as the preserve of the mother, and moreover as hormonally driven, Joseph's depression at the baby's birth was legitimately post-natal. The predicament he faced is typical for countless mothers who have learned to live making great sacrifices, remaining in intolerable, sometimes violent relationships, at huge personal cost 'for the sake of the children'. Tragically sometimes contracts with oneself cannot be re-drafted until the child is grown.

Caroline, by contrast, although juggling three conflicting contracts managed to find a way to reconcile them. The breakthrough came when she re-examined her idea of how 'good mothers' fulfil the role. And finding the middle way she learned to redefine her mothering role so that it was no longer so all-consuming, completely eclipsing her own personal needs.

Wendy's difficulty, following on her own experience as a child, centred around her absolute dedication to the idea of mothers always being able to cope. She had to learn to make allowances for the difficult circumstances she was facing, a husband who travelled, leaving her the full brunt of responsibility for much of the week. Her conditioning had taught her to unnecessarily fear the responsibilities of motherhood, and in therapy she was able to draw distinctions between her mother's desperation as a widow with no support whatsoever, facing many financial burdens, and herself, an experienced neonatal nurse. Her depression lifted once she began to share more of her concerns with her husband, overcoming her fear that her intrusive thoughts were an indication of some serious illness which would render her children motherless, her worst fear.

ACCESS CONTRACTS

Post-natal depression should be seen as transcending clinical definitions, gender, and time-span. This is self-evident where relationships break down and custody and access battles rage. Estranged parents can be plunged into depression and unspeakable torment which can last a lifetime. The adversarial legal process involved can cause parent alienation and destruction of such magnitude that desperate measures such as child homicide and suicide occur. In the hysterical emotional climate generated by the 'wronged' parent's indignation, every card in the pack is played with ruthless intent. The children become unfortunate pawns, used as instruments to inflict wounds, or avenues to convey anger. Everything from protection orders, barring orders, accusations of sexual abuse, unfaithfulness, neglect, addictions and psychiatric instability are used to fabricate a profile of the other parent as someone to whom access to their children should be denied, limited or supervised.

Some solicitors and barristers, untrained in family therapy, and therefore lacking psychological knowledge of human dynamics, run the risk of turning family law into nothing more than a thriving financial industry and bringing their entire profession into disrepute. Some behave not as legal eagles, but as vultures hovering over the battlefield looking for easy pickings. As each side fights it out, in an atmosphere of mounting distress and time urgency, enormous fees change hands, usually crippling the 'loser' and the so-called 'winner'. It is not unknown for children to find their homes sold over their heads to pay legal costs, in the name of indulging one hurt parent's thirst for revenge. It is rare to find 'good counsel' given to such a parent, cautioning them to rein in their anger in favour of prioritising their 'beloved' children's needs.

Suddenly, parents who were up until then considered safe and adequate, find themselves considered a danger to their children, an unfit parent. They find themselves being assessed by some willing psychologists and psychiatrists, acting as hired guns, providing reports as to their suitability as parents, blatantly favouring the paymasters. How can judges be expected to make just rulings in the fog of such a war is a miracle, faced with a tide of skilfully presented, sanitised and carefully selected facts, backed by the evidence of 'expert' witnesses. In fact, the rise of legal lying in the name of the 'truth' is now common place.

A parent's image is systematically destroyed in the name of proving him or her to be rotten to the core, when in fact it is their failure as a husband or wife which has become the issue, not their parenting. Somehow they must be made pay, and the cost is the children's alienation from them, which can be life-long. When the battle is over and the spoils divided, devastation is the legacy. Many regret that they allowed themselves to be steered by their legal team in this way. Some realise too late, that they were manoeuvred and bullied into taking positions from which there was no coming back. 'Let's take the bastard to the cleaners', 'Let's teach the bitch a lesson', 'Let's get every penny'. (It is not uncommon practice for a legal team to try on the issue of custody and access in straightforward separation and divorce cases, in order to up the stakes, and put the frighteners on the other side. The agenda is to generate as much fear and conflict as possible, a side effect of which is more fees.)

Emotional chaos can possess the parent who has been ob-structed from fulfilling their private contract to their children. In a climate of overplayed adherence to timing of visits, slam-ming down of phones, awkward silent Sunday afternoon meals in fast food restaurants, tearful departures, Christmas days spent apart, and threats of further legal action – depression, hope-lessness and despair thrive. Now with nothing to lose, with no purpose to their lives, feeling totally alone and consumed with mental and emotion turmoil, irrational actions can be embarked on. Some fathers sever all contacts, some commit suicide, while some mothers kill their children and then themselves. One father recently resorted to pouring petrol over himself in a soli-citor's office, setting himself on fire, such was his frustration at not being taken seriously. These tragedies fill our newspapers and should beseen for what they are, failures of the legal system instead of a psychiatric illness. Such medicalisation allows society to shirk its responsibility and avoid putting in place a truly humanitarian system of justice. Good legislation works. Models of such exist in other countries, in particular New Zealand where the orientation is towards the well-being of the children.

CHAPTER 12

Suicide – The Black Swan Approach

ALL SWANS ARE WHITE UNTIL A BLACK SWAN COMES ALONG

Suicide – intentional self-killing – has been used by human beings for aeons to bring an end to intolerable suffering. We are the only form of life that is self-conscious, can hate and loathe ourselves to our very bones, and can plan and execute our own death. Suicide has always been part of the repertoire of human solutions to human problems.

There is an abundance of material floating out there on the subject; statistics, personality profiles, preventive measures, deficiencies of neurotransmitter substances, psychological post mortems, etc. All white swans, with many shared attributes in common. We would like to introduce the black swan.

It is not our intention to present the definitive interpretation of every aspect of suicide, from its conception right to its execution. Or indeed to offer the ultimate or perfect solution. There can be none. Why? Because suicide, like birth, life and death is very personal, no two can be the same. Add in that aspect of us we call our essence or our soul, and it becomes even more inaccessible to outside interpretation and analysis.

We can never fully understand the motives of another human being, or their thinking, for consciousness is by its nature immeasurable and unpredictable, and beyond the reach even of the instruments of science, themselves a product of it. For this very reason any objective predictions of suicide and absolute methods of control are impossible. It is with this inherent limitation in mind that we can offer merely an option, to be considered by a potential suicide: an invitation to re-examine their stance and entertain something novel.

POISED ON THE BRINK

You have come to the point where the only control you feel you can bring to bear on your mental and emotional turmoil is to obliterate yourself and end the suffering. To date you may have gone down the route all desperate people go, that of 'trying everything' in your search for peace of mind; self-help books on depression, different cocktails of anti-depressant medication, second and third medical opinions, counselling and psychotherapy, self-development workshops, alcohol and recreational drugs, or filling your life with distractions. You may even have attempted suicide before, either on the spur of the moment or following months of careful planning. Or you may, as is equally common, have said nothing to anyone and taken none of the above steps. At this point you may have already worked out precisely your suicide route to the last detail – the method, the day, the time, the hour, making sure to have no interruptions. You have possibly even composed your suicide notes and played the video in your mind of people's reaction on finding them.

READY, STEADY ...

- Your mind is ceaselessly stalking your problem and looking at it from every possible angle, frantically seeking a solution, obsessively playing over and over the same images, videos, tapes and programmes.
- Having passed the threshold of what you feel able to endure, you are desperate to end the torment right now. You are absolutely convinced that you cannot go on living any longer, with your life as it is, with this much anxiety, or with such despair. You are beyond the dark night of the soul.
- Feeling deeply hurt and disillusioned by some crushing betrayal, loss, rejection or abandonment, your mind is spinning with a variety of bottom-line conclusions:
  'Nothing I do is going to make any difference.'

'I don't belong here, the sooner I'm gone the better.'
'I can't go on with this charade any more.'
'No one cares about me.'
'No one understands me, I'm on my own with this.'
'This is the only way out.'
'I'm such a failure.'

- With your mind in the driving seat, consuming all your energy, you have become disconnected from your body, no longer caring about food, rest or pleasure.
- With an increasing distance between you and the world, you're ignoring all efforts by others to engage you, merely going through the motions, without much feeling or empathy for them.
- Your heart is closed. Hope, compassion, forgiveness, acceptance and love have all become things of the past.
- Helpless, with your will paralysed, it's hard work finding the energy and motivation to do anything creative or new. Hurt by the world, you have recoiled into yourself, becoming locked into your inner world. You are now interfacing only with a movie screen reflecting back to you nothing but your own ineffectiveness, in which you see no hope of ever creating a place for yourself again in the outside world.
- You are consumed by a conviction that someone or something is to blame for your misery, and the fires of resentment, bitterness and anger burn brightly. Someone must pay. Once you've branded the culprit your mind plays the video of the impact your death will have on them, that moment when they'll realise they have driven you to suicide.
- Guilt, shame and the pain of past wrong-doing have eclipsed all purpose or reason to go on. Your anger and self-loathing has reached the point where paying the ultimate price is the only form of suitable punishment to suit your 'crime'. You are the judge, jury, prosecutor and are now planning your execution.

God, the ultimate rescuer, for abandoning you to
ery, cynical thoughts reign supreme. You see life as
lost all meaning, value or moral order, where chaos
is in a pointless void.

- You feel the serenity of commitment, of having made your
  mind up, other-worldly with providence on your side, floating free of your problems and your old life, disconnected
  from it and keen to be entering your new one.

PRESS PAUSE

We have established that there is a complex process involved in
you arriving at such a serious decision as ending your life. You've
obviously given it a lot of consideration. You've arrived at the
point where the pain of continuing your life far outweighs the
fear of ending it, and have made a decision to go ahead.

How did you come to make such a judgement? For most important decisions which are going to have serious consequences
you would usually go through a format. You'd gather in as much
information as you could, arrange it all out so you could see the
entire picture in as full a way as possible, and having given due
consideration to the pros and cons, you'd make an informed
choice. Let's look at what 'informed' means.

What difference would it make if you were a bride at the alter,
about to marry your beloved, to receive at the eleventh hour
some new information you hadn't known of before – that he is
in fact already married, and father to two children living in another part of the country, or that he is gay and always has been,
or that he will later on refuse to have children, having always
disliked them?

What if you were a potential investor about to entrust your
nest egg, hard earned over decades of conscientious work, in a
new venture suggested to you by someone you hardly knew. Would
you make a different decision if you knew that in fact the com-

pany was in name only, a complete fiction existing only on paper, and that hundreds of others had lost life savings through it, like you were about to do?

The point here is that for any decision-maker such as yourself, having the full picture could change everything. To make an important decision from a restricted vantage point makes you vulnerable to making a mistake which you may regret later, and forever pay the price for.

Marriage and investments are trivial choices compared to that of taking your own life, which is the only truly irreversible one there is. The fact is that there are relevant factors at play in the moment of choice, which you are unaware of; pieces of information which even at this late hour we invite you to consider.

As an individual on the brink of suicide your mindset has one flaw, one well hidden from you. Your mind has become skewed, and as such is primed to make a serious error. 'Not so!' you will object, 'Only I know the full story, you haven't walked in my shoes, lived inside my skin, felt my pain. If you had you wouldn't be so quick to suggest I'm making the wrong decision. I've been fucked over and over and I just can't take it any more. I'm out of here.'

The legitimacy of your argument and the way you feel go without saying. But on what is your judgement based? Your mind? Is it wise to depend for your solution on the instrument which has been the very source of all your distress, a piece of software containing a virus? Could you trust it? No doubt the bride and the investor trusted theirs too, until the point at which those hidden facts were revealed. If their mind remained skewed in favour of doggedly maintaining their course – love is blind after all, and the smell of quick money can eclipse clear thinking – this would render them beyond all sensible cautions to pause and reconsider.

It is fair comment to say that your mind has taken absolute control. It is as if your personhood and sense of being has been taken over by a dictator. One which, like all dictators, be they Caesar, Hitler or Mao, will tolerate no questioning or dissent. Can you trust such a mind not to send you on a suicide mission in its name? What if it was wrong?

UNPLUGGED FROM THE MAINS – THE STATE OF DISCONNECTION
Suspend your thinking temporarily and consider plan B. Central to the black swan approach is a non-intellectual solution to your predicament, which bypasses your mind.

Your state, your suicidal state, is a reflection of a closed or malfunctioning energy system. (Those who work in vibrational medicine are familiar with such a state, its symptoms and its causes. This will be elaborated on later in Appendix 3.) If your energy was in the open state you would not be experiencing such a profound sense of shut-down to life. Consider what happens in the morning when people awaken, there is a build up of energy in the body which animates it for the day ahead. No matter how tired they had been the previous night, this surge is miraculously there for them, allowing them to act out all the various roles they need to during their day. All life forms experience this surge, be they your dog, your cat or your canary, and it is ultimately connected to the universal life-force itself, the same source which energises the daffodils to appear reliably each year and the sun and moon to faultlessly rotate.

If one office computer isn't turning on while all the other ones are, it's more than likely because it's not plugged in. Your suicidal status, obviously different from your contented family and friends, is trying to tell you something: it's a messenger telling you you're disconnected. When that current of energy isn't flowing this is how you'd feel:

- Our survival drive is instinctive and present in all life-forms. We are plugged into the life-force just as surely as all the machines in our kitchen are to the mains. This allows us to keep going, to keep functioning at all costs, no matter how immense the fear, the effort required, the mountain to be scaled. Our record at surviving life-threatening events is legion. We are human beings, and we are here to be, right to the final curtain. In your case your survival drive has been eclipsed by the opposing strength of your convictions to terminate and abort the mission.

- What about feelings? We all know some emotionally intelligent people – they're sympathetic and the feelings of others matter to them. Because of their empathic nature their orientation is towards the group, the collective, having 'we' more than 'me' energy. They are just as mindful of their own needs, and never self-destructive, instead seeking out pleasurable and sensuous experiences, ranging from nice food to sexual intimacies. They are both givers and receivers. Without such energy you'd be feeling numbed down and walled off to the world of feeling. In this state, self-mutilation could be a practice that you might have engaged in as the only way of breaking through the numbness, through feeling the pain and seeing the blood.

- Willpower and motivation come easily if one's energy is flowing. Tasks get done, ideas are implemented and follow-through occurs in the direction of one's life purpose, hopes and aspirations. One is effective, with a strong sense of personal identity. In your disconnected state, frustration, irritability, ineffectiveness and paralysis of will are commonplace.

- Let's take love. We locate its energy in the heart, and you have not being experiencing its benefit. Think of someone with an open heart. They possess the qualities of acceptance, trust, hope, non-judgement, forgiveness, compassion, which appear to spontaneously flow out of them. We would even regard them as having a lot of 'soul'. Heart energy says 'anything is possible' and is open to new things. In order to be on the brink of suicide your heart energy has to be shut down.

- Your creative drive is the charge behind all forms of communication and expression. It facilitates free, open and authentic communication, the ability to listen, to tell our story, and to put form on what arises in our imagination. Since your creative juice has dried up, a staleness sets in, where novelty is rare and ways of communication blocked. And therefore you favour silence and secrecy.

- Flexibility of mind is essential on any journey, as it allows you to make necessary adjustments in the face of obstacles which arise along the way. As such, you make judgements and decisions as to how best to deal with new demands: 'Let me see, how will I tackle this?' In a state of rigidity, with hardening of your attitudes, tunnel-vision, and with only a one-track mind to guide you, your range of manoeuvrability has shrunk. The irony is that you still unshakeably believe that you are absolutely correct in your judgements and intolerant to any view to the contrary.

- Having a map of where you are going in life, you develop beliefs and convictions as to how best to make that journey possible. Realising your dreams, becoming the person you want to be, and creating the kind of world you want to live in, give meaning and purpose to your existence. Since you have lost your connection with your path, all your expectations have evaporated, grinding your life to a total standstill. Such has been the meltdown in your outer world, that you've lost the plot. The only thing you now know is that you need to unplug permanently from the life-force.

DOWN WITH THE DICTATOR – MAKE A LEAP OF FAITH

Healing comes in many forms, many of which you have already tried. We invite you to rebel, to overthrow your dictator by partaking in the practice of energetic healing methods and other essential actions.

Because your mind has ceased relating to your body, it now wants to part company with it and we have established that the best persuasive arguments are not going to alter its view. So we're not going to work directly with the mind. We're going to take an action approach. Quite simply we are going to connect the body again to the mind and not allow it to 'go it alone' any longer, holding forth, ranting on, ignoring the body's right to a voice. It's been the dictator for too long, silencing your emotional world, and leaving your body out in the cold. Our intention is to facilitate you to bring the body centre stage, and by doing so to create new emotions, and to eliminate the virus in the software of your mind, by laying down new circuits.

MOVE YOUR ENERGY BY DOING SOMETHING PHYSICAL

Every day, set your alarm clock, and get out of bed, splash your face with cold water, and get out of your house as quickly as possible, and start moving. Whether it's walking or jogging. Whether it's on a footpath, on the beach, in a forest, or in a field: just move. Get ahead of your mind, don't give it time to warm up.

AFTERWARDS – TAKE A SHOWER

Alternate it from being as hot as you can bear, then as cold as you can bear. Do it for as long as you can.

ENERGETIC BREATH-WORK.

Creating stillness through the breath: Breathe in, making your inhalation last to a count of eight, filling your entire lungs. As you do so, support this in-breath with the statement 'My inhalation brings silence'. Hold for a count of four. Then exhale for a count of eight, and as you do so support the out-breath with the statement 'My exhalation brings peace'. Pause again for a count of four. Repeat this cycle for three minutes.

Six-directional breathing: Sit in a quiet room, on an upright chair, feet planted on the ground, hands in your lap. Close your eyes. Visualise the air around you as gold which you are going to breathe in. Start with the front of your body. Take a deep breath, and visualise that you are drawing the air in through the front of your body through tiny pores, as if the skin all over your body was a lung, exhaling out through the back. Now reverse the process by drawing the gold air back in through pores on the back of your body, exhaling it out through the front. Repeat this twice more.

Next breathe in through the left side of your body, exhaling out through the right, then back in through the right side, exhaling out through the left. Repeat this twice more.

Now inhale the gold air through the top of your body all the way down, to exhale it out through the soles of your feet. Repeat this twice more. And finally, inhale the gold air through the soles of your feet, right up through your body, exhaling it out through the top of your head. Repeat this twice more.

SOUND WORK – CHANTING

Focus your attention in the area of your heart (centre of love and compassion), at the centre of your chest. Take in as deep a breath as you can, and as you exhale make the following sound using the syllables: HUM – AH – EEE – OLA – OM

Repeat this eight more times, nine in all, all the time focusing on your heart area.

Focus your attention on your solar plexus (centre of will), in the area at the end of your breast bone. Take in a deep breath, and as you exhale repeat the same chant nine times.

Now focus your attention on your mid-abdomen approximately two fingers distance below your navel (centre of feeling). Take in a deep breath, and as you exhale repeat the same chant nine times.

CASTING THE BURDEN – SHARING THE PROBLEM
First imagine handing over your problem into the care of a higher power. This can be your spirit, your inner divinity, the universal life-force, or your version of God, whatever you feel represents that concept for you. Now, repeat over and over in your mind the following statement, making whatever adjustments you need to until it fits for you: 'I cast the burden of my pain and suffering (or the issue of … or my problem with … or my difficulty about …) onto my inner divinity (or your own alternative) so that I may be free to give full expression to my potential. An example might go like this. 'I cast the burden of my lost relationship onto my spirit, so that I may be free to give full expression to my potential' or 'I cast the burden of my tormented mind onto God so that I may be free to give full expression to my potential'.

CATHARSIS – EMOTIONAL DISCHARGE
Find a way to discharge the destructive energy inside you. Break the circle, stop it going round and round gathering momentum.

Empty your mind of it somehow:
- turn the music up loud in your car or house, or drive to the beach or the country, and scream your head off until you're exhausted.
- call the Samaritans.
- get an immediate acupuncture session – today – it opens the closed circuits in your body and acts like a release valve on a pressure cooker.

REFLECTION

Repetition of these practices is vital. Initially you won't feel like doing them. Your mind is afraid now of losing its grip and will try to sabotage you by asking what difference they're making, suggesting reasons to give them up, but these can't be entertained.

The first-thing-in-the-morning activity is non-negotiable, it must be so to unseat the mind from its habit of taking over your very first thought. Moving of your energy or 'chi' can be undertaken in a layered manner. Start by a minimum of a half hour walk if you're unfit, then work it slowly upwards, then see if you can progress to a slow jog, then make it more vigorous, and for longer, as time goes on. If a different activity such as cycling or swimming attracts you more as a substitute, embrace it.

The breath and sound work ideally should be done three times a day.

Casting the burden is a way of giving the mind a break from having to be the sole problem-solver, and can be repeated over and over, particularly when the suicidal thoughts and the wagging finger and taunts of the dictator are most active.

Catharsis as a means of discharge is as old as time. Be creative, find a way.

FOLLOW-UP

All of the above practices are something you can do on your own. You will find that you will notice a shift in the days and weeks following their implementation. When you've decided to give life another chance, when you've stepped back from the brink, the momentum needs to be kept up, otherwise your mind will gain the upper hand again.

YOGA

The term comes from the Sanskrit word meaning union. It stands out as one of the only forms of body movement which has as its explicit intention the unification of the mind, body and spirit in a quest for physical and mental well-being, and a sense of tranquillity. The very act of going through the series of postures achieves this. Yoga classes are widely available and the input of a trained teacher in the beginning is invaluable. At a later stage, your yoga practice can be carried on by you at home and there are numerous videos and DVDs to help you.

ACUPUNCTURE

Acupuncture is an ancient form of energetic healing. It restores the free flow of energy which has become blocked and stagnant in depression. With the reactivation of the life-force, the heart opens and the vital qualities of hope, compassion and calmness emerge, paving the way for new beginnings.

HOMEOPATHY

In the hands of a skilled practitioner, homeopathy can be a powerful adjunct in the dark times when one contemplates self-annihilation. The following are some of the main remedies homeopaths use to assist patients in suicidal states, together with the symptom patterns relevant to each:

Anacardium: Paranoid states; torn between two wills; profound melancholy and angry despair.

Arsenicum album: Restless with great mental anguish, fear; obsessed with order; suspicious; oversensitive.

Aurum metallicum: Sense of utter worthlessness, self-condemnation; overburdened with responsibility and guilt.

Cimicifuga: Enveloped with despair; darkness and confusion; sense of impending doom; often hormone-related.

Hyoscyamus: Suspicious, paranoid delusions; hysterical reactions; delirium; jealous rages.

Ignatia: Full of suppressed grief; feels hopeless; hysterical states; loss of loved ones.

Kali bromatum: Everybody conspiring against him; disgust for life; delusionary states; hallucinations; feels abandoned by all, even God.

Lachesis: Anguished; lost control of mind, tongue; sexual/ religious conflicts; feels poisoned, hated, despised.

Mercurius: Weary of life; suspiciousness; full of irrational impulses; self mutilation.

Natrum muriaticum: Sensitive and reserved; prolonged, unexpressed grief; desires solitude; dwells constantly on past hurts.

Natrum sulphuricum: Constantly struggles with suicidal impulses; deep melancholy; solitary; depressed, suicidal after head injury.

Nitric acid: Hopeless despair; full of anger about past troubles; hard and vindictive.

Picric acid: Exhausted, burnt out by life's stresses; mentally unable to think, concentrate.

Psorinum: Despondent, despairs of ever recovering; feels abjectly alone, a failure; feels forsaken by all.

Sepia: Worn out by constant demands; emotionally, physically drained; total indifference to life and loved ones.

Veratrum album: Religious delusions and despair; mania; sullen indifference; frenzied excitement.

HANDS-ON WORK
Chiropractic work, cranio-sacral balancing or deep-tissue massage – to release tension from the spine, joints, ligaments, muscles and connective tissue.

COMMUNITY SUPPORT
The track record of organisations such as Recovery, Grow, Alcoholics and Narcotics Anonymous is beyond dispute. They are accessible, user-friendly, and most importantly accepting and

supportive. You will not be alone for long, they have heard versions of your story many times. If a reconnection with a higher power helps you, shop around and find an outlet that meets this need, church services, prayer meetings, etc.

PSYCHOTHERAPY

Get a psychotherapist who is skilled to take you beyond hand-holding and the tissue box, reconnecting you to your survival instinct, your feeling world, your will and motivation, your heart, your creativity, your insight and the bigger picture. Get a psychotherapist who is a soul attendant. If you can find one who can help you appreciate that you are a spiritual being having a human experience, then you have found gold. At the most pivotal moment of your life you need someone who is open hearted and totally accepting of you, no matter what it is you have to say. Someone who will take you at face value without the slightest hint of judgement, disapproval or disquiet. Someone who you can trust and who will be absolutely confidential, in other words whatever you tell them stays in the room.

Behind the drive to take your life could be one of the following reasons:

- You're overwhelmed with guilt and shame over something you've done, which may inevitably become public knowledge and for which you may be punished or cause your family great distress.
- You may have had a bad experience with recreational drugs, leaving you paranoid and convinced that you're going mad and will spend your life in a psychiatric hospital.
- You may worry that because you were sexually abused as a child you will turn into a paedophile and abuse other children.
- You may be misinterpreting panic attacks – racing heart, diffi-

culty breathing, dizziness, sweating, fear of dying and escalating levels of anxiety if you can't get out of a place easily
– thinking they are the first signs of a mental illness.

- You may imagine that in a moment of loss of control you
could harm another person – stab them, strangle them, or
even run them down in your car – and that everyone is safer
if you're off the planet.

- You may be the target of bullying, sexual harassment, sexual
abuse or intimidation, in seemingly inescapable situations.

- You may be addicted to a substance like heroin and can no
longer carry on with the endless cycle of stealing, lying,
prostitution, fending off menacing dealers and mounting
debts.

- You may be confused about your sexual orientation, and for a
variety of reasons unable to cope with being gay, fearing the
repercussions of coming out.

- You have experienced an episode of sexual inadequacy and
fear that it may be life long, failing to realise that such occurrences are a common temporary side effect of performance anxiety, alcohol and some recreational drugs.

- You may have had your heart broken by the love of your life,
and without them have no wish to continue living, so great
is your pain.

- You may have reached the limit of your endurance in terms of
psychologically distressing symptoms, which have been
diagnosed as part of a life-long illness for which you have
been told you will always need medication and periodic
hospitalisation.

- You may be taking SSRI (selective serotonin re-uptake inhibitors) anti-depressant medication such as Seroxat, Lexapro, Efexor and Prozac.

- You may be overwhelmed by the responsibility of crossing the
line into adulthood and having to take care of yourself –

find a job, a place to live, and to totally fund yourself.
- You may be crippled with social awkwardness, feeling that you will never make friends or ever have a boy or girlfriend.

If you have experienced the psychiatric services as an ill wind, don't re-expose yourself to them simply because you feel you've run out of options. There are always more options.

You need to map out your future relationship with life in a new way, one that you could consider committing to instead of wanting to disengage from. The process of reconstructing yourself cannot be done overnight. A boat which must remain afloat has to be repaired a plank at a time. A good psychotherapist can help you do this. Alternatively, if circumstances allow, it may be an option to repair it on dry land – taking time-out in a retreat centre, a healing sanctuary, a monastery, a meditation centre. Somewhere you feel safe, comfortable and cradled, with willing support available to you. Having given yourself 'space in the brain' you may still need psychotherapy.

Time-out is not unlike the frog in the pot story. If you put a frog into a pot of hot water, it will jump out. However, if you put it into a pot of cold water and slowly heat it one degree at a time, the frog will stay where it is and die. What's the difference between the two scenarios? Awareness. The heat in the first pot is such a shock to the system that the frog knows beyond doubt what it has to do to stay alive. The second pot fools it, since the heat builds up too slowly for its radar to even register that it's in trouble until it's too late.

Psychotherapy, while it can help you to repair, rebuild and heal yourself, also has an extra dimension – one that is in the direction of personal liberation, where you can rebuild yourself into a form which you can approve of and accept, no matter what your faults.

CHAPTER 13

Psychotherapy – Personal Liberation

Psychotherapy derives from the Greek *psyche* meaning soul and *therapeia* meaning attendance. It's a science of personal liberation. One that holds the belief that we can be more than bundles of conditioned reflexes, capable of transcending the very worst that life can fire at us. It offers the prospect of inner peace, self-love, spiritual awareness and interconnectedness.

Peter, a thirty-five-year-old businessman, was passed over for promotion in a computer company. Since he had been working towards the position for years, he became deeply depressed, disappointed that he would now not have this opportunity to prove himself. Although his job was still secure the news made him feel like leaving, because of his sense of embarrassment and wounded pride. It opened up past wounds – a relationship with his father fraught with criticism and verbal abuse, and a teacher who had bullied and humiliated him in front of his other classmates. Self-criticism was always a mental habit with Peter, fed by the constant need to prove himself, and leading to him setting excessively high standards for himself, his staff and even his children. He felt misunderstood and alone, made all the more difficult by the fact that his wife criticised him for overreacting, and rebuked him about not getting over it, as it was affecting the entire family.

Sarah, age forty-three, a mother of three teenagers, wasn't altogether surprised when she discovered that her husband John was having an affair. It had happened before and like the previous ones Sarah waited for this one to blow over. What shocked her was the fact that this time he had fallen in love with his new girlfriend and wanted to move out of home, which he did. They had been childhood sweethearts and her heart was broken. She withdrew from the world, weeping for hours and spending all her time alone, and because she wasn't sleeping, drinking heavily towards evening. Her mother advised her to see her family doctor, who prescribed anti-depressants which gave her some more energy to re-engage with others, but didn't help the pervasive sense of emptiness and hopelessness that she'd ever feel happy again. The happier she saw others being, the angrier she became at her new situation.

Patricia, a fifty-one-year-old single woman working as an executive in a ministerial department of the government, after a recent promotion found herself the target of bullying by her new boss. This highly qualified, confident woman had always had a track record of excelling at her job. Her area of expertise was in conflict resolution and labour law, and aided by her prior experience as a trade union official, she had through the years negotiated many successful outcomes in challenging situations. She was stunned to find that her boss related to her as a threat, and had set about mounting a campaign to undermine her authority. He used every opportunity to question and devalue her work, even using group meetings to humiliate her. Every effort to defend herself was met with silence from their superiors, and an increased effort on his part to crush her. Constantly feeling frustrated, vigilant and alienated, after eighteen months her health wore down, with frequent infections, migraine headaches, a rise in blood pressure and chronic insomnia becoming the norm. She could think of nothing else but him, playing over and over in her mind conversations they had had and situations of reprimand and humiliation. Nightmares followed high levels of anxiety, and she was ultimately diagnosed with post-traumatic stress, her cardinal symptom of that being depression.

Martin, a twenty-two-year-old college student, got his first panic attack at a party following a rock concert, as a result of taking over a hundred magic mushrooms. He was overtaken by a wave of intense fear, feelings of dizziness and unreality, worried that his heart would explode it was beating so strongly. He couldn't breathe properly, and hurriedly left the party. In the following days and weeks he remained in a state of constant vigilance, convinced he had done some permanent damage to his brain, so paralysed and paranoid was his thinking. At college, and in crowded places he continued to have panic attacks, and found himself having to run out of pubs and lectures, finally avoiding them altogether. He saw his future as being altered for ever, shunned as a 'weirdo', friendless and dependant. This bleak scenario deeply depressed him, and he began contemplating suicide. He had decided that one day when the house was empty he would hang himself.

KNOW THYSELF – WISDOM CHIPS

From ancient to modern times, human beings have intuitively sensed that inner disquiet and distress could be transcended by the acquisition of certain wisdoms and behaviours. The awareness that inner turmoil affected interpersonal relationships and ultimately the cohesion and co-operation within communities, spurred on the search for 'the' answer to this perennial problem. Gurus, high priests, shamans, prophets, philosophers, religions and spiritual practices, facilitated the search for a solution, making inner wisdom their goal.

The ancient Greeks probably came the closest to offering an answer. Over the entrance to the temple at Delphi, where intellectuals and leaders consulted with the Oracle, the voice of the gods, was the inscription: Know Thyself!

This is not an invitation to bask in the sun of our own ego, marvelling at our special talents and attributes, but more importantly to acquire a knowledge of our entire personality including our prejudices, inadequacies and shortfalls. Obviously we are better equipped for life if we know our strengths as well as our weaknesses – what impels us forward and what holds us back. Knowledge of the workings of our inner life is ultimately the rock on which we build our self. It leads to the growth of inner wisdom, personal control and a power base on which to rely as we work in the external world, in a sense providing psychological air-bags to buffer us against setbacks. These are the core building blocks of healing.

The cases above are typical of many distressed people who make their way to our consulting rooms seeking help with a predicament or life issue. By that time all of them have crossed a line in their life, after which they became aware of no longer being able to handle the roadblock in front of them. From that moment on, either their previous ways of engaging the world seemed inadequate, or the impact of the trauma simply became so overwhelming that it left them in a state of paralysis and hopelessness. Either way, in order to re-engage with the future again, they need help to find some new avenues of movement, and some even to create a new identity completely different from their old one. In this sense psychotherapy truly is 'soul attending'.

Psychotherapy has the objective of assisting individuals such as these in the following key ways:

- By creating a safe, compassionate, non-judgemental listening space where they can unburden themselves and work through a grief, a loss, a disappointment, etc.
- By helping them to develop more effective coping skills to deal

with difficult situations or people, such as a bully at work, a violent husband, an unsuitable school.

- By enabling them to find contentment and peace of mind through fostering a healthy, non-judgemental, loving relationship with themselves.

By the time Peter presented himself for psychotherapy, plagued with self-loathing and shame for having failed, he was haunted by his father's words 'You will never amount to anything'. He spent his days visiting the various exhibits in the museum of his mind. Past failures and setbacks – the time a teacher humiliated him in front of his class for making a mistake, when he didn't make it onto the football team, when a girlfriend left him for his best friend, and when his father beat him for having his bicycle stolen. He was obsessing over what he'd done wrong to have missed the promotion, and all the qualities that the new guy had that he felt he lacked. He simply saw himself as a bad provider, a bad husband and a bad father.

All reassurance from his wife to the contrary fell on deaf ears. Peter had just about managed over the years to hang on to some version of himself as capable and competent, but the new development had changed all that, exposing him as someone whose self-esteem and sense of his own worth was fragile, and far too dependant on his performance in the various roles.

The task he and his psychotherapist have to undertake together is to peel back the layers of hurt which have put in place some of his thinking habits, and which have resulted in him relating to himself as a worthless human being, undeserving of compassion or forgiveness. In order to do this, he must first be helped to understand some of the dynamics of how the mind operates.

Mind Works

Self-consciousness – How I See Myself
   'I hated myself for letting them down.'
   'I was so ashamed of myself for screwing up.'
   'I'll never forgive myself for being so stupid.'

Peter is all too familiar with such inner judgements. Yet if he stopped to examine what was happening he would see that there are two parts of him talking to each other– 'I' and 'myself'. Which is the real me? Both.

What sets us apart from any other form of life is our ability to symbolise, to think in words, to reflect, to compare ourselves to others, in other words to be self-conscious (from the Latin *conscious* meaning to know within oneself). This implies the faculty of seeing oneself, and of being self-aware as though we were standing back observing another part of ourselves. As we've seen above, each human being has effectively two aspects to this self-consciousness, namely that of the observer and that part which is being observed, which we will call the performer or actor. All of our inner dialogue occurs between these two. This is known as the intrapersonal relationship.

These two partners in our mind can get along or be constantly at war. If this relationship is tranquil, then inner peace and self-love prevails. In other words there is harmony and non-judgement. If on the other hand they're at each others throats all the time, how dramatically different life is for the poor performer. Now every action is scathingly judged, compared unfavourably to others, and ridiculed, with respect and approval withheld by his tormentor. This mental situation was observed by Milton: 'The mind is a place which of itself can make a heaven of hell, or a hell of heaven'.

THE CRITIC – THE OBSERVER WITH A BAD ATTITUDE

When we are born we are in a sense parachuted onto the stage of life into a role with a pre-determined script defining how we should live it. None of us had the opportunity to sit down with God and chose whether to be born, our time of arrival, gender, looks, nationality, family, religion, level of intelligence and so on. Leaving aside the notion of karma and pre-birth choice, many of us feel we are living a life which we have not chosen, but paradoxically are held responsible by our observer for being the way we are, blamed as if we had a choice in the matter.

According to our scripted role, the observer will imply that one of our first duties is to make our parents happy. A hideous expectation, given that all the resources are on the parental side in terms of power, control and know-how. Not only are we expected to be pleasing to our parents, but also to our siblings, relatives, peers and later our teachers, employers, partners and so on. To ensure that we fit into this formula, society subtly moulds our observer through an unconscious conditioning process – a brainwashing. Our observer emerges from this convinced that it can only love and approve of us as long as we meet society's conditions. If we don't, loving care and attention, so vital for any young person, will be withheld.

Over the entrance to every home, school, and workplace should be inscribed the prophetic words: 'As you are perceived by others, so shall you perceive yourself'. Put simply, if as a child you are repeatedly told 'you're no good, you're no good, you're no good' then eventually you will believe it, internalise it as the voice of your observer, and find yourself automatically thinking 'I'm no good, I'm no good, I'm no good'. In other words our observer takes up the stick with which we've been beaten, and beats us in equal measure. In this way the critic is born. This is the kind of observer which Peter has developed, one who is hostile, judgemental and who makes his life a misery. In extreme circumstances such an onslaught might encourage some to take their own lives. This state is self-loathing at its most destructive.

Saying it another way – let's return to the analogy of the stage of life and the drama of being a child. Instead of our observer being in the front row applauding our performance as an admiring friend, many experience a heckler who throws abuse and rotten eggs. It seems as though their observer had been taken to the back of the theatre, and brainwashed by agents who represent different societal schools of thinking and conditioning, then returned to the front row instructed in how to give you, on the stage, a hard time. This heckling makes the performer begin to doubt himself and forget he is doing his best with the resources available to him. Then he takes the criticism to be true. Within this model for those whose observer has been trained to be such a critic, it means that a part of them is pitched against themselves, much like having a hand which is unceasingly trying to choke them. They are sleeping with the enemy, but it's inside them. It seems unbelievably that we can actually end up with a mind that is assaulting us.

Contrast this with a child who has been cherished by loving parents, their efforts praised, and failures and difficulties understood and allowances made. This paves the way for the development of a loving, peaceful, intrapersonal relationship between the observer and performer, and ultimately the notion of unity where both are on the same side.

It is self-evident that the quality of our relationship with ourselves dictates in like measure the quality of our relationship with others. If I don't like myself I can't genuinely like others, if I don't love myself I can't genuinely love others. There is no track record of generosity of spirit.

Rate the severity of your own critic on a scale of 0–10.

THE WITNESS – YOU CAN'T CHANGE WHAT YOU'RE NOT AWARE OF

Before we can liberate ourselves from the tyranny of the critic we must first become aware of its presence and the stranglehold it has over our life. We can have no doubts that it enslaves us to a life of misery and mental turmoil, and that ultimately it prevents us from reaching our true potential, finding our life purpose and connecting to our higher self.

In the very act of standing back, as you would when watching yourself in a video, objectively and from a distance, your witness or higher self is born. It is only with the witness in place that the critical observer can be systematically dismantled to allow the development of the supportive and loving friend we deserve.

Within the stage analogy, the witness can be seen as the director. That part of us that sits in the gallery, watching the self-conscious performer from a distant viewing point. The witness can make a clear distinction between the performer and the observer. It can appreciate that the performer is 'dancing as fast as they can'. It can understand that the harshness of the critic comes from having internalised the voices around it, perhaps through the whole of their childhood and teenage years, voices which were judgemental, perfectionist, impossible to please, unloving and unsupportive.

Unfortunately for many, such is the fusion and enmeshing of the critic and the performer, with its inherent turmoil, that neither the space nor the time is available for the witness to emerge. This tragic situation obliterates any possible awareness that the words of the critic are untruths, resembling the propaganda used by any tyrant to keep their subjects ignorant, fearful and powerless. This state ensures that access to the higher self is denied and that personal evolution is totally eclipsed.

The witness position is the gateway to personal freedom. By cutting us loose from the critical observer, it frees us to make

WITNESS

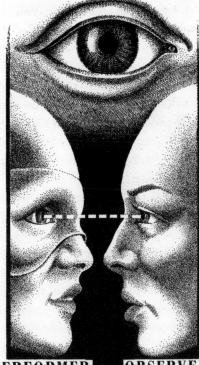

FRIEND
OR
CRITIC

PERFORMER   OBSERVER

INTRA-PERSONAL
RELATIONSHIP

THE STAGE
OF
LIFE

realistic assessments around relationships, the contexts in which we function, life purpose and quality of life. The burning questions our witness may then encourage us to ask can include 'Are my lifestyle and belief system growth-promoting, and in the direction of compassion and inner peace?'

Peter, Sarah, Patricia and Martin all need to acquire the ability to witness before they can be free to evaluate what has happened to them. When Peter develops the ability to witness, he will be able to say to himself 'Don't be so hard on yourself, you're doing your best. Can you not see that it's OK to choose your own standards, even if your father wouldn't approve?'

In Martin's case the witnessing needed to be from a position informed with the true facts about panic, instead of the inaccurate catastrophic predictions he was making, and which were actually escalating his fear levels. He needed to realise that panic is not a mental illness, is not the result of some damage the mushrooms did to his brain, and that he could in fact be shown the skills to control and eliminate them by a psychotherapist familiar with this specialised territory. Through learning to apply the brakes to his overly aroused nervous system, with specific breathing techniques and thought disciplines, an alternative future scenario emerged, one in which he no longer needed to fear the attacks, nor avoid them. With the seemingly inescapable fear no longer looming so big, his suicidal thoughts abated.

PUBLIC OR PRIVATE OPINION – WHO RUNS YOUR LIFE?
The pressure to conform is growing in our society. The expectations which are placed upon us to be a certain way, to play a certain role, begin early. If you don't play the game, approval is withdrawn. Climbing the ladder of success, whether it's in the family, at school, college, or in the world of work, is a programme in our mind, pushing us to achieve a status that is held to be right and true by the dominant consensus opinion. Rightly

or wrongly our parents are the initial and primary agents of this process. It's continued by our teachers, our peers, our social group and mainly by the media. We find ourselves shaped and sculpted to reproduce in our own lives cloned versions of the examples held up to us as ideal. This becomes the context in which we develop our attitudes, values and expectations, which in turn conditions us to move in certain directions and away from others, approval being the bait. It is therefore a fear-based process, playing on our vulnerabilities and our unmet needs.

The two main players are our observer, us looking at ourselves, and the public gaze, the eye of the other looking at us. This viewpoint of others is a creation of our culture, and is the main propaganda tool of the socialisation process, how to be and how not to be. It is omnipresent, and always prepared to judge, criticise and draw comparisons between you and others. 'Why can't you be like everybody else? Why do you always have to be different?' In time the weight of these criticisms with their implications to let go of your individual nature and conform like everyone else, is internalised and becomes the voice of your observer.

At a micro level the public gaze will enquire 'Do you have the right look, partner, clothes, friends, car, job, apartment, etc?' It tracks us to the grave. The essence of psychotherapy is to make us aware of how moulded we are by this conditioning process, and to put in place the tools with which to liberate ourselves. So rather than blindly and compulsively always 'having to' prove ourselves as the perfect daughter or son, the best mother or father, the most successful provider – we would feel freer to make them 'want tos' and to ask 'Can I trust these "have-tos" and "shoulds" if they're not making me happy?' (At a macro level the public gaze shapes our sense of nationalism, religious convictions, political views, opinions on racial issues, gay rights, abortion, stem cell research, etc. We now know that the invasion of Iraq was supported by a powerful worldwide propaganda effort.)

How many people give over their entire lives to satisfying the demands of the public gaze, killing themselves to do well, and at the end of the day losing all connection with who they are, or why they're here? They have become empty shells with nothing inside. Peter, Sarah and Patricia have, to varying degrees, been held hostage to their roles. Patricia all the more so because, as a single career woman, her job became her sole identity, and without it she has little to fall back on to fulfil her. Sarah to a lesser degree has invested heavily in her role as wife, and is finding it hard to redefine herself as a single woman.

They've been reading someone else's script, rather than being their own author, and understanding what it is to be truly authentic. Such people have led a life where their reference point for how to think, what to say, how to behave, and even what to wear is outside themselves, measured against some arbitrary scale devised by others for them. They live in fear of failing to reach these fictional targets, and their critic keeps them perpetually vigilant of any shortfall through constant bulletins as to the likely consequence – the unquestioned disapproval of the public gaze. Daily they are beset by doubts, recriminations and mental assaults – the territory of the depressed. Peter is a classic example of this.

People who panic like Martin are susceptible to the burden of the stigma surrounding any form of mental illness, which he worried he might have. His fear levels were escalating whenever he thought he might be seen having an attack, and his feeling of powerlessness lessened once he could move from 'What if they see me?' to 'So what!'

THE TRIANGLE OF BEING – YOUR EVOLVING PERSONALITY
The concept of personality can best be seen as the interplay between three aspects, namely – thinking, feeling and behaving. How you think influences how you subsequently feel and be-

have. How you feel in turn affects how you behave and think. Likewise how you behave determines how you feel and think.

An everyday example might be a person who holds the general belief (thinking) that being late for a meeting of any kind is inexcusable given the consequences for others – 'one should always be on time'. One day on their way to a meeting they encounter a long tailback on the motorway which is going to delay them. Such a person will begin to experience feelings of guilt, frustration, anxiety and possibly anger. The physiological counterparts follow – they feel hot, sweaty, tense and possibly panicky. Behaviours such as honking the horn, cutting in on other drivers, drumming fingers on the steering wheel and the frantic use of the mobile phone go with this state.

If one does not have such rigid thinking around punctuality, feelings such as these will not be aroused and behaviours will be more in the direction of 'making the best of it'. This might mean listening to the radio or a favourite CD, and the feeling of calmness which follows might allow the person to make a relaxed explanatory phone-call.

Within the triangle of being it is easy to understand how escalation can occur, creating an intense downward spiral which gathers momentum as it moves through all three points of the triangle, each feeding into and fuelling the others. The reverse is also true, by the conscious introduction of a creative change in your thinking patterns, feeling state or behavioural tendencies, a desired positive result can be brought about.

Depression is an emotional state in which one is overwhelmed by feelings ranging from hopelessness to despair and desolation. In such a state the belief that 'nothing I do makes any difference' has strongly taken root, a belief which sabotages change. Once an emotion is backed up by the mind's logic 'After all the terrible things that have happened to you, you have every right to be depressed', a very potent ally has now been brought on board, empowering the right of the emotion to exist, and the notion that it should go on and on without interruption. Now the fixation becomes self-perpetuating, enough is never enough, you will always want more of the emotion. Social withdrawal and dependent behaviours cement the symptom logic in place. Without an awareness of the relationships within the triangle, a downward spiral is inevitable.

By contrast, by focusing less on your feelings and consciously putting in place behaviours which cause an opposite feeling, you will demonstrate to yourself that 'I can do things which make a difference', and a gradual erosion of the sabotaging belief occurs.

Behaviours such as taking exercise, having a massage, or learning yoga can, albeit temporarily, show that you have been instrumental in causing a shift in your inner world. Over time, with repetition of such effective behaviours, the original powerless mindset is dissolved, and replaced by a more empowering one – 'I can help myself'. This inevitably leads to a feeling of hope, control and self-mastery.

For Sarah and Patricia, moving away from the constant preference for hurt feelings and ruminating thoughts about the past is a vital step, by seeing these as practices which are destructive and can only increase their distress. By interrupting them with behaviours which are incompatible with both, an alternative avenue of movement is created. Martin also learned that certain behaviours made his attacks worse, like restless pacing around and excessive drinking, and others helped it, like breathing slowly and diverting his mind to other things.

CO-CREATION – YOU'LL SEE WHATEVER YOU'RE LOOKING FOR

Whatever is to the forefront of our mind, we'll see it in the world we perceive. If we are thinking about changing our car to a particular model we will automatically see more of them. If we're looking for a new winter coat, or a new mobile phone they seem to pop up everywhere in the world around us. Sometimes we marvel at coincidental occurrences which seem to happen as if by magic – you're planning a holiday and you meet someone who has just been there.

There is a natural law at work here – you selectively draw forth from the world whatever your mind is focused on, both within and without. A fundamental law of consciousness is that whatever we focus on expands. To illustrate this for yourself look around the room and count how many things you notice that are red in colour. When you are finished, and without looking around again, ask yourself how many things were blue. If you don't know how many, it's because you weren't looking for blue at the time. By virtue of the fact that you were searching for red, you were unconsciously excluding blue. The implications of this simple experiment are awesome, as it demonstrates how value judgements and prejudices are so loaded in favour of one direction even though others exist.

> The mind becomes that which it contemplates.
>
> Shelley

If you are depressed and thinking 'I'm useless, there's nothing I can do, people don't care, life's too difficult' then you will selectively highlight your faults, seeing only what's wrong with your life. The opposite is also true – if you make a conscious decision to really examine if any aspects of it are working, then you'll find there are some. It's a case of whether you see a half-full or a half-empty glass. In other words you construct the world from behind your eyes.

Depression reflects a state in which the mind has foreclosed on any new ideas. All thoughts, feelings and behaviours are being filtered through a helpless and bleak mindset. Rather than take in new information, all you experience is the stale repetition of tormenting memories of a self leftover from yesterday. There is no evolution, no new co-creations, only stagnation, disorder and decay. Like looking for only the colour red, those with a dark and hopeless outlook on life only draw in evidence which is commensurate with that. In other words in this brain-locked state misery sees only misery.

Your stream of consciousness is made up of thoughts which are either supportive and user-friendly (positive thoughts) or critical and hostile (negative thoughts). These latter thoughts are largely fed to your mind by years of conditioning. With an awareness that thoughts can influence both how you feel and how you behave in either a positive or negative way, if you wish to feel and behave in ways that benefit you rather than harm you, it makes logical sense to eliminate the negative thoughts. This process involves learning to examine your stream of thoughts as they flow by your window of perception. From this perspective you have a choice to make.

Either you allow the flow to continue willy-nilly, and download every thought into your triangle of thinking, feeling and behaving, without discrimination, or in your own best interest you consciously decide to intervene. From the passing flow, you might now choose to separate the positive thoughts from the negative, allowing the latter to flow on by without reacting. In this way you are guaranteeing that the thinking part of your triangle is relating to as many positive thoughts as possible, screening out negative influences from going on to adversely affect the other two aspects of the triangle. If you begin to notice negative thoughts which say that 'you're a loser' (conditioned by your father's or mother's voice) then wouldn't you be ill-advised to entertain them, if you're hoping to build up your self-esteem and feel more contented in yourself? Would you invite your worst critic to sit in your company all day, and wonder why you felt awful at the end of it? Would you tolerate a radio station or watch a soap that you intensely dislike?

We exercise free will constantly in every respect but relative to our thoughts, we operate under the premise that we have no choice at all but to react to every passing thought. In fact the position is that we allow many thoughts to go by without reacting to them. The rules of the road are a trivial example of thought discrimination or editing. Despite having the momentary inclination to do so, we choose not to run a red traffic light, exceed the speed limit or ignore the old lady on the zebra crossing. Entire schools of philosophy are based on the practice of thought management – the use of 'right thought' is fundamental to many spiritual traditions. Shakespeare was a pragmatic realist in this regard: 'There is nothing good or bad but thinking makes it so'.

Because Sarah sees her husband as a 'total bastard' she feels utterly abandoned by him. What she fails to acknowledge is that he is still a very good father and provider, resources which she can rely on. This perspective would make her less helpless, but the trade-off for feeling this means that she would have to give up indulging her wish to remain a victim. Peter has to learn to derive self-esteem from areas independent of activities in which he proves himself, where he can value himself for who he is rather than what he achieves, the yardstick his father used to measure worth. He has to learn to appreciate qualities which he never valued before, such as his sense of humour, loyalty, creativity, adventurous spirit and love of nature and music. Martin had to discipline himself to concentrate on the medical evidence that he had been given that a panic attack can never harm you, and to take his focus off the worse case scenario, such as collapsing or losing control, which were not factual at all.

ACCEPTANCE – THE PREREQUISITE FOR CHANGE

Acceptance has got bad press, many taking it to mean acquiescing, putting up with things, being a doormat. Yet paradoxically no change is possible unless there is acceptance of things exactly as they are now, the way they have unfolded, contrary to what you might have thought possible. Wishing things hadn't happened changes nothing. No matter what painful things were done to us, no matter how unjust, or by whom, the fact is they have happened, and nothing can change that. As we move through the stages of loss – denial, anger, bargaining, depression – trying reluctantly to integrate the event as irreversibly now part of our personal story, we frequently stall at the last stage: acceptance.

Often the losses are subtle and internal, rather than external and obvious like death. Loss of an illusion or dream we had – that we would be successful and happy, that love would last forever, that we'd always have our health – means our game-plan vanishes, and stunned, we struggle to integrate its demise. Disillusionment is in this sense an inseparable and integral part of depression, the helplessness in the face of the inescapable reality that our bubble has burst, a fact we cannot accept. The emotional response of depression is triggered as this awareness dawns on our rational mind. Often a deep reviewing of our contract with life itself is on the cards now. We begin to ask the big existential questions, and the disillusionment becomes more global as it draws us into our past, where we re-view similar setbacks. Do I want to go on living in a world that continues to deliver such shocks? What else might be in store?

Many people experiencing depression turn over and over in their mind certain turning-point behaviours, which if they had not done them would mean 'it would never have happened'. It's as if the compulsive reviewing process might air-spray out of existence the initiating step of the entire experience:'If only I hadn't been so trusting … If only I'd never met him … If only I hadn't listened to so-and-so's advice ...' All these statements have in common an underlying non-acceptance of past events, as if one could undo them. This denial also leads on to tremendous levels of anger, but more importantly to certain bargaining policies for future prevention. These range from never, ever trusting anyone again, to never taking the advice of others again.

Acceptance doesn't stop you hoping the future will be different. To do so is healthy, and is also a prerequisite for change. But acknowledging things as they are now, not as you wish they were, comes first. Acceptance is the most radical position a human being can take as it creates a starting point – a new beginning.

In the words of the Serenity Prayer:

> God grant me the serenity
> To accept the things I cannot change,
> The courage to change the things I can,
> And the wisdom to know the difference.

This wisdom can often be difficult to achieve on one's own, such are the roadblocks placed by the conditioned mind, but it can be achieved in psychotherapy. Patricia has to acknowledge that contrary to her plans, or to what she would ever have dreamt possible, her career has indeed taken an unfortunate turn. She will not move on until she can let go of the notion that she can change her bully, expect support from more senior colleagues and admit that the department's 'bullying policies' have no teeth. Likewise acceptance is critical learning for Peter, and even more so for Sarah if she is to progress through the stages of grief for her lost marriage.

SYMPTOM AS MESSENGER

Just like thoughts, feelings and behaviours, symptoms are another important aspect of you which, if you learn to witness them, can yield vital information which can point you in the direction where change is needed. Symptoms are expressions of imbalance in our lives. In much the same way as a pain in our big toe draws our attention to an ingrown toenail, likewise your depression is not there by accident, but is trying to draw your attention to an underlying problem.

Imagine pasting over the flashing oil light on the dashboard of your car. Doing so is perilous, because now the need for lubrication goes unheeded and unmet. To anaesthetise your depression with emotional painkillers, attempting to medicate it out of existence is an unwise move. Its valuable message will be missed, if the underlying cause is not explored in psychotherapy.

If your feelings of depression were to be seen as messengers, what would they be telling you?

BECOMING A RESPONSIBLE CHOICE-MAKER

What does it mean to take responsibility? The word derives from the Latin *respondere* which means 'to undertake to perform our part in a solemn engagement which is expected of us'. In other words to come up with a creative solution to the task at hand. And not to do the opposite which is to despond, meaning to abandon, to lose or to yield. Responsibility means standing one's ground, taking it on the chin, thinking creatively, and choosing to do what one wants and needs to do, rather than what one 'should' do or has been told to do by others. A sense of responsibility for oneself instils the notion of personal agency, the ability to act on your own behalf.

In many other areas we acknowledge and accept that it is up to us and us alone to act. If our car breaks down we don't sit in shock at the side of the road letting the hours tick by, hoping someone will notice and do the necessary for us. Instead we take steps to get it to the garage. If we run out of milk we don't keep checking the fridge every couple of hours to see if by some miracle it has filled up with milk – we go to the shop.

Only when you've learned to stand back and witness, can see how your conditioning has shaped you, and when you've managed to accept the situation you face now, only then can you become your own agent, an informed choice-maker. This paves the way for freedom, flexibility and personal growth. With these in place you no longer have to behave like a bundle of conditioned reflexes that are constantly being triggered by people and circumstances into predictable outcomes of behaviour, where you respond mindlessly as if you were a performing seal.

If you want to move in the direction of personal liberation, you have to accept that you are the creator of your own emotional responses to situations and predicaments. No one can be to blame for how you have chosen to respond. Within this framework statements like 'He made me so angry I had to hit him' are invalid. A responsible reading of the situation would be that he pressed some button in me which made me feel angry, but since it's my button, and I own it, if I want to I can choose not to hit him back. Only with a witness in place can you see that this choice could be a more conscious one, rather than an unconscious trigger-hair reflex.

According to Deepak Chopra: 'If I were to insult you, you would likely make the choice of being offended. If I were to pay you a compliment, you would most likely make the choice of being pleased or flattered. But think about it: it's still a choice ... I could offend and you could make the choice of not being offended. I could pay you a compliment and you could make the choice of not letting that flatter you either'.

Feeling you are a victim of circumstances and blaming others for your distress *ad infinitum*, is a frequent feature of the depressed state. This blocks change and healing as it limits us to just one emotion, diverts our hope for change to an outside agent, putting the control in someone else's hands. How many depressed individuals hang their liberation from such an emotion on the apology of their perpetrator? If Patricia's healing is going to depend on the acknowledgement by her bully of his actions, then she, as his victim, is paradoxically giving him more control, because her state of mind now depends on him, and as such she is in danger of never moving forward. She has been victimised but she can choose not to remain a victim forever. Sarah might usefully ask herself if all the fault did indeed belong with John, or was she partly responsible? Might she have lost touch with him through her over-investment in the children, and her failing to see the cracks in the relationship when he embarked on serial affairs? To do so will move her out of the victim role and back in control of her emotions.

Personal Boundaries – Our Psychological Skin

We're all aware of the need to set boundaries in physical areas – closing the front door of our house for privacy, knowing to stop when we've eaten enough food, choosing an early night if we're getting up early, not drinking if we're driving, etc. Self-regulation is a fundamental principle of life, a concept known as auto-poiesis, deriving from the Greek *auto* meaning self, and *poiesis* meaning maintenance.

Even a plant will discriminate in favour of hydrating itself and taking in adequate light, by putting out roots or inclining itself away from shade. Pollen distribution in a flower garden depends on the discriminatory faculties of a bee as it visits certain plants and not others, making deliberate survival choices based on their nectar content. The amoeba, a tiny unicellular organism living in water, has a cell membrane which is semi-permeable and takes in what it needs directly from the water bathing it. If this boundary or skin is too closed, it will fossilise and die, if too porous it absorbs too much and bursts. The dynamic balancing act to keep it alive, maintaining the status quo, is known as homeostasis.

We humans are frequently less aware of the necessity to discriminate in favour of our basic needs for sleep, nutrition, security or love. Nor are we aware if that mechanism has become distorted, and our psychological skin has become too tight or too permeable. Too tight and we can't give and take, or allow others in. Trusting, delegating responsibility, accepting advice and sharing don't come easily for those with closed boundaries, whose belief in controlling everything themselves is their fortress against fear, keeping all new ideas out, making them as laws unto themselves. Since certain life circumstances dictate that in order to go on you must change your previous policy and lean on others, let them support you, trust them to take over if you're exhausted – if you can't do this, depression inevitably follows. Without the ability to let others in, your sense of isolation grows and no new avenues of movement open up.

The leaky boundary is also common in depression. Too open, you take in and take on the problems and issues of others far too readily. Unable to set a boundary by saying 'no', you become 'all things to all men', and begin to feel overwhelmed and trapped.

It's not as straightforward for us humans as it is for the amoeba. The ideal boundary situation is a synthesis of both, neither too closed or too open, in other words semi-permeable, flexible, and with the control over it negotiated from within. This type of boundary allows that there will be time for us to give our energy to projects, loved ones, and routine daily chores in a measured way which acknowledges that there is a finite reserve of energy, after which no will have to be the answer to requests. (Learn to keep a personal boundary management diary – see appendix 1.)

Without such a managed boundary, the notion of a balanced life, personhood, and selfhood cannot emerge. Stretching the metaphor of personhood to nationhood, it means that each nation has the right to have its own identity and constitution, the right to protect and negotiate across its boundaries, the right

I CONTROL WHAT COMES IN

I CAN ASK AND BE HEARD

I CONTROL WHAT I GIVE OUT

I CAN SAY NO AND BE HEARD

I CONTROL WHAT I GIVE OUT

LIAM DELANEY.

to fly its own flag, have its own anthem, and control itself from the inside through its laws and legislation.

Frequently working against the freedom to say no and protect yourself from overload are the labels of selfish, lazy, uncooperative, not a team player, etc. If you see yourself as a nice person, then you'll be reluctant to discommode or hurt others, which you may have to do to meet your need for time-off, and to prevent yourself from being constantly hoovered by the demands of others. This creates a conflict inside, and you're liable to give in, so that your opinion of yourself as a nice person remains intact, no matter what the cost. Basic assertiveness is a skill which many depressed individuals have never learned to be adept at.

Your conditioning, both cultural and within the family, may have placed restrictions on your ability to feel comfortable defending your needs over those of others. 'Good' mothers, 'nice' people, 'conscientious' workers, earn these accolades precisely by not rocking the boat or discommoding anyone, but the trade-off is that their own needs go unmet.

Many depressed people have little sense of what these needs even are, because they have never been encouraged to treat them as valid or legitimate. Psychotherapist and author Alice Miller clearly outlines the shaping of this tendency in children, who grow into adults who can never be too perfect or too nice:

> In what is described as depression and experienced as emptiness, futility, fear of impoverishment and loneliness, can usually be recognised as the tragic loss of self in childhood, manifested as the total alienation of the self in adulthood.

Only when the conditions of approval are met, do they feel they deserve to address their own needs. Many can't even identify what these are, or if they can, will always automatically give way to someone else's, rather than risk disapproval by asserting themselves. This is the reason why so many depressed people find it hard to engage in self-loving and pleasurable behaviours, whether it be from enjoying a long leisurely bath as opposed to a quick shower, or to treating themselves to a delicious meal as opposed to resorting to junk food or not bothering to eat at all. For many sex is a thing which never crosses their mind.

Psychologically, an awareness of having a pressing need or desire is our way of ensuring that the level of one commodity essential for our survival is maintained at all costs – energy. This life-force resource is our 'mains supply' which runs all the other millions of physiological subroutines, right down to cellular interactions involved in respiration, digestion, immunity and many more. Each day is a balancing act of which we are not even aware. At all times we are presenting our mind with a hierarchy of needs jockeying for position. Whatever is top of our list wins the allotment of energy. 'Should I exhaust myself keeping all the balls in the air, keeping everybody sweet, or should I acknowledge that I'm tired?' isn't even a question which crosses our mind. If your overriding need is to see others happy, and grateful to you, then awareness of being tiredness won't even surface.

Unlike the amoeba or the bees, the skill of energy banking is absent in many depressed individuals. Nothing tells them if theirs is 'in the red' or 'in the black' at any given time, what drains it or acts as a resource. It's as though two buckets are balancing on each end of a see-saw. Certain beliefs we hold, feeling states we indulge in, and roles or activities we commit our energy to, can squander our energy budget, filling our drains bucket to overflow. Learning to plug these drains is a first step, but unless we rapidly offset this situation by filling our resources bucket, *energy bankruptcy* is inevitable. If you're depressed, ask yourself if in your case the unmotivated bottom of the barrel state could be the result of the burn-out which such overspending brings. Plugging drains and identifying resources may be new territory for your personality, but one which you can learn in psychotherapy, and which will increase your sense of control over your energy account, leaving you less vulnerable to outside forces. (Appendix 2 will help you get started.)

How do you go about plugging drains? The word to assert means to claim a right to something. Many aren't aware it's even a choice, that it is actually everyone's right to turn down requests, and to leave others to handle their own problems before rushing in to ease their distress. If this conviction is not well developed, you can feel helpless and powerless to influence your situation. Always saying yes, as the superman or superwoman martyr does, means an overwhelming number of tasks, and usually a depletion of energy.

If the ability to set boundaries is absent as they were for Peter, then depression is the inevitable outcome. Psychotherapy and the development of the witness position would help him to identify his leaky boundary, which doesn't know how to prevent incoming demands from flooding him. Then he could decide for himself if he had done enough to prove himself as his father's son, as a husband, parent, and employer, and if he could accept himself as he was, adopting realistic standards, and thinking of what he needed for a change. This is the point when Patricia decided to jump ship, that 'enough is enough', to seek a severance package, and that no matter what the implications she needed to honour herself, and leave. Sarah discovered she had more control than she thought by setting limits on John's turning up at the house whenever he chose, by changing the locks. She also set a limit on her own exhaustion by insisting he give her some free time without the children, and reduced her financial worries by seeking the advice of a solicitor to help them plan out the future.

Learning to access previously untapped resources means a re-education of your senses, a process in which you learn to appreciate the value of down-time, being a receiver of support for a change, and seeing companionship and love as a source of pleasure rather than an obligation. While we may have ideas about what may or may not be a resource, in the name of creating new avenues of movement, experience rather than discussion is the ultimate teacher.

THE CYCLE OF EXPERIENCE

> No wind is favourable unless you know to which port you are sailing.
> Seneca

Part of the depressive experience is feeling lost on the high seas, going around in circles, with no sense of direction. The old port has vanished, swallowed up in the wake of the trauma or setback. What was once viable no longer is. Sarah's entire future has been altered irretrievably, and the job of psychotherapy is to help her see a new one. For this she may need to formulate a new identity or life purpose, and having done so to strike out in a direction which complements it. She needs to realise that there can be life after divorce, that the individual who was there before she married is still there, capable of reinventing herself, achieving things, managing her life, perhaps meeting someone else, and even being happy again. Sarah will initially have doubts as to whether this is possible, but her psychotherapist will encourage her to experiment nonetheless. Only by risking and trying, will she test out if her doubts are valid, and this information will lead her to discover a port which she finds is worth pursuing.

She is now engaging with the cycle of experience, where she is trying things on for size, looking for the right fit for her. This cannot be done by merely talking but must be discovered through action, a step which so many depressed individuals find impossible to initiate.

George. A. Kelly, the father of personal construct psychology, saw human beings as scientists oriented toward the future, forever testing predictions, anticipations or theories, in an effort to constantly create new avenues for growth. In his eyes, every human being was a work in progress, who was making certain anticipations which were growth-restricting, such as 'That'll never work' while for others, 'Why not?' propelled them forward. He saw the experimentation process as the only way of testing out which was which, with completion of the cycle as the teacher. Kelly felt there were often yawning gaps between what we anticipated would happen, and what actually did result. He pushed constantly for us to measure the outcomes against the predictions, and to stop repeating cycles which had been invalidated – to notice errors of thinking – when we thought something would happen and to our surprise it didn't. In other words to stop cooking the books, to end the denial, and to get on with revising our future action plans accordingly.

Consider a child who has a fear of water and cannot join his friends in the swimming pool because he thinks that he will drown. Some schools of therapy might spend a considerable time examining the sources of his fears, their validity, and his resistance to change. They will scrutinise his relationship with his swimming coach, and make him aware of his lack of courage and what he is missing out on. In Kelly's terms, the solution lies in the actual experience of the water. He would construct a graded swimming programme, which while acknowledging the fears, nevertheless begins a non-threatening, gradual exposure to the water, perhaps via the baby pool and with the use of swimming aids, until the child felt comfortable to engage with the bigger experiment, which is joining his friends in the pool. It's through the experience of feeling safe in the water and the gradual falling away of his fears that the way opens for the fun and enjoyment of swimming. Through this continual use of the cycle of experience his anticipations would change from fear of drowning to enjoyment and belonging.

Martin's catastrophic predictions of a panic attack causing him to collapse or lose control were contributing to a policy of avoiding certain triggering situations, leading him to feel more and more depressed and hopeless. Instead, he decided to take the risk of testing out what his therapist had told him, that if he stayed and used his new skills, he could ease the attack that way, and feel safe, instead of running. He found it worked, and more effectively each time, as he slowly chipped away at the belief that he was in danger and could never feel safe if he stayed.

Sarah, like many depressives, and millions following a divorce, held the unshakeable expectation that she would never be happy again, and for that reason she could think of nothing else but restoring the past to the way it was, which, since that can't be so, makes her withdraw altogether from social contact. Such beliefs suggest to her the futility of attempting to rewrite her future, since she sees her happiness as being dependant solely on John's presence. This is patently untrue and she must find this out, but that knowledge will only occur if she takes the risk and ventures out again, with a sense of pro-activity, as the one responsible entirely for her own happiness. In time, through trial and error, she will learn where her new sources of happiness lie, and eventually begin through the pleasure principle, to have feelings of enthusiasm for repeating the same actions she did to bring that about. Likewise Peter learned that he could derive feelings of pleasure, as opposed to achievement, from activities not tied to having to prove himself.

As Ludwig Wittgenstein said: 'It makes sense that if you don't like the direction in which you are headed, you had better change direction, or you will end up in the direction in which you are headed'.

Blocked Feelings – Emotional Flooding

It is through our feelings that we define what new experiences mean to us, by the emotions they elicit. A situation which vaguely unsettles one person could instil abject terror in another, so absolutely unique are our interpretations. A life which fulfils some may be found by others to be stultifying.

Some depressions creep in slowly, insinuating themselves into the foreground without much apparent drama externally, nothing concrete appearing to have changed. Yet there is a pressing-down feeling, where the sky is no longer the limit and it dawns on you that the ceiling of possibilities seems lower, your spirit cramped, your job a straitjacket, your marriage stifling, youth has fled, the tide's gone out, resignation now the only option. You've made your bed, but you might as well be lying in a coffin.

Victor Frankl, psychiatrist and survivor of the Nazi death camps, made man's search for meaning his life's work. He tells the following story, as a tragic illustration of this type of depression:

> Imagine a happy group of morons who are engaged in work. They're carrying bricks in an open field. As soon as they have stacked all the bricks at one end of the field, they proceed to transport them to the opposite end. This continues without stop and every day of every year they are busy doing the same thing. One day one of the morons stops long enough to ask himself what he is doing. he wonders what purpose there is in carrying the bricks. And from that instant on he is not quite as content with his occupation as he had been before.
>
> I am the moron who wonders why he is carrying the bricks.

More commonly, depressions follow periods of intense distress, a tidal wave, swamping you with layer upon layer of new material, a jumble of impressions and feelings to be integrated and reconciled in your mind. You battle to sift through them, to figure out what it all means, the implications for your future, and what it says about the world you have to go on living in. Before you have time to rally from one wave of emotion, another is already upon you, hurling you into another spin cycle. Finally, like the shipwrecked, you are washed up on the shore, lifeless and beaten. Even years after the loss of a loved one, many still find new layers of distress surfacing which they hadn't confronted before.

In such a state of overload, as you flounder around trying to stay upright, there is often no room for considering the feelings of others alongside your own. Any more emotion on board and you feel you might implode. Your need for time on your own when others need you may seem selfish, but is self-preserving, side-stepping the exhaustion that more 'putting out' brings to an already depleted system.

In the depressed state your feeling world is like a sink with the outlet blocked. No longer able to allow your reactions to events to flow through, no cleansing occurs, and the same old thoughts and preoccupations go round and round seeking a way out. Since even the word emotion describes our processing of movement and change in our life, in the event of that mechanism being disabled, only staleness and numbness is found in its place.

Expressing your emotions to others performs certain important functions, and allowing them to dam up competes with others which are seeking expression. At a very basic level you may simply need to have your emotions witnessed by a fellow human being in a compassionate non-judgemental way, even if what he meets is cynicism, melancholy or self-loathing. These cause distress in close family and friends, who remember you in better times, and most likely discourage you from airing your negativity. An impartial sympathetic psychotherapist can allow you the space to do this.

The Navaho, a North American-Indian tribe, have a custom whereby following a trauma it is your right to call the tribe together and ventilate every detail of your distress, receiving their unreserved support. This you may do on three occasions. On the fourth time the tribe gathers, and as the circle forms, they all turn their backs to you. This gesture is to convey to you that they see any more expression as sapping your power, a commodity which is relevant to them since you are a valuable member whose input is needed, and an act which the tribe can no longer afford to condone. In current times, many a psychotherapist takes on the role previously played by our 'tribe', validating us and giving our emotion the recognition it deserves. Yet the wise therapist knows when to move you on to the next stage.

Every emotion has an agenda in a social sense. Notice how a child who has hurt themselves looks around to locate mummy before bursting into tears, and in the event of finding her absent will hold on until she returns to open the floodgates.

Anger, fear and depression although seemingly very different emotions, are closer in terms of what simulates them than you might think. Anger as an emotion says 'something I value has been threatened, but I feel I can protect it'. Fear says 'something I value has been threatened but I'm not sure if I can protect it' and depression says 'something I value has been threatened and there's not a thing I can do about it'.

Often the thing we're angrily trying to protect is our self-image, our continued view of ourselves in spite of what our adversary is suggesting – that we are lazy, inconsiderate or inadequate. Our emotion shifts to fear if on the other hand we worry that we might not be able to keep intact the thing we value, if our job truly is about to go, if our relationship does indeed look like it's over, or if we believe that the next panic attack will make us lose our mental stability completely. Depression takes hold as our perception grows that the horse has bolted, there's nothing more to be done, it's a *fait accompli* and we've lost the battle.

Sometimes there can be confusion in what we feel, depending on how we have read the situation. At times of great emotion psychotherapy is invaluable to sort out our reactions and bring perspective. In Patricia's case, her therapist helped her to see that her anger was fruitless, it wasn't ever going to change her bully and achieve what she thought it would. Anger can be like throwing hot coals at the enemy, in the process you get your own hands burned. She had to learn that in order to win the war she had to lose that battle and let go. In Martin's case, finding out that he could learn anxiety-lowering techniques helped to ease his fear. The added reassurance by his therapist that his panic symptoms were not the first signs of a mental illness meant his future might be OK after all, and helped his depression lift.

The benefit for Sarah came from another of the functions that expressing emotions has. A reality check occurred whenever she told her therapist how helpless she was and how much of a victim. She expected this position to be supported, and her therapist to agree, but instead she was gently asked why she was holding back from taking measures which could make her feel more in control, and was challenged to confront her own actions which were sabotaging her progress.

CLOSED HEART – NO HOPE

> Too long a sacrifice can make a stone of the heart.
> W. B. Yeats

In many cases, in tandem with emotional overwhelm, your heart can close also. It is through your open heart that you experience feelings of acceptance, trust, hope, non-judgement, forgiveness, compassion, balance, harmony, interconnectedness, oneness, peace, spirit and soul.

The open heart is associated with Buddha and Christ consciousness. It acts as a counterpoint to your mind which is set up to be bipolar and discriminatory, and whose operational software is taken up largely with analysing, evaluating, making judgements, strategising, forward planning and perpetually scanning for danger. Vital to your survival, your mind advises you what to go towards and what to avoid. 'This car is coming too fast, wait until it passes before you pull out', 'This food is gone off, don't eat it', 'If you don't get a move on, you'll miss the plane'. It also marks your cards 'You shouldn't have done that, you screwed up', 'What kind of stupid fool would have done that?' The inner dialogue of your mind (the conversation between your observer and performer), while reflecting instinctive survival information, on the whole relies on information fed to it through social conditioning rather than inherent wisdom. It takes a position, excluding one course of action as it favours another.

Your heart, by contrast, is inclusive, and its nature is entertain both sides of any argument, to accept that many views could be valid, that more than one version of events could be possible. Your open heart will acknowledge that it is possible to have a happy childhood, but also not out of the question to be abused for years by a close relative. Both can happen. In essence the heart says 'anything is possible'. Today you could win the lotto, or get knocked down by a car. It's a position reflecting innocence and wisdom at the same time. While the mind forecloses, the heart is always open to new things.

When a series of traumas are experienced, the naivety and innocence of continued openness can look less like wisdom and more like sheer stupidity. Your mind will say 'How could you have let that happen again? That's it – no more trusting people', silencing heart consciousness. Unopposed, the mind with no counterpoint has free reign. Its black-and-white dictums squeeze hope out, replacing it with cynicism, victimhood, blame, self-criticism, withdrawal and defeat: 'Why try? It's not going to work, the cards are stacked against you.' This is dangerous territory, because with the emotions flooded and the heart closed to compassion and forgiveness for one's self, many find that the promptings of the tormented mind to end it all begin to take form. It's as if when the pain of living outweighs one's sense of obligation to others, and with hope gone, and the fear of dying receding – suicide becomes a viable way out.

Sarah has become cynical, bitter and sees no hope of ever trusting anyone again – her heart is broken, and she will need an opportunity to grieve. A psychotherapist will spot the policies which her closed heart will be peddling: 'Don't trust, don't let the guard down, and don't take any chances'. A psychotherapist will work to dissipate shame, guilt and hopelessness by encouraging individuals to see a bigger picture, entertain other options, to trust enough to take risks, and to abandon the restrictive ways of living which their mind has been recommending.

The heart can be encouraged through many avenues, by specific energetic exercises (see appendix 3), by homeopathic remedies and by acupuncture.

THINKING OUTSIDE YOUR BOX –THE GATEWAY TO THE SPIRITUAL

With your witness in place it is possible now to view yourself from a distance, looking on from the position of your higher self. You are able to see yourself as a self-conscious performer, on the stage of life acting out your numerous roles, inescapably embedded in your triangle of being, your personality, your ability to manage your boundaries. You are also able to see that these are all in turn inseparable from your ever-changing context, which is constantly shaping you. Context is a combination of things: the home you come back to each evening, the school or job you go to each morning, your urban or rural environment, your community, your culture, even the climate you live in. Your context is in essence the space you inhabit in its broadest sense. It directly affects how you think, feel, and behave. It can be growth-promoting or restricting. We all know the benefits of a change of environment on holiday, a change in job or a house move. You'd be hard put to maintain your traditional way of thinking, feeling and behaving if you had to go and live in Darfur when you're used to Beverly Hills.

Thinking outside your box is a viewpoint from which your higher self can begin to appreciate the interconnectedness of all the elements of your life, bringing with it the highest level of clarity. This is free will in its truest sense – the most liberated position from which you can ever hope to operate. Free of your box, it allows you to take a bird's eye view of your life, seeing it for what it is, untainted by prejudice and bias from all your past experiences and free of the influences brought to bear on your view by your present context. From here you can see that nothing is forever fixed, that your future is up for grabs and that ongoing re-examination ensures that you remain a work in progress, never finished evolving. This is the fertile ground for new ideas, actions and behaviours. Ultimately you can set the measure of your own freedom or your own bondage by the many ways in which you can choose to conduct your life – that you can create your own alternative approaches to the reality in which you operate, no more held hostage by circumstances, a victim of fortune.

George A. Kelly said: 'No one needs to paint themselves into a corner; no one needs to be completely hemmed in by circumstances; no one needs to be the victim of his biography. We call this philosophical position constructive alternativism ... It implies that man can enslave himself with his own ideas and then win his freedom again by reconstruing his life'.

In Patricia's case it would have made a world of difference to her had she changed her context sooner, once the tide had turned against her, before her health broke down. Her context was affecting her from all angles – thinking, feeling and behav-

ing. For the lack of the ability to witness she couldn't see clearly enough how toxic it was until it was too late.

Without a witness, Peter couldn't see the conditioning at work which had turned his observer into a tormentor, a hyper critical slave-driver using him as a tool with which to secure his father's approval.

Sarah had for years stopped seeing herself as anything but a wife and mother. Without a witness to prompt her, she lost touch with herself as an individual, as she did with John.

By helping Martin to stand back and view himself outside his box, and view each panic attack happening, he learned that they were not in fact dangerous, although very unpleasant. This gave him room to decide whether to run or stay, and with more control, to see a way out of his dilemma.

Thinking outside your box creates a certain level of detachment, without implying aloofness, which allows you to operate in the world with greater and greater freedom. Your spirit finds a voice, blossoming under the luxury that only freedom from enmeshment can afford. A gateway opens now to a deeper level, your spiritual dimension. Up until now megabytes of your consciousness have been consumed by the overriding needs of your roles, the public gaze, your conditioning and the process of recovering from traumas and hurts implicit in living life. There is little left over for reflection on the bigger questions, such as life purpose and our spiritual journey. It is from this perspective that you can begin to appreciate that you are a spiritual being having a human experience.

> All day I think about it, then
> At night I say it.
> Where did I come from, and
> What am I supposed to be doing?
> I have no idea.
> My soul is from elsewhere,
> I'm sure of that,

I intend to end up there. This drunkenness began
In some other tavern. When I get back around
To that place, I'll be
Completely sober. Meanwhile,
I'm like a bird from another
Continent, sitting in this aviary.
The day is coming when I fly off,
But who is it now in my ear,
Who sings my voice?
Who says words into my mouth?
Who looks out with my eyes?
What is my soul?
I cannot stop asking.
If I could taste one sip
Of an answer, I could break out
Of this prison for drunks.
I didn't come here of my own accord,
And I can't leave that way.
Whoever brought me here
Will have to take me home.

Rumi

Rumi's words resonate with an all too common experience summed up by 'What am I supposed to be doing? I have no idea'. Without such answers we might find ourselves joining a queue to climb a ladder which is against the wrong wall! Rumi's lines 'my soul is from elsewhere, I'm sure of that, and I intend to end up there' reflect a vague sense of spiritual longing somewhere in the recesses of our awareness. Rumi is asking basic questions – which voice should we be listening to, the voice of our soul or the voice of our conditioning: a socially programmed hypnosis, an induced fiction which we have all collectively agreed to create? 'If I could taste one sip of an answer, I could break out of this prison for drunks.'

CHAPTER 14

Mounting your own Anti-Depressant Response
Whose Life is it Anyway?

The central premise of this book is that depression is an emotion, a natural response to our experiences of life, just like fear, anger, sadness, love and joy. The word emotion derives from the Latin *movere* meaning to move. If somebody pinches you, who feels it but you? Nobody else. Nor does anyone know what it's like to wake up inside your head, with your unique thoughts, moved by your feelings, and inside your skin.

Like a fingerprint, we are all once-offs. We come into the world by ourselves, and we leave it the same way. For the duration of the journey in between, we are extremely fortunate if we are able to raft up with a number of close friends, soul mates who we can share the journey with, and who empathise with our unique experience of it.

Since your uniqueness is therefore a given, the responsibility for how you live your life – the ability to respond to it, to become your own personal agent and come up with creative solutions to the many situations which arise – rests solely with you. Life is not a dress rehearsal.

> We cannot put off living until we are ready.
> The most salient characteristic of life is its
> coerciveness: it is always urgent, 'here and
> now' without any possible postponement.
> Life is fired at us point-blank.
>
> Jose Ortega Y Gasset

To put off playing your part, is what happens when you define your depression as a disease. Now you immediately find yourself on a well-worn conveyor belt, like a can of beans, an object, a thing being moved along through a predefined process identical to all the others. No place here for uniqueness or personal journeys. The moment of diagnosis, 'you have a chemical imbalance, which can be rectified with an anti-depressant', and the passing of the prescription across the desk marks a major turning point. You now have a sick brain.

From this point on, it is the job of the pills, your emotional painkillers, to fix you, and your doctor's responsibility to oversee that process. You move into the passive state of waiting and watching. 'Did the doctor say they'd kick in at three weeks or six weeks?' In a disorder which is in essence a disempowered state, you have now placed your locus of control inside the bottle: 'What's happening? They don't seem to be doing their job? Maybe I need stronger medication? Or does it mean I have something more serious.'

Once you're on the sick-brain conveyor belt, a series of different anti-depressants will be prescribed, with or without sedatives or sleeping pills. A psychiatrist may offer a more elaborate cocktail with a suggestion of a hospital stay if these fail to provide the lift you're hoping for. If all fails, electro-shock therapy may be recommended, the endpoint of the conveyor belt.

BECOME YOUR OWN AUTHOR – BITE THE BULLET

At the core of life is the central issue of being authentic, which derives from the Greek *authentikos* meaning to be your own author – to write your own script. This stance is proactive. Those who live life from this perspective know that in times of difficulty there is no ultimate rescuer to wait around for, no cavalry about to appear over the hill ready to save the day. Such people accept that life can be turbulent, with distressing times built-in, and that depression can be one of the responses to such times. Never-

YOU CAN'T STOP THE WAVES
BUT YOU CAN LEARN TO SURF

theless, they also appreciate that ways can be found to negotiate such difficult periods without going under. Their motto would be 'you can't stop the waves, but you can learn to surf'.

They understand the deal. In the interest of rising to the challenge and mounting a campaign to change their unhappy state – their feelings of depression – then the responsibility will have to be shouldered by them and them alone. They also factor in that; risks will have to be taken, appropriate back-up support found, and crucial new information entertained as to what will enhance their healing and what will sabotage it. They are crystal clear that their depression is a messenger, an experience which should be listened to rather than silenced, and its information used to initiate change.

Those who have had a near-death experience, life-threatening illness, or 'road to Damascus' moment, are forever changed by it, and they find that every aspect of life is re-prioritised. Suddenly and dramatically they 'get it'. From then on, life is a journey imbued with meaning and purpose, one which may include a spiritual aspect, where each second of it is precious and not to be wasted. For such people there is no longer any room for complacency.

> You are what your deep driving desire is.
> As your desire is, so is your will.
> As your will is, so is your deed.
> As your deed is, so is your destiny.
>
> Upanishads

These lines take no prisoners. Unless your 'deep driving desire' is to find ways of getting well, then your destiny is to remain depressed. Once that desire is your top priority, then the will and motivation will be there to take the necessary steps to make absolutely sure that happens. If it isn't, if you want to avoid making changes more than you want recovery, if you want to blame others more than to feel inner contentment, if you want to get well without spending any money on the venture, if you prefer the role of poor me rather than personal liberation; then continued depression will be your lot.

Throughout this book we have repeatedly put forward the notion that depression is a messenger, a wake-up call, announcing to you over and over to dig deep, to trawl to the depths of your being for solutions. Such depth can give birth to a newly developed awareness that you are a spiritual being having a human experience, and that your spirit, if tapped into, can infuse your life with meaning, purpose and a sense of your destiny. Thereafter nothing can prevent your will and your actions guiding you towards that destination. Then you will know the port to which you're sailing.

MOUNTING YOUR OWN ANTI-DEPRESSANT RESPONSE

> Healing is cumulative and everything only works some of the time.
> Walter Makichen

There are many roads leading to depression, and there are as many leading out of it. We are inviting you to consider methods of healing depression which we have personally found to be invaluable. We run a holistic practice and have seen through the years what works and what doesn't. What always strikes us is the unique healing effect which can result when the correct match is found between sufferer and healer, and where the timing is right. We have witnessed individuals who for years have been caught up in the psychiatric or counselling treadmill, who suddenly cross a line after an intervention which to everybody's delight has clicked with them.

Healing the emotion of depression can sometimes happen miraculously in an instant. For others it can be a pilgrimage through a variety of methods and therapists. The most important person in the healing process is the sufferer and us professionals are merely the handmaids. The sufferer has the biggest investment in the outcome, and if their intuition tells them to pursue a certain healing avenue, then they should be supported in that, and criticisms and detractions of their chosen method not thrown in their way. The healing power of desire and intention cannot be underestimated as a force in its own right. Given the weight of opinion which sufferers place on medical recommendations, vigilance is required by their doctor lest their disapproval close a door, outruling the benefits for their patients. Clichéd scientific jargon such as 'don't bother with that, it's not evidence-based' have no place, particularly if that person has not been helped by conventional approaches and they see some ray of hope in the new intervention. In the scientific world the power of the placebo response is so appreciated that it is now being seen as a healing intervention in its own right. Comparative studies between the effectiveness of medications and that of sugar-coated pills (the placebo) bear this out. The response occurs at the level of consciousness and emotion, qualities which cannot be measured by science. Evidence for precisely how healing occurs still eludes us. What we need to respect is that it happens. Without being trivial, there is many a lotto win which would lift a serious depression.

1: Off Duty – Time for Sanctuary

Depression is a wound. It can cut to the very heart and soul, and the wounded need sanctuary to allow healing. The first stage of treatment for a broken leg is rest and weeks later, gradual mobilisation. The limb is not expected to function normally, and we allow ourselves to be cared for by others in every way.

The same urgent need for rest and time out from their responsibilities applies to some of the depressed. Many somehow manage to keep the ship afloat, struggling hard not to give in, yet paying a high price on a daily basis. However just as many reach a point where they no longer have the energy or the will to struggle any more. This can come early on, in the initial stages after a trauma, or later when they've become burnt-out by the effort of dealing with their distress over months or years. Regardless of cause, a moment is reached when the need for sanctuary, and for permission to be off-duty becomes pressing. It affects equally those whose depression arose following some distinct emotional incident or those for whom it emerged gradually without any obvious reason.

One aspect of this stage of depression which is shared by all, is the overriding impulse to recoil from the world, batten down the hatches, crawl into their shell and disconnect. One of the difficulties in our modern quick-fix society is that such time-out is often not an option. The unrelenting treadmill beckons, propelling us from behind to keep moving forward, and to keep the juggling act going. Mortgages have to be paid, children cared for, job prospects have to be considered and the stigma of a stay in hospital factored in. Like the story of the frog in the pot we need to jump out of the boiling water, but often can't.

Yet a stay somewhere is exactly what many need. At present the only available version is the psychiatric hospital, which may turn out to be a far from healing experience. Many are posttraumatically stressed by their stay, terrified by the 'Cuckoo's Nest' antics of some co-habitees, particularly those who have been involuntarily detained. Others become distressed by the dumbed-down feeling which accompanies the excessive medication regimes, rarely seeing their doctor, and the realisation that they are now on that conveyor belt. And perhaps most despairing of all is the fear that they might eventually join the population of revolving-door patients who they meet – those who for years have been on every possible combination of medications and perhaps had electro-convulsive shock therapy, yet still are no better.

This scenario can be avoided, and with the compassion, good-will and support of others, a sanctuary experience devised elsewhere:

A *restful safe environment:* This can be provided in one's own home, the home of a friend, or some other suitable place where support is available – a spa, a meditation or healing centre, or any place of retreat.

Supportive minders: Supportive in the sense of not being critical, not pushing advice, and allowing the individual to access and articulate their needs in their own time. Depressed individuals need to feel that the minder's presence is unconditional and compassionate, and the legitimacy of their experience is validated instead of questioned. Exhortations to do this or that, helpful as they may seem to the minder, are counter-productive as they can put pressure on an already overloaded individual, and interfere with a process which has its own unique time-frame.

A minder's role is to take responsibility for all the individual's basic needs: shopping, cooking, family duties, and managing the boundary relative to visitors, phone calls and work-related issues. In other words keeping the world out, offering companionship without intrusion, and essentially providing a cotton-wool experience.

Sleep therapy: To restore normal sleep patterns through sedative medication, the general practitioner can be invited to become a co-participant in the project. Many with depression have an element of anxiety which is associated with racing thoughts, ruminations and vigilance. Sleep is nature's balm, and allows the restorative properties of the life-force to flow unimpeded.

Body therapies: Massage, reflexology, acupuncture may be particularly appropriate as home visits to rekindle the individual's own healing response.

We are made to connect. In the depressed individual this essential need has been sidetracked resulting in further isola-tion. By the time depression reaches its peak, the individual has often distanced from those around them to the extent that touch, affection and sexual intimacy rarely occurs. Yet touch is what anchors us into life. At this point, touch with a loving intent could be our most potent healer, but is often unavailable, or not availed of, such is our estrangement from loved ones.

At such a time professionals can provide a vital link back to that anchor, through bodywork. It has the added advantage that, at a time when energy is low, nothing is required of the in-dividual but to receive.

Time: The body has its own optimum heal-by dates for a vari-ety of traumas and illnesses. In the case of the broken leg, if re-mobilisation is delayed, then healing is disrupted and things go backwards. Unused muscles atrophy, skin degeneration occurs, blood supply stagnates, and weight-bearing becomes impossible. In the case of an emotion such as depression, the natural healing responses are also arrested if re-engagement with life fails to occur. For this reason the time-out stage, like the immobilised leg, should be limited. Gradual *re-engagement with* the world is critical – through gentle exercise, incremental social contact, and the re-establishment of basic routines. In the same way that re-mobilisation with the broken leg is lengthy, difficult and ini-tially painful, so can be the depressed individuals first forays out into the world.

The bridge into the future: Consideration, where appropriate, must be given to in-depth psychotherapy, grief counselling, marital counselling, mediation, career changes, retirement, financial re-structuring, etc.

2: EXERCISE

Depression is a state in which your mind and body become disconnected. The mind rules supreme, with its dark, hopeless, pessimistic and self-loathing thoughts. The body's energy is at an all-time low, and it has lost the ability to feel pleasure. Studies have established beyond doubt that regular exercise affects all these for the better, most immediately by increasing energy levels through its overall stimulating effect on the 'chi' or life-force.

No matter what age you are there is a form of exercise to suit you. It can include solitary exercising, such as gardening, fishing, walking, cycling, jogging, swimming or going to the gym. If you've played social sports before, such as tennis, golf or five-a-side football, you could recommence them, without necessarily having to play at a high level. If the exercise is a type which involves being out in nature, then that's an added bonus. There can be an immense sense of exhilaration when one connects with an activity that is associated with good times, jogging old memories such as those from summer holidays by the sea, which are timeless and ageless, emphasising that you are more than your depression. Alice in chapter 10 found her turning point in this way.

All exercise puts a halt, at least temporarily, to the flow of thoughts, which are rarely found to come up spontaneously during the activity. If they do, dislodging them is easier during exercise, because you can redirect your attention to the sound of your feet pounding the pavement, or the movement of your limbs through the water as you swim. Your mind is put aside as you are drawn to the sensations in your chest as you breathe faster and faster, or the pounding of your heartbeat. Many people describe an almost meditative stage in their exercise where they become less aware of themselves, and go into a zone where they lose themselves, and they spontaneously feel moments of positivism and joy. In moments like these the old stagnation can give way to creative ideas and solutions.

Depression can as well be defined as the absence of pleasure as the presence of sadness, which is undoubtedly why exercise is so well known to have an anti-depressant effect. It leads to a release of endorphins, such as serotonin and other neurotransmitters. Normally, when artificial psychic energisers are used for some time, the receptors in the brain become less responsive to them, and for the same effect you need to take more and more. Moreover, because the receptors become less and less sensitive, normal pleasures such as sex, lose their pleasurable feeling. Exercise-induced endorphins do the exact opposite, and working on the pleasure principle, the more this natural mechanism of producing these pleasure molecules is used, the more effective the mechanism becomes. Exercisers simply get more pleasure out of life.

Exercise, like meditation, is a practice and if it can it should be done every day. If that's not possible at least on the weekend. The effects build exponentially. One cannot continue feeling like the walking dead during exercise, the two states are simply incompatible, and with time cancel each other out. Everything about exercise is in the opposite direction to the medicated depressed state.

3: A Nutritional Programme to Improve your Mood
As the saying goes 'You are what you eat', so it follows that it's worth looking at your diet and considering all the current information relating to depression that is now available. If you think you could improve the quality of your diet, then here is a brief outline of areas you might look at. We would suggest you take it further and consult with a nutritionist. To facilitate clarity in the vast field that nutrition has become, we sought the knowledge and guidance of Brenda Duffin, who trained with Patrick Holford, author of *Optimum Nutrition for the Mind*.

Feeling depressed can lead to a series of bad eating habits which can put a strain on an already low energy system. Eating the right foods will boost your energy and so increase your ability to make changes in your life.

Our brain uses up to thirty per cent of all energy from the foods that we eat. The billions of cells in the brain form a complex, not unlike the worldwide web, allowing communication with each other through chemical messengers, such as serotonin, noradrenaline and acetlycholine. If this finely tuned mechanism becomes unbalanced it can result in depression, anxiety, panic attacks, insomnia, lack of concentration, poor co-ordination, and memory deficits to name but a few.

A pioneer in the field of mental health and nutrition was Dr Carl Pfeiffer, an American doctor and biochemist, whose work is being carried on by Patrick Holford, the nutritionist. Types of mental illness were identified that could be influenced by particular nutrients and diet. They pay particular attention to:

Omega 3 and 6 Fatty Acids
Since two thirds of your brain is composed of fatty acids, the entire range of depressive symptoms improves with a good blood level of omega-3 and omega-6 fatty acids. If blood levels are low, depression, lethargy and poor motivation are common, along with an inability to relax, memory deficits and difficulty concentrating. The capacity for pleasure is reduced.

As omega-fats decrease in the diet of any population, as it has in the west, depression rises. Sadness and fatigue, decreased libido, and persistent thoughts that life is not worth living, insomnia and anxiety, can be influenced as you rebalance these fats.

Nutritionists say that our brains are akin to sophisticated race car engines which are meant to run on highly refined fuel, but unfortunately are being asked to get by on diesel. Fish eaters are less prone to depression. Why? Because fish is the major source of omega-fats, specifically herring, sardines, salmon, tuna and mackerel. In countries where fish consumption is high, such as Asian countries, the rates of depression are considerably lower than in the west. Certain seeds, and eggs are other equally good sources.

You can influence how you feel, both your energy level and your mood, by giving yourself the ideal quantity and type of protein every day. Hippocrates said 'Let your food be your treatment and your treatment your food' as far back as 2,400 years ago. For most people their diet is the main source of these vital substances. While foods such as fish, seeds and eggs, is the best natural way to get enough of these essential amine acids, supplementing them is the surest way to ensure you're taking in enough of them. Many reporting depression have significantly lower blood levels of these fats which can be rectified by taking supplements

Omega 3 doses: Within this family of fatty acids the two essential ones are DHA and EPA. In order to obtain the anti-depressant effect you must consume a combination of at least 240mg of DHA and at least 340mg of EPA a day. Check the concentrations on whatever product you settle on. Cod liver oil capsules in fact contain low amounts of the fats, so chose fish oil concentrates instead to create the level required to influence mood. The liquid forms, such as Eskimo-3, are absorbed more directly, but may be found unpalatable by some.

Omega 6 doses: Within this family of fatty acids the essential one is GLA. The best source is starflower oil or evening primrose oil, and you need at least 100mg a day.

Tryptophan
Tryptophan is an amino acid precursor of the much talked-about neurotransmitter, serotonin. In some individuals it can be lack-

ing which leads to various signs and symptoms. Serotonin plays a role in the female hormone cycle. It's generally lower in women, which may explain the moodiness, irritability and sensitivity to pain experienced by some women before and/or during their menses. 'Women with low serotonin are more likely to express their anger inwardly, with depression and even suicidal behaviour. Men with low serotonin are often violent and can even engage in dangerous criminal acts. Alcohol and drug users also turn out to be low in serotonin' (Holford, *Optimum Nutrition for the Mind*).

In order for tryptophan to break down into serotonin, adequate levels of vitamins B3, B6, folic acid, vitamin C and zinc are required. The following are good examples of meals high in tryptophan: Oat porridge, soya milk and two scrambled eggs, baked potato with cottage cheese and tuna salad, chicken breast, potatoes *au gratin* and green beans, wholewheat spaghetti with bean tofu or meat sauce, salmon fillet, quinoa and lentil pilaff and green salad with yogurt dressing. If you're taking this in supplement form, you'll need 500mg twice a day.

Blood Sugar Balance

Signs of blood sugar imbalance include depression and crying spells, irritability, dizziness, insomnia, excessive sweating (especially at night), excessive thirst, blurred vision, lack of concentration, forgetfulness, drowsiness after meals, unexplained fatigue and/or craving specific foods such as chocolate and sweets.

Junk food has little or no nutrients in it. Having ingested it there is an initial sugar surge, which is followed by a release of insulin, the hormone which clears it from the bloodstream for absorption. However this clearing process causes an energy low, a trough which in a depressed person comes on top of an already depleted system. The dip makes you feel you need a top-up, which if it's more low quality sugar will repeat this peak/trough cycle again. The end result is that you never end up holding on to the high energy feeling for long.

A nutritionist will direct you towards the kind of foods which release energy slowly. The scale that scientists have created to describe this process is called the Glycaemic (or GI) index. If you want to keep your energy at a constant level without peaks and troughs, then eat foods which have a low GI index. The bookshops and libraries have an abundance of material on optimum nutrition.

Alcohol and Recreational Drugs

The association between alcohol use and depression is irrefutable. While its use is understandable as an anaesthetic to ease anxiety or help insomnia, or as a means of temporarily lifting the mood, the effect several hours later is a lowering of energy and a dampening of the spirits. There are often maudlin or melancholic elements to this, with the nostalgic bitter-sweet tendency to revisit past times. More often than not this inevitably opens the door to sadness, a sense of loss, missed opportunities, regret and ultimately self-loathing and hopelessness. Alcohol acts as a tipping point triggering suicide.

Add to this the actual toxic effect of the alcohol by-products as they are broken down in the blood-stream over the next twelve hours or so; sluggishness, lethargy, and a slowing down of all the mental processes. Sleeping through breakfast, the day kicks off with you in an already low energy state before it has begun. The hangover state creates a vulnerability which brings on panic attacks. Your body inevitably will be suggesting you stay in bed a couple of hours longer, and put off going out and interacting with the world until you feel more up to it. As another futile day passes, possibly notched up as a sick day from work, your critic takes a reading, and begins its work of reminding you what a waster you are. And as evening approaches the cycle will need to be repeated. At an interpersonal level alcohol destroys relationships, robs childhoods, depletes finances and turns users into selfish individuals. Nobody likes living with a drunk.

The aim of all recreational drugs is to create a high, but what goes up must come down, so an inevitable low follows, having a greater effect on someone who is already depressed. This is common knowledge to any user. If you want to create an anti-depressant response, cut them out.

Exponents of optimum nutrition such as Patrick Holford, give good evidence-based reasons for including folic acid supplements in that minority whose depression is due to low folate levels, and recommend ruling out a possible congenital histamine imbalance.

4: HOMEOPATHY

In our book *Going Mad?* we extensively covered the role of homeopathy in all forms of mental distress. We have found that in depression, some of the remedies can have the most profound effects, at the very deepest of levels. In our experience *Ignatia* facilitates the healing of a broken heart, *Stramonium* benefits many cases of sexual abuse and physical violence, and *Aconite* helps where fear of death is paramountfear of death is paramount. For the purposes of this chapter we discussed the homeopathic treatment of depression with Declan Hammond, a director and co-founder of the Irish School of Homoeopathy in Dublin. His two cases below illustrate the effect the remedies *Arsenicum Album* and *Aurum Metallicum* can have on depression. He has also contributed to chapter 12, recommending remedies which are relevant to the suicidal state.

The homeopathic approach recognises that all symptoms of ill health, whether physical, emotional, mental or spiritual, are merely expressions of an underlying cause – an imbalance in the patient's energy. We all have an in-built mechanism for healing, which when blocked or imbalanced gives rise to what we call disease. This imbalance can be triggered by many common factors – genetic, upbringing, social status, trauma, etc., but our reaction to these is uniquely personal. No two individuals will suffer from depression in exactly the same way, nor present with exactly the same symptoms.

To a homeopath these symptoms are the mechanisms a patient has developed for survival and need to be handled with great care. Suppression of these mechanisms chemically or behaviourally can be extremely damaging and leave a patient at great risk of developing more serious symptoms and ultimately prolonging their suffering.

Rather than controlling or indeed suppressing these symptoms with powerful, mind-altering drugs, the homeopath will prescribe safe, natural remedies. These are individually selected and dispensed in minute doses, to stimulate the patient's energies and thereby rectify the underlying imbalance. The homeopathically prescribed remedy stimulates the energy, then the body/ mind wisdom, the inbuilt healing mechanism, takes over and continues the healing process.

By treating the underlying source of depression in this way, patients experience a return to health in a gentle gradual manner, without the potential complications or dangers of conventional medication. Emerging from their healing journey energetically stronger and more resilient, they will be more robust on all levels and better able to manage oncoming life setbacks.

Anna, a single woman in her late sixties, presented for treatment with a diagnosis of depression and anxiety. She was suffering from chronic insomnia; terrifying panic attacks; intense restlessness; a compulsive need for order and cleanliness; constant diarrhoea with abdominal cramps; trembling with weakness in her limbs and heart palpitations. She was taking five different prescribed medications to treat anxiety, depression, irritable bowel syndrome, blood pressure and insomnia and had been drinking up to a half bottle of whiskey every night to get to sleep.

She is retired from professional life and had been the sole carer of her aged mother, a long-time sufferer of Alzheimer's. While under Anna's care, her mother had a serious fall, was taken into hospital and will remain there for the foreseeable future. Anna had a mini breakdown at that time and all her symptoms started soon after.

Anna was treated homeopathically with the remedy *Arsenicum album*, a remedy often required by people experiencing intense anxiety, arising from a deep sense of insecurity and inability to adapt to life's changing circumstances.

The treatment lasted six months, at the end of which Anna had come off all her conventional medication. Her blood pressure and bowel function were normal; she slept 'like a baby'; was free of panic attacks; only drank socially. Most importantly for her was a newfound zest for life. Instead of feeling depressed about her own and her mother's circumstances, she now sees her life in terms of opportunity and is excited about what the future holds for her.

Barry, fifty-six, was CEO of a publishing company. He described himself as 'a born leader' and was at the top of his profession for the last decade. Despite all the evident signs of success (top of the range car, expensive clothes and exclusive address), he was deeply depressed and suicidal. His life was not worth living and the only thing that had kept him from suicide was the deep sense of responsibility he felt for the family he would leave behind.

He worked from an early age, had always been driven to succeed in his career, to work hard, to achieve the highest goals. But having achieving all that he had striven for, he found it meaningless. Suffering from regular angina attacks, with elevated cholesterol levels and dangerously high blood pressure, Barry despaired of ever getting well and felt that a heart attack was imminent. He had not told his family or friends about his condition. This was his responsibility alone. The fact that he was so ill had proven to him that he was really a failure in his life. He was responsible for taking care of his family and employees, was consumed with worry and guilt about what would happen to them when he was gone and constantly berated himself for not having been strong enough to shoulder it all.

Barry's homeopathic treatment was daily doses of the remedy *Aurum metallicum*, metallic gold, renowned for its ability to bring people out of deep, hopeless, often suicidal, depression and a treatment for a wide range of serious heart disorders. Patients needing this remedy often experience life as an unbearable burden that they alone must carry.

During his treatment, Barry recognised that his depression stemmed back to the death of his mother while he was in his teens. Instead of grieving, he had thrown himself into his work and buried all the pain of her loss. Over the year he was treated homeopathically, he went through an intense period of grief and shared this with his wife and close friends. When he came through this he decided to take early retirement from his job. Much to his amazement his family were delighted at this. An incredible weight had lifted from Barry's shoulders and he felt that his life had just begun. To his cardiologist's amazement, Barry's heart and circulation symptoms had disappeared and his medication was discontinued.

A first consultation with a professional homeopath will last about an hour. During this time a case-taking will include details of all current body/mind symptoms, as well as general questions about the patient's personality, temperament, dreams, personal and family medical histories. Lifestyle, diet, stress levels and causative factors will also be touched upon.

Typically one remedy will be chosen to cover all of the above and patients will be seen at regular intervals to monitor treatment and results. Frequency of consultations and length of treatment will vary according to individual needs and circumstances.

The results of homeopathic treatment are surprisingly rapid and can also be very profound. A patient can expect to experience not only an amelioration of presenting symptoms and a return to health but also greatly increased energy and a heightened sense of life purpose.

5: ACUPUNCTURE

Newly returned from a residency in China, Declan Phelan, who has focused his practice on the area of psychological medicine, brought us up to date on the current uses of acupuncture in the area of depression.

Acupuncture operates on the principle that if a state of imbalance has arisen within the body's flow of energy, the 'chi', which is disseminated throughout via twelve meridians or channels, the energy will be blocked or weakened. Since this affects all the levels of our being – mind, body and spirit – the imbalance is widespread. The way is opened for physical disease to gain a foothold once the body's immune resistance is thrown off, and mental and emotional turbulence is the form of expression in other cases of imbalance, with depression, anxiety, irritability, mood swings, insomnia, mental confusion, memory deficits and concentration difficulties.

These energetic highways can be stimulated by very fine acupuncture needles at predetermined points in ways which have beneficial effects on depression and anxiety:

– by *blocking* the regions of the emotional brain that are responsible for the experience of pain and anxiety, lessening such feelings.

– by *stimulating* the secretion of endorphins, the feel-good substances which have morphine-like actions.

– by *balancing* the two branches of the autonomic nervous system, increasing the para-sympathetic side which is the physiological brake and decreasing the activity of the sympathetic side, the accelerator.

Energetic stagnation can be caused by injury, trauma, lifestyle, drugs, alcohol, stress, shock, fear, loss, alienation, bullying, work-related difficulties, and environmental factors (such as toxic chemicals, heavy metals, etc.), to name but a few.

In traditional Chinese medicine, opposing forces, such as heaven and earth, darkness and light, hot and cold, weakness and strength, activity and rest, influence balance. They are called yin and yang. With our lifestyles today it is sometimes easy to allow one to dominate the other.

In western physiology, emotional and mental processes are attributed to the brain. In Chinese medicine, these processes are interlinked with the functioning of internal organs. The relation between each organ and a particular emotion is mutual: the state of the organ will affect the emotion and the emotion will affect the organ. Thus the heart relates to joy, the liver to anger or irritation, the lungs to sadness and worry, the spleen to pensiveness, and the kidneys to fear, shock, willpower and the will to survive.

These emotions usually only become a cause of imbalance when they are excessive or prolonged.

Fear and its Effects on the Kidneys
Living in fear for a prolonged time will cause the kidney energy, the powerhouse of our being, to become weak and damaged.

Fear of financial problems, of family breakdown, of abandonment can manifest in the form of lower back pain, corresponding to the physical location of the kidneys.

The kidneys control the knees, ankles and feet, and problems in these areas are frequently found in those who are afraid
of moving forward in life. Chronic bladder problems usually indicate insecurities, and can often be seen in young children suffering from bedwetting.

Controlling worrying or catastrophic thoughts takes much
effort, and can be exhausting. Those whose kidney energy is
stimulated through acupuncture will notice a reduction in such
racing thoughts without having to fight so hard to achieve it.
Insomnia becomes less of a problem as the burden on the mind
to be constantly vigilant lessens.

Joy and Happiness and their Effects on the Heart

Deficiency of heart-felt joy can also become a cause of disease
with mental restlessness, depression, anxiety and insomnia.

Since the mind in Chinese medicine has its home in the
heart, then healing the heart will have an overall effect on our
mental and emotional well-being. The most efficient re-balan-
cing therefore for our heart is love, beginning with loving from
within. Acupuncture stimulation of the relevant meridians can
start that process, by opening the flow of energy in it' direction.
If it has proven supremely difficult to override your mind's
'logical' suggestions to loathe yourself, then you may persuade it
to relinquish its hold if you use acupuncture to 'send' the energy
there instead.

Anger and its Effect on the Liver

Anger taken in the broad sense includes other emotional states,
such as resentment, repressed anger, irritability, frustration, rage,
indignation, animosity and bitterness. Long-term depression is

often due to resentment or repressed anger. This may show as sadness and grief but anger is often their travelling companion, since it is part of the range of emotions we experience when we encounter loss. When a person cannot allow themselves to feel angry, either because they are afraid of it or feel it is inappropriate, it can result in depression and other symptoms: outbursts, impatience, restlessness, insomnia, violent dreams, agitation, headaches, blurred vision and tightness of the chest.

The liver is in charge of the direction of life. If the liver is healthy a person will be fearless and decisive. In a state of blockage we may act like a loose cannon ball, not knowing which direction to take.

Acupuncture can work hand in hand with psychotherapy, counselling, homeopathy, bodywork and other holistic practices.

6: YOGA

Our advice on this discipline came from Ciara Cronin, who sees beyond the use of yoga for fitness and exercise, and was able to inform us of its many values in the healing of depression.

Yogic philosophy interprets states of depression holistically 'as a kind of psychic constipation blocking our energy flow, manifesting as our inability to be present for the experience of life, and at its root, signalling a difficulty with being itself.' Patanjali, one of the fathers of the yoga tradition, describes the four pathological states that accompany the obstacles to inner awareness – depression, anxiety, trembling in the limbs and unsteady breath. He believed that in a variety of practical ways yoga can help someone suffering from depression to return to their true self – by caring for themselves, through the physical practice of the yoga postures, through the use of certain prescribed breathing techniques, and through the healing practice of relaxation and meditation.

The Postures

The physical practice of the postures, or *asanas*, is often the first avenue of treatment of depression through yoga. Due to their mental preoccupation, coupled with not enough physical exercise, depressed people have become detached from their bodies. Their energy resides in the upper energy centres and never grounds through the core and legs. Healthy people by contrast are balanced energetically, the energy flowing through the entire body.

Yoga postures, breathing and the use of sound, by the repetition of certain chants, is a powerful recipe for positively altering the body's biochemical and hormonal balance, since all affect the body through energetic means, which bypass the mind. By increasing the amount of oxygen in the bloodstream, and by causing the master glands of the brain, the pituitary, pineal and hypothalamus, to release hormones: alertness and concentration levels are boosted. The stimulation and relaxation of the endocrine glands of the body, where our hormones are produced, which occurs during yoga, positively affects mood and thinking, directly altering a person's perception of reality.

The balance of stimulation and relaxation achieved through yoga practice stimulates the pituitary gland to release endorphins, while the peripheral glandular system produces adrenaline and noradrenaline, the hormones which help us to meet challenges and which stimulate brain activity. The blood levels of cortisol, the hormone of defeat, drops, and oxygen consumption increases, reducing the muscle tension and easing the anxiety which often accompanies depression. Following a two-hour yoga class the alpha waves (relaxation) and theta waves (unconscious memory, dreams and emotions) can increase in the brain by up to forty per cent, with the stress hormone cortisol significantly dropping.

Yoga postures for a depressed person can be tailored to their individual needs depending on the stage they are in, and a good match arrived at between the troublesome symptoms and the treatment programme. One-to-one classes can be arranged initially, where your teacher is tuned in to your specific needs. Depression can be broadly characterised into two energetic states: excessive tiredness, lifelessness, apathy, intense introversion and inferiority, or by contrast agitation and anxiety, with high levels of muscular tension due to unreleased emotion.

A vigorous programme of postures, focusing on backbends and sun salutations, will keep the person externally focused, while avoiding forward bends and postures that promote too much introspection. At other stages, once some energy has returned to the system, and they are not so tormented by their thoughts, there may be benefits to holding the introspective postures to explore, experience and clear the underlying feelings and perhaps gain insight into the cause of their depressed state. Inverted postures are particularly useful as they alter the flow of blood, lymphatic drainage and cranial sacral fluid. This increases the availability of oxygen and glucose in the brain required for the creation of the feel-good neurotransmitters of norepinephrine, dopamine and serotonin.

Other specific variations can be added, such as keeping the eyes open in those whose habit is to dwell in their destructive inner world too much, or postures encouraging abdominal deep breathing if they are shallow breathers, which many depressed people are. There are specific postures which invigorate and give a feeling of hope by opening the chest, such as backbends, if closure of the heart energy centre is a factor. Others promote relaxation rather than stimulation if anxiety is more of a feature, such as seated forward bends which can be helpful in calming an agitated mind. Standing poses help ground energy, elevate mood and build confidence.

Practising the postures in different sequences can make a difference in particular forms of depression. Chronic depression sufferers benefit from beginning their practice with quiet chest opening postures and progressing to more active, energising poses. Someone suffering from an anxiety-based depression may start with a series of active poses to release excess energy, then follow them with some calming, restorative poses.

This only-way-out-is-through philosophy of some schools of yoga sees the yoga mat as an appropriate place to explore the darker feelings that characterise depression. Students are encouraged to move slowly, deliberately holding postures while staying present to the emotions that may arise, and by doing so anchoring the mind in bodily sensation. With the body no longer sidelined, a deep relearning happens, and a profound level of healing can occur. All the practices in yoga are simply tools to strip away the layers of armouring that keep us feeling separate from ourselves and others. In this way witness consciousness is cultivated so a deeper acceptance of reality can take place.

Breathing Practices
Breath is often described in yogic tradition as the bridge between the body and mind. These practices can have a powerful effect on a depressed person – elevating mood and consciousness by directly increasing the flow of *prana*, or life-force through the entire system. By consciously controlling the breath, the amount of prana in the body may be channelled, either energising or calming the system, depending on the practice. The internal state of a person can be revealed by close observation of their breath. Upper-chest breathing of shallow, short breaths into the tops of the lungs characterises people who are out of their body and in their head. This type of breathing can become a vicious cycle, further locking tension into the body rather than allowing it to release. Many depressed patients actually immobilise their diaphragm, unconsciously trying to control powerful feelings of fear, resentment or sexuality.

Simply teaching a depressed person how to breath evenly and deeply can have a profound effect on their mental state. Deep diaphragmatic breathing fully exposes the blood in the capillaries to air, and circulates the oxygenated blood to the lower parts of the lungs. Deeper breathing brings a more grounded feeling of being in touch with the body and its feelings. With the breath more grounded in the body and the diaphragm relaxed, the body often begins to allow repressed feelings to emerge. Feelings of anger, fear, resentment, grief may surface and need to be held, integrated and processed either on the yoga mat or with a properly trained psychotherapist.

Specific pranayama techniques may also be taught to depressed students. As depression is seen as a state of imbalance, many yoga teachers recommend alternate-nostril breathing, to balance the right and left hemispheres of the brain and increase the flow of oxygen to the brain. Right-nostril breathing has a stimulating effect, good for sluggishness and lethargy, while left-nostril breathing has a calming effect on restlessness and anxiety.

Meditation Practices

A valuable aspect to the practice of yoga in its fullest form will take in practices to still the mind. Mindfulness meditation is a way of cultivating awareness by slowing and quieting the active mind. By meditation on the experience of the breath, the sensations or feelings in the body and by simply passively watching thoughts pass through the mind without judging or engaging with them, witness consciousness is cultivated. From this position a person may become aware of patterns of behaviour or thought. Simply observing the never-ending traffic flowing past our inner screen can teach us how fleeting each experience in life is, whether it's internal or external, and how irrelevant many of our thoughts are. Acceptance of their transient nature can help us to accept painful experiences, knowing they cannot be

prevented and will soon end, while not becoming over-identi-
fied with them.

Meditation practices can also be varied as the predominant
symptom requires. Depression impairs our ability to focus, and
the practice of one-pointed awareness, an open-eyed concentration on an object can be taught, can help centre and calm the
mind, giving it a break from having the problem as centre stage.
Sufferers of post-traumatic stress syndrome who may experience
overwhelming images and flashbacks of abuse that they may not
be ready to integrate, may benefit from the less introspective
practices to cultivate meditative states, such as the postures or
the use of sound in chanting. These stimulate the occipital cortex of the brain while deactivating the prefrontal cortex, thereby tempering distressing images.

Regular Practice

A crucial prerequisite for successful treatment of depression
through yoga is by having regular practice, which will give more
profound results. It can be difficult to motivate a depressed person to do anything and not to increase their sense of failure if
they fail to live up to the demands of a daily practice. But if
through the gentle guidance of an understanding teacher they
can feel safe and empowered it is hoped that the results will in-
crementally grow and the tangible benefits will promote the
desire to engage more and more with their yoga practice.

7: BODYWORK – ROLFING

If depression is allowed to persist over extended periods of time,
with energy levels already low, and therefore little movement
occurring, this powerful emotion becomes woven into the bodily
structure as a self-protective holding pattern which consumes
energy. William Reich, the psychoanalyst refers to this as character
armour. Since energy is already in short supply, the body starts

to shut down and the connection to the world dims. Deeper still, it becomes incorporated even into cellular life, affecting its basic functions such as immunity, reducing the killer-cell (T-cell) response by up to fifty per cent. Other systems are affected too, such as the cardiovascular, endocrine and locomotor.

With this awareness in mind we have worked over the years with a variety of body-workers from different disciplines. Rolfing has been the one which we have found to be the most effective. We discussed the value of using this technique in treating depression with therapist Gillian Duffin.

Whenever negative emotions are expressed, they are accompanied by a simultaneous shortening of flexor muscles. A chronically flexed body has to expend a lot of energy just to hold itself up, continuously adding energy to that body to keep it going, leading to chronic fatigue, a common feature of depression. Like a crooked building that puts stress unevenly throughout the structure, poor alignment increases stress in all body parts, especially through the joints. The breath also suffers and the delivery of our life-force to the being is diminished. Feelings of physical imbalance may not be perceivable to most of us: we do not connect our backache to the underlying support that the feet and legs give to the back.

Just as laughter releases tension and opens up the body, short- or long-term feelings of depression are visible as a closing in or down of the body – the slumped shoulders, head down-turned, with the vision of our horizon lowered. Where the depressed look with their vision is where they go in their feelings ... down. The body and mind can therefore be looked at as different expressions of the same thing, two sides of the same coin, and inseparable. A person's performance is enhanced when their physical structure improves, changing towards a more orderly and energy-efficient arrangement of the whole body. As the body begins to feel more balanced and secure, this is reflected in the individual's personality and sense of well-being.

To realign the body, Ida Rolf designed the ten-session process which she termed structural integration. It involves the application of specific pressure to the connective tissue and the muscles held within its web, releasing the energetic holding patterns.

8: PSYCHOTHERAPY AND EMOTIONAL EXPRESSION

Depression involves a relationship between the rational and the emotional minds. The painful emotions felt in depression are registered in the emotional mind, but are not always relayed and made conscious in the rational mind, making way for interpretation and the possibility of integration. We therefore often remain unaware, sometimes for life, of what the initial impact was – neglect, abandonment, physical violence, sexual abuse – but fully aware of its effect, depression and other symptoms of distress. You know you feel depressed, you just don't know why.

Talking out one's distressing emotions with someone, psychotherapist or not, is critical to finally putting your emotions in word-form, the language which your rational mind understands. Finally being able to put words on feelings which have been crippling your life, realising what the full story is, and being able now to make sense of what has been going on, is a liberation. It can begin the process of releasing the energy of deep-seated depressing emotions which have held you hostage sometimes for years. The chapter on psychotherapy elaborates how that process works.

The track record of organisations such as Recovery, Grow, Alcoholics Anonymous and Narcotics Anonymous is beyond dispute. They are accessible, user-friendly, and most importantly accepting and supportive. Fellow travellers, they understand your story well, and you will not feel alone for long.

***

THE JOURNEY TO THE SELF – YOUR YELLOW BRICK ROAD

The modern fable of *The Wonderful Wizard of Oz* centres on the human struggle for empowerment and personal liberation. Dorothy, the orphan comes to know her innate courage and power, through a series of challenges strewn in her path, and with the help of various fellow-travellers. Swept up by a cyclone on a farm in Kansas, she loses consciousness, and finds herself alone, lost and frightened in a strange far-away land called Oz. She is told by the inhabitants that the Wizard will magically solve all her woes and send her back home to Kansas.

She sets out on the hero's journey to find this guru, only to discover after many trials and tribulations, that he is in fact an illusion. On the point of despair, she has an important real-isation, which comes in the form of the good witch of the north. She is told that she had the power to go home all along, but didn't know it. All she had to do is to click the heels of her ruby slippers and chant the mantra 'there's no place like home, there's no place like home'. Within seconds Dorothy wakes up in her bed, with the same foster parents with whom she had been so disenchanted in the beginning of the story, only now she embraces them whole-heartedly.

The parallels with the journey through depression are ob-vious. Alone and rudderless, the depression experience distances you from all sense of power. In such a frightened and vulnerable state you look to others for a solution, placing the locus of con-trol outside you, in experts of various forms, seeking their magic. The journey to discovering that they have none is a huge learn-ing curve, painful and rocky. The final realisation can come only from your inner voice, but only if you're listening. At that moment it can be both a shock and a joy to find that you had the power within you all along. Once you know that, you're in the home stretch. To your immense relief, home – your entire being, mind, body and spirit – is a thoroughly acceptable place which you can happily live in.

Not unlike Dorothy, the adult character in Mary Oliver's poem *The Journey*, finally became aware that they were drowning in their lives, that responsibility for change rested with them alone, and so they decided 'one day' to end the suffering, by empowering themselves to change. With many obstacles on the path they knew it was not going to be easy. However the very act of initiating some avenue of movement connected them to their own inner voice which gave them the confidence to keep going in the direction of liberation and healing. Neither had to leave home – but simply cease listening to the advice of others, and instead take their cue from their own intuition, and sense of spirit.

The Journey

One day you finally knew
what you had to do, and began,
though the voices around you
kept shouting
their bad advice ...
'Mend my life!'
each voice cried.
But you didn't stop ...

CHAPTER 15

Medication and Electro-Convulsive Therapy
Time for Change

À LA CARTE MEDICATION

It is beyond the scope of this book to discuss in depth the variety of medications currently being used to treat depression. Broadly they can be divided into those which elevate the mood, psychic energisers or uppers, and those which suppress the mood, sedatives or downers.

UPPERS:

- Tricyclics, (such as Tryptisol and Prothiadin)
- Monoamine oxidase inhibitors (MAOIs) such as Parnate
- Selective serotonin re-uptake inhibitors (SSRIs) such as Prozac, Seroxat, Efexor and Lexapro

DOWNERS:

- Anxiety-lowering drugs, the benzodiazapines such as Valium, Xanax, Lexotan
- Anti-psychotics such as Zyprexa, Rispiridol and Seroquel
- Hypnotics for sleep, such as Zimovane, Stilnoct and Rohypnol
- Anti-epileptics such as Epilim and Tegretol
- The salt Lithium, in the form of Priadel and Camcolit, also has a suppressing effect on mood

It has been our position throughout this book that depression is an emotion and is secondary to our interaction with life. Part of the expression of any emotion is a change in our physiological and chemical state. We have stated that this change is not a disease created by a sick brain, and should not be treated as one. Our fundamental position on the current use of medication is that it should not be presented in the way it currently is to patients – as a cure for an underlying fault or deficit in the hardware of their brain. In truth their distress is the result of a shift in their software programme – their thoughts and feelings.

OUR SIMPLE PLEA IS FOR HONESTY

If a doctor wishes to prescribe an anti-depressant, rather than saying to the patient 'you are suffering from a chemical imbalance, a deficiency in serotonin' and giving the impression that there is something seriously wrong with their brain's functioning, it would be more appropriate to say 'you are going through a difficult time because of your circumstances, and I will prescribe something to give you a lift'. No one is arguing that in some cases anti-depressants can create that sought-after lift in mood and enhance a person's feeling of well-being. So can other uppers such as amphetamine, cocaine, ecstasy, etc., which all do so by acting on the same serotonin pathway. None of these however claim to cure any underlying imbalance, but simply to make one feel good. As most regular cocaine users would agree 'there's only one thing better than a line of coke, and that's another line of coke'. Helen described what it did for her – 'it filled me with energy, I felt I could get things done, my thinking was clear, I was confident and relaxed interacting with people, and it made me enjoy life'.

Amphetamines were widely used for the treatment of depression in the 1950s and 1960s, but in a straightforward and honest fashion. If you were down, you took an upper (amphetamine), and if as a result you became too speedy and couldn't sleep, you took a downer, usually a barbiturate. In those days nobody spoke of diseases of the brain. Amphetamine and barbiturates, both of which worked effectively to influence emotions, were withdrawn from general prescription because of their addictive qualities.

Doctors should inform patients from the beginning of possible well-known side effects, such as loss of libido and other sexual dysfunctions, insomnia, dizziness, nausea, constipation, dry mouth, and many others. Among the more serious are self-mutilation and suicidal thoughts.

The third untruth, by way of omission, is that doctors neglect to inform patients that the anti-depressant can be addictive, and that severe withdrawal effects may be experienced when they attempt to come off them. Some people, after many unsuccessful attempts to quit, have to remain on them for years. What patients might like to know is that in the process of artificially elevating their mood, the medication suppresses the body's natural ability to manufacture neurochemicals such as serotonin. While the artificial substance is being taken, that natural process is suspended and in time the body forgets how to produce them. Should the substance be withdrawn, there is an inevitable gap in production, and the catch-up to normal levels may never kick in, hence the inevitable dependency or addiction.

If anyone has any doubts as to the side effects of anti-depressant medication, look at the Seroxat saga, which stands out as the most problematic of the SSRI group. Its link to suicide, self-mutilation, and addiction is now well established, to the extent that it has recently been withdrawn for prescription in the under-eighteen age group. Notwithstanding this information, because of mass marketing and the withholding of negative trial results, it continues to be the most widely subscribed worldwide. The head of Seroxat's manufacturing company is quoted as saying, as he commented on the wide range of illnesses that they could get licensing for; 'there's a lot of runway space out there, lets get the planes down'.

From a doctor's perspective, reading the 'prescribing information' associated with the use of psychiatric medication is a
cautionary exercise. Headings like special warnings and precautions, contra-indications, adverse reactions, undesirable effects, drug interactions, renal impairment, hepatic impairment,
over-dosage, etc., leap out at you like tigers from the small print
informing you that just about anything is possible on swallowing
one of these pills. Potentially no cell, no normal bodily function, no organ is safe from harm – from passing urine to the
regularity of your heart beat. And the dangers dramatically go
up when cocktails of medication are ingested together – poly-
pharmacy. It's not uncommon to see patients taking up to seven
or eight different types of psychiatric medication every day,
some of which are to offset each other's side effects, others to
compensate for thyroid function which has been destroyed by
the use of Lithium. And yet, often decades later, they are still
depressed. Naïve patients are sometimes stunned to hear that
they are taking uppers and downers at the same time. One has
to wonder about the logic: don't they cancel each other out?

Threats to life are boldly stated on the prescribing information leaflet, and we are not just talking about suicide. One drug
company declared that its product can actually cause mortality,
and that 'this information is derived from clinical trials'. In a
Dear Doctor letter we received dated 8 March 2004, we were
thus informed of the deadly dangers of Olanzapine, better know
as Zyprexa. 'While taking Olanzapine, elderly patients with
dementia may suffer from stroke, pneumonia, urinary inconti-
nence, falls and have trouble walking. Some fatal cases have
been reported in this group of patients.'

The letter came from the Medical Director, Eli Lilly & Co
(Ireland) Ltd. (This drug company are also the manufacturers of
Prozac.) Zyprexa is widely used in the treatment of schizophrenia
and in certain depressive disorders. What is most disturbing in

their alerting of doctors about these fatal side effects, is the implication that they have then discharged their duty in merely issuing such a warning. Surely the appropriate response would be to withdraw it instantly, and for the Irish Medicines Board to immediately suspend its use in all age groups, not just the elderly! If Zyprexa were a car, it would be recalled without question, lest even one fatality occur.

There is a common misperception that anti-depressant medication is specifically designed for the human brain. The truth of the matter is that it is widely used in veterinary medicine. Polar bears in the zoo are prescribed it to help them cope with their inappropriate surroundings, and horses and greyhounds are given it illegally because it enhances performance.

HUMPTY DUMPTY SCIENCE

Elements of the pharmaceutical industry has hijacked science, and piggybacked its efforts onto the neurochemical model of illness for profit motives, marketing the sick-brain model of depression, and coming up with emotional painkillers as the antidote. They manipulate statistics to its own ends, tells lies, and selectively withholds the negative results of trials putting peoples lives at risk. With vast sums of money at their disposal they have managed to turn lies into truth. As Humpty Dumpty said to Alice in Wonderland 'when I use a word it means just what I choose it to mean – neither more nor less'.

If we choose to stand back we can see that while anti-depressant medication may have helped some, it has failed many in terms of offering relief and freedom from their symptoms. The thousands of revolving-door patients bear testimony to this – their life a balancing act where the juggling of doses of corrective medication has become a life-long process. In Ireland there were 7,545 patients admitted for depressive disorders in 2003, and sixty-eight per cent of these were readmissions. This warehousing of suffering human beings would be a thing of the past if anti-depressants delivered what they claim to.

TOXIC PREGNANCIES

It is a common misperception that there is a vast difference between the nutritional needs of a day-old baby on the mother's breast, and one on the threshold of birth, its nutrition arriving through the mother's placenta via the umbilical cord. Everyone is agreed that toxic substances are bad for babies. Would any mother in her 'right mind' give a day-old baby alcohol, a cigarette or Prozac?

Pregnant women have a right to be informed that studies are now finding that newborn infants are manifesting symptoms similar to the infants of crack-cocaine-addicted mothers; seizures, muscular rigidity, jitteriness, abnormal crying, respiratory difficulties such as going blue on feeding, some requiring hospitalisation. What mother, if she knew of such dangers, would persist with a drug simply to make her feel better while her baby was at risk? Given that she may already have taken precautionary measures such as giving up cigarettes, alcohol, junk food, sleeping pills and even painkillers.

INTOXICATED BABIES

The nine-month journey from a fertilised egg through the process of cellular specification (when cells go on to specialise, differentiating into bone, muscle, nervous tissue, heart, eyes, ears, etc.), and into the trillions of cells of a fully mature baby, is a phenomenon beyond comprehension. The entire journey is backed up by hundreds of millions of years of the DNA story. This delicate finely-tuned developmental ecosystem – the foetus – the goal of which is to become a unique human being, can be diverted off course by the slightest alteration from normal in any of the variables affecting this act of creation. We must understand that every cell in the foetus is bathed in a fluid which delivers the oxygen that is inhaled into its mother's lungs, the amino acids that come to it through the mother's gut, and the hormones produced by her endocrine glands, etc. Similarly, less natural substances reach the foetus, such as nicotine, alcohol, pesticides and other environmental toxins and drugs, streetwise or otherwise.

The Thalidomide scandal of the 1960s shocked the world. Innocent mothers were prescribed medication for nausea during pregnancy. Tragically thousands of babies were born with limb deformities, and the drug was immediately withdrawn. In the aftermath no pregnant mother could be persuaded to even take a paracetamol for a headache lest it harm her baby. All trust had been lost in the pharmaceutical industry's reassurances that certain drugs were safe in pregnancy. The discovery of foetal alcohol syndrome, which was accompanied by retarded growth and intellectual impairment, alerted us to the detrimental effect of even small quantities of alcohol reaching the baby in utero. Likewise the link between low weight and intellectual developmental delays in the babies of smokers.

Current research shows that there is a strong link between attention deficit disorder (ADD) and attention deficit hyperactive disorder (ADHD) following exposure in the womb to the SSRI group of anti-depressants. Buzzed-up intrauterine babies are primed to need a similar substance after birth to function optimally. Enter the amphetamine Ritalin. Once started on the amphetamine route, research now shows that eighty per cent will be on some version, prescribed or otherwise, for life.

We live in an age where women are giving serious consideration whether to even have a child at all, and if they do they will go to any lengths to ensure its safe delivery. Many prepare their bodies for the pregnancy to make sure that the foetus is not developing in a toxic ecosystem; they give up smoking, take up yoga, eat only organic foods and cultivate optimal nutrition, etc. Some in order to achieve a pregnancy, go down the tortuous road of years of IVF. When they do get pregnant, they continue the healthy approach; watching their sleep, maintaining their health, cutting down on stress, and getting the best anti-natal advice. The primary focus is the baby – whether they will breast feed, have a home delivery, underwater if it helps, or a maternity hospital with the neonatal backup if it makes for greater safety.

Some are even seeking advice as to how to go about every step in the most conscious way possible, from the conception onwards, learning ways of communicating with their unborn child, with a view to its transition into the world being optimal for all concerned. Books such as *Spirit Babies*, by Walter Makichen, reflect this growth in consciousness in this group of highly motivated and aware mothers. It seems unbelievable that after all this effort, during a visit to their doctor where they complain of moodiness or irritability, they will allow themselves to be prescribed an anti-depressant. Why? Because they are assured it is safe.

Take Lexapro, the most prescribed anti-depressant for newly diagnosed patients in Ireland. In its abbreviated prescribing information under the heading 'pregnancy and lactation' it states 'As safety during human pregnancy and lactation has not been established, careful consideration should be given prior to use in pregnant women. It is expected that escitalopram will be excreted into breast milk. Breast-feeding women should not be treated with escitalopram.' (In case you're confused, escitalopram is Lexapro.) This information implies that the drug reaching the baby through the mothers breast milk is different than when it is delivered to the baby from the placenta via the umbilical cord. The fact of the matter is that if it is not safe during breast-feeding, then it is not safe during pregnancy, since the developing foetus is even more prone to damage than a newborn. Surely this is Humpty Dumpty science at its best.

Another group of women, already on anti-depressant medication when they became pregnant, continue to take them, innocently assuming it is safe. Some, who are taking a cocktail of medication which may include Lithium, may not realise that even in adults, male or female, it destroys the thyroid gland and compromises kidney function. What effect must it have on the developing foetus? Are pregnant women informed that Lithium causes congenital defects, the heart being most affected?

DRUG DRIVING
At the scene of an accident after someone has crashed into you, do you ever think to ask the other driver, 'are you taking anti-depressant medication?' Does the garda who arrives at the scene, apart from breathalising the offending driver, ever ask the question either? Are blood levels ever taken for prescribed drug analysis?

Pilots are instantly grounded when prescribed anti-depressants, due to awareness of the responsibility of their job relative to other's safety. Should mothers displaying 'baby on board' stickers not also be? Or bus drivers, taxi drivers, truck drivers, or any citizen driving a moving vehicle while 'under the influence'.

Clearly, the warnings on the prescription bottle – 'Avoid alcoholic drink. May cause drowsiness. If affected do not drive or use machinery' or the proprietary PIL (patient information leaflet) approved by the Irish Medicines Board – are not taken seriously by consumers of these drugs. This is not their fault. The warnings hardly qualify as such. They have a purely advisory tone. Compared to the fearsome warnings of death and serious illness on tobacco products, they constitute no warning at all.

Then there is the question of whether people read the PIL that came with their medicine with any great degree of attention. As with a cigarette package, the box is the place for a serious warning against potentially fatal consequences, and the warning should not mince words.

It should state, bluntly and clearly:

> Do not drive at all while taking this medication. This pro-
> duct could be responsible for a fatal accident or serious in-
> jury if you drive while taking it.

Doctors have access to information on the dangers of medications through the 'prescribing information'. The abbreviated
prescribing information relating to Lexapro under the heading
precautions reads 'driving and operating machinery: no direct
impairment of psychomotor function. However, as with other
psychotropic drugs, patients should be cautioned about the risk
to their ability to drive or operate machinery.' What exactly are
they saying? They seem to be saying there is no impairment, yet
there is a risk in driving ability. More Humpty Dumpty science.

Relative to Zyprexa (a major tranquilliser frequently used in
combination with SSRIs in the treatment of manic depression)
under the heading driving, etc, it elaborates 'May cause som-
nolence or dizziness. Patients should be cautioned about operating hazardous machinery, including motor vehicles'. What does
cautioned mean? That you should drive more carefully? That
your insurance may not cover you if you have an accident? Surely most people already drive with caution. The manufacturers of
Seroquel, a drug also used in the treatment of depression, under
the heading effects on ability to drive, inform us of their
concerns – 'Patients should be advised not to drive or operate
machinery until individual susceptibility is known'. Does this
mean you have to crash before you know you are susceptible?

If psychoactive medication can cause dizziness, sleepiness,
poor concentration, slow reaction time and other deficits in
higher intellectual functioning, as alcohol does, then surely the
person on medication should be suspended from driving as the
alcoholically-intoxicated are, lest even one road traffic accident

results? We can argue about where responsibility lies, but ultimately we feel that since doctors are the gatekeepers to accessing prescribed medication, it is our ethical responsibility to embrace the Hippocratic oath which enshrines the notion 'First Do No Harm' by exercising the power of the pen and ceasing to prescribe medication of such toxicity and potential for death on the road. The time has come where doctors need to make it clear to their patients that if they prescribe psychoactive medications that they should inform both their car insurance company and the licensing authorities. One can be absolutely certain that in this litigious age the pharmaceutical companies have covered themselves with respect to liability.

ELECTROCONVULSIVE THERAPY

If a psychiatrist believes that depression results from a sick brain, and medication has failed to cure a patient, what is their next step? The same one that a gastroenterologist would take when conservative medical treatment of a bowel disorder such as Crohn's disease or ulcerative colitis fails – the last resort is considered, surgery. For a biological model psychiatrist, the end point of the sick-brain conveyor belt, is ECT. In many respects it resembles a surgical procedure.

An electrical current of between 70 and 400 volts is passed through the brain of the patient with the intention of producing a grand mal or major epileptic seizure. The voltage is typically as great as that found in the wall sockets in your home. If the current were not limited to the head, it could kill patients through inducing a cardiac arrest, the cause of death in electrocution.

Electrodes are placed over both temples. The electric shock is administered for as little as a fraction of a second to as long as several seconds. The electricity in ECT is so powerful it can burn the skin on the head where the electrodes are placed. Because of this, psychiatrists use electrode jelly, also called conductive gel, to prevent such burns. Because a shock-induced seizure is typically far more severe than those suffered during spontaneous epilepsy, in early times, unless the shock patient's body was paralysed by pharmacological agents, it would undergo muscle spasm sufficiently violent at times to crack vertebrae, break limb bones and damage teeth. To avoid this, current practice involves sedation with a short-acting intravenous barbiturate, followed by muscle paralysis with a curare derivative, and artificial respiration with oxygen to compensate for the paralysis of the patient's breathing musculature.

The shocks create an electrical storm that obliterates the normal electrical patterns in the brain. They are administered in a series over a few weeks, up to an average of from six to ten sessions, to ensure the procedure 'takes', that is, alters the electrical activity of the brain sufficiently so that the individual will not remember, at least for several months, the depression that they were experiencing before the shocks. In our practice we have met a number of patients who over the years have been administered upwards of 100 ECT sessions, and are no better.

In essence ECT is a closed-head electrical injury, typically producing a delirium with global mental dysfunction (an acute organic brain syndrome). Following it the individual is dazed, confused, and disoriented, and therefore cannot remember or appreciate current problems. The changes one sees when electroshock is administered are completely consistent with any acute brain injury, such as a blow to the head from a hammer, a concussion.

The greater the brain damage, the more likely that certain memories and intellectual abilities will never return. Memory deficits, retrograde and anterograde (before and after the event), are among the most common early signs of traumatic brain damage, and are seen in virtually all cases of ECT. Events which follow an ECT session are forgotten completely, such as visitors calling,

phone calls received, speaking with their psychiatrist, etc. Overall, the studies of autobiographic memory confirm widespread and devastating losses, extending to even the major events of their previous lives. Memories are foggy about details of personal history such as family weddings, graduations, jobs, etc. As the mind is the place the memory calls home, such deficits are extremely anxiety-provoking and disorienting; one's very identity is being altered. Autopsy studies of animals and some of humans show that ECT causes severe cellular damage, including cell death.

Anne Marie, a twenty-three-year-old university graduate working in IT, was admitted to a Dublin psychiatric hospital with a diagnosis of mania. She was slow to respond to medication, and to accelerate the process six sessions of ECT were administered over a two-week period:

> I was a shell, a shadow of my former self. I was so drugged up, or affected by the ECT treatment, I don't know which, that my concentration levels were at zero. I slept, or wanted to sleep anyway, all the time. The only comfort I took from life was food and I ate that in abundance. My short-term memory was affected also. I hated going to the outpatient clinic as I was terrified of the doctors: imagine, twenty-three years old at the time and terrified of doctors. It was like I had regressed back to my childhood. I used to make my mother come into the doctor's with me. I saw somebody different every time so there was no consistency in the care.
>
> It took me six months to start feeling anyway 'normal' again. I was utterly depressed and wanted to die. The panic attacks were the worst. Dreadful, frightening, debilitating, I never want to go through those again. I finally went cold turkey on my anti-psychotic medications as I felt so drugged up. I managed to bounce back to my former self, the self that I thought for a while was lost to me forever.

Brigid, a sixty-nine-year-old ex-nun, recalls how, at the age of thirty-five, she became unsure of her vocation and considered leaving the order. Depression was diagnosed, and ECT eventually prescribed in an effort to 'bring back some perspective'. Her family on a Sunday visit to the convent in the country, discovered that she had been hospitalised three weeks earlier. On arriving to the hospital, they were shocked to find her disoriented and dispirited, and took her home immediately. She had received over twenty sessions of ECT. Over the following months, with her family's encouragement she decided to leave the order. While she regained physical health, certain intellectual deficits became apparent. She had been a secondary teacher in a convent school, and her presumption was that she would resume this career, seeking a post locally. To her horror, she found that many of her prior skills relative to teaching had vanished, and she had to accept that it would not be an option. Exploring alternative vocational avenues, she decided to develop healing skills and trained as a nurse, finding that she was still able to learn new material. To this day she still suffers from memory blanks extending as far back as her early childhood.

If a woman like Brigid came to an emergency room with the same symptoms, perhaps from a short circuit in her kitchen, she would be treated as an acute medical emergency. If the electrical trauma had caused a convulsion, she might be placed on anticonvulsants to prevent a recurrence of seizures. If she developed a headache, stiff neck, and nausea – a triad of symptoms typical of post-ECT patients – she would probably be admitted for observation to the intensive care unit. Yet ECT delivers the same electrical closed-head injury, as a means of improving mental function.

Elderly women, an especially vulnerable group, are becoming the most common target of ECT. Veronica, a ninety-two-year-old woman, became extremely distressed following a burglary to her home and was admitted to hospital. She had a long psychiatric history which began following the death of her husband twenty-five years previously, and had been on various cocktails of medication over the years. She failed to respond to an increase in her medication and ECT was suggested by her psychiatrist. The family sought a second opinion and a decision was made to bring her home and provide home nursing instead. With the combined support of her family and her general practitioner she rallied and regained her previous levels of functioning. One has to wonder what the outcome would have been for such an elderly woman lacking family backup or interest.

Arguments put forward as to the benefits of ECT have to be examined with extreme caution for several reasons:

- It is fundamentally traumatic in nature.
- Many of the patients are vulnerable and unable to speak up for themselves.
- It is administered to many involuntarily due to their having being committed against their will.
- Most controlled studies of efficacy in depression indicate that the treatment is no better than placebo.
- It perpetuates the illusion that depression is the result of a disease of the brain rather than an emotional response to life events as in the case above.

As they attempt to recover from ECT, patients frequently find that their prior emotional problems have now been compounded by ECT-induced brain damage and dysfunction that will not go away. If their doctors tell them that ECT never causes any permanent difficulties, they become further confused and isolated, creating conditions for further depression and in some cases suicide.

In other areas of medicine where practices have been shown to be harming the patient, they have been deemed no longer viable and have been discontinued. Why has the same questioning of ECT as a procedure not occurred? There can only be one of two answers. Either the psychiatrists using it are misguided enough to still believe that the dubious benefits outweigh the well-established risks to their patients, or a cover-up is occurring where once brain damage to patients is acknowledged, law suits will follow.

LET WISDOM GUIDE

This is the motto of the Royal College of Psychiatry, who unequivocally support the use of ECT. The following is from their patient information on-line service:

> Repeated treatments alter chemical messages in the brain and bring them back to normal. This helps you begin to recover from your illness.

> *How well does ECT work?*
> Over 8 out of 10 depressed patients who receive ECT respond well making ECT the most effective treatment for severe depression. People who have responded to ECT report it makes them feel 'like themselves again' and 'as if life was worth living again'. Severely depressed patients will become more optimistic and less suicidal. Most patients recover their ability to work and lead a productive life after their depression has been treated with a course of ECT.

> *What ECT cannot do?*
> The effects of ECT will relieve the symptoms of your depression but will not help all your problems. An episode of depression may produce problems with relationships, or problems at home or at work. These problems may still be present after your treatment and you may need further help with these. Hopefully, because the symptoms of your depression are better, you will be able to deal with these other problems more effectively.

> *What are the side effects of ECT?*
> Some patients may be confused just after they awaken from the treatment and this generally clears up within an hour or so. Your

memory of recent events may be upset and dates, names of friends, public events, addressees and telephone numbers may be temporarily forgotten. In most cases this memory loss goes away within a few days or weeks, although sometimes patients continue to experience memory problems for several months. ECT does not have any long-term effects on your memory or your intelligence.

There are literally hundreds of scientific papers written on the dangers and inappropriateness of ECT, not to mention the thousands of personal testimonies published as to its barbaric effects. The enormous conceit shown by the Royal College in the face of such feedback, while patients continue suffering, should not be tolerated any longer. Even the information above which it issues to patients is full of contradictions, fudging the issue of damage to mental function, seeking still to justify it. While it accepts that brain damage occurs, why does it continue to trumpet its value? Is it saying that brain damage is a reasonable price to pay? This position is a farce and is reminiscent of the movie *The Eternal Sunshine of the Spotless Mind* which tells the story of a company called Lacuna (meaning gap, space or cavity) whose services are available to individuals wishing to erase unpleasant memories through a brain-washing procedure.

The Royal College minimises ECT, making it look like a routine dental procedure:

What will actually happen when I have ECT?
For the treatment, you should wear loose clothes, or nightclothes. You will be asked to remove any jewellery, hairslides or false teeth if you have them.

The treatment takes place in a separate room and only takes a few minutes. Other patients will not be able to see you having it. The anaesthetist will ask you to hold out your hand so you can be given an anaesthetic injection. It will make you go to sleep and cause your muscles to relax completely.

You will be given some oxygen to breath as you go off to sleep. Once you are fast asleep, a small electric current is passed across your head and this causes a mild fit in the brain. There is little movement of your body because of the relaxant injection that the anaesthetist gives. When you wake up, you will be back in the waiting area. Once you are wide awake, you will be offered a cup of tea.

Note 'small current' and 'mild fit'.

THE PROCRUSTEAN BED

In Greek mythology Procrustes, otherwise known as 'The Stretcher', would capture innocent travellers and compel them to stay the night. To satisfy his sadistic humour he would insist they sleep on his iron bed, and would stretch the ones who were too short until they died, or if they were too tall, would cut off their limbs to make them short enough. Either way, the bed remained the same size in spite of those sacrificed. His name has survived him as a byword for cruelty and obstinacy.

The Royal College is taking a Procrustean position regarding ECT, tailoring statistics and the term 'wisdom' to fit the outcome they desire. Like Procrustes, the cries of whose victims fell on deaf ears, the college declines to hear information which begs to differ. In doing so the college is guilty of creating a false consciousness: a hideous lie, using 'wisdom' and bad science to create their version of the 'truth'. In effect they have led us to believe that a mathematical formula exists: wisdom + science = truth.

The eminent American psychiatrist Thomas Szasz wrote:

> electricity as a form of treatment is based on force and fraud and justified by 'medical necessity'. The cost of this fictionalization runs high. It requires the sacrifice of the patient as a person, of the psychiatrist as a clinical thinker and moral agent.

In their paper 'Time to Abandon Electroconvulsion as a Treatment in Modern Psychiatry' the authors Youssef and Youssef (1999) state:

Is ECT necessary as a treatment modality in psychiatry? The answer is absolutely not. In the United States, 92 per cent of psychiatrists do not use it, despite the existence of an established journal entirely devoted to the subject to give it scientific respectability. ECT is and always will be a controversial treatment and an example of shameful science. Even though some 60 years have been spent defending the treatment, ECT remains a revered symbol of authority in psychiatry. By promoting ECT, the new psychiatry reveals its ties to the old psychiatry and sanctions this assault on the patient's brain. Modern psychiatry has no need of an instrument that allows the operator to zap a patient by pressing a button. Before inducing a fit in a fellow human being, the psychiatrist as clinician and moral thinker needs to recall the writings of a fellow psychiatrist, Frantz Fanon: Have I not, because of what I have done or failed to do, contributed to an impoverishment of human reality?

Let us not forget the Health Research Board statistics: 'the 2003 data show that 859 patients received ECT in Ireland'. We the authors take the position that this is 859 individuals too many, and that ECT should be banned on the grounds that it is no longer medically sustainable and is dehumanising for all concerned. We invite the psychiatric profession to consider the words of Alfred Adler:

The truth is often a terrible weapon of aggression. It is possible to lie, and even to murder for the truth.

APPENDIX 1

Personal Boundary – Management Diary

At the end of each day, set aside some time to become aware of your feeling state and to record the answer to the following questions in your diary.

Question 1 *How do I feel right now?*

For example, do you feel anxious, angry, frustrated, irritable, overwhelmed, taken for granted, disillusioned, depressed? Or contented, peaceful, happy, energetic?

Question 2 *What thought, event, or interaction caused me to feel like this?*

For example, intrusive thoughts of the past could lead to you feeling sad, regretful or guilty. Persistent worrying thoughts about the future, such as health, work or relationship concerns, could mean you are too anxious to enjoy the present.

An event such as being late for an important meeting, an unexpected bill or an extra deadline to be met.

Interactions with people who were intimidating or pushy, may result in you being cornered into taking on tasks you didn't want to. Others may have wasted your time, leading to frustration, or may have bullied you, leading to escalating levels of fear.

Question 3 *What strategy do I need to put in place in order to prevent a recurrence?* (tomorrow being another day)

Intrusive thoughts can be interrupted by distracting yourself through another activity, like doing a breathing meditation, by handing the thought over to your higher self (see casting the burden in chapter 12), taking exercise, or making a cup of tea, etc.

Events can stop being a cause of turbulence if you spot the theme. Instead of continually blaming the traffic for your lateness, take responsibility and get up earlier. If your finances are in disarray make an appointment to talk to your accountant, or start cutting back on spending. To avoid the panic of last minute deadlines, negotiate a more reasonable time scale with your boss, request extra help or let go of the reins and delegate more.

Interactions are the most common source of emotional distress. Basic assertiveness and communication skills can go a long way. For example, if you hope to be listened to, rule number one is not to threaten the other party's ego by using ridicule or sarcasm ('you call that help!'). Asking for what you want should be done in a precise, specific way, so people are clear. When you say 'no' it needs to always be said in a clear, respectful, understandable manner. Non-verbal body language is crucial, such as making eye contact and putting your feelings clearly in words, rather than slamming doors, sighing or rolling your eyes. Space-invaders or toxic people can be discouraged by deflecting their phone calls and no longer entertaining their negativity by minimising your exposure to them – even if they're family. Seek help with dealing with a bully.

If you feel isolated or overwhelmed you may need to allow others to support you, showing them your vulnerability and admitting you need help rather than struggling on feeling depressed and alone.

After keeping the diary for a number of weeks, you will notice that there is a clear cause and effect relationship to your feelings and that the same causes tend to recur. In other words there is a pattern or theme for which it is your responsibility, and yours alone, to manage. If you don't feel you are able to manage your own boundaries, a psychotherapist can help you gain the skills.

Drains and Resources – Energy Banking

The amount of money we have in our bank account is finite. If expenditures outweigh deposits we go into overdraft. The thoughts, feelings and behaviours which accompany being 'in the red' are radically different from those of being 'in the black'. For example, when you are thousands in deficit, a routine domestic bill may throw you into disarray, leading to you feeling guilty, worried about the future, and may fill you with self-loathing thoughts. It's obvious that if your account is healthy the bill has little impact.

People rarely relate to their energy as being finite and constantly push past the point where they should stop putting out and start conserving. Below are two buckets balanced on a see-saw, one representing the drains (withdrawals) on your energy and the other the resources (deposits).

If your drains bucket is heavier than your resources one, you will go into deficit and begin feeling tired, sapped of energy, irritable, anxious, overwhelmed, depressed, etc. This deficit situation is incompatible with feeling peaceful, contented and in control. It can be avoided by learning to plug the drains on your energy and to compensate by topping up on your resources. You have to be proactive about this, rather than waiting passively for things to improve.

Question 1 *What experiences, situations or people do you find drain you of energy?*

Make a list (i.e., excessive drinking, sleep deprivation, high maintenance or difficult relationships, bullying, deadlines, financial worries).

Question 2 *What experiences. situations or people give you energy?*
Make a list (i.e., time out, sleep, pleasurable pursuits, sporting activities, or exercise, the company of certain friends).
Question 3 *What actions have you yourself taken in the last week or month to plug these drains and stop them recurring?*
Make a list.

Question 4 *What actions have you yourself taken in the last week or month to make sure that your resources stay topped up?*
Make a list.

Having energy to spare can pay dividends at times when unexpected demands are made on you, making the difference between you coping with them or becoming depressed by them. When your energy is up and you are in good form, it is easier to incorporate a setback into your schedule and not be thrown off balance emotionally. When it is low, it's easier to reach that tipping point where the next small drain renders you feeling out of control and depressed.

APPENDIX 3

The Chakra System

It is beyond the scope of this book to cover the chakra system in any great detail. What follows is a brief outline of its basic principles.

The chakras are centres or vortices of electromagnetic energy found within the body at clearly definable anatomical positions. Because they move in a constant circular wheel-like motion, ancient Hindu healing texts have named them 'chakras' meaning spinning wheels or disks.

The seven major chakras run along the central axis of the body from the base of the spine to the crown of the head. As electromagnetic storage units of information vibrating at different frequencies, they interact with the energy field around the body. This contains our memory, thoughts, feelings, emotions and dream frequencies. The mind is not confined to the brain. It's a necessary processing organ which, if damaged makes conscious retrieval of thought forms impossible. In this way the brain can be seen as a central recording depot which logs all the emotions and thoughts in our history and then transmits them to the energy field for storage.

This bio-energy field also contains the blueprint for the entire body, shaping such things as cellular development, replication and repair. The pattern of disease is first imprinted here, before it manifests in the body as pathology. In the near future diagnostics and healing interventions will 'operate' at the level of the energy field, building on the current use of ultra-sound, lasers and radiation. It will finally blur the boundaries between psychological distress and physical disease in terms of the way in which energetic disharmony manifests itself. When this day comes the only distinction between a panic attack and a heart attack will be the energetic level at which they present.

The chakras are step-down transformers or transducers, which process electromagnetic waves of frequencies which are outside of the range of the other five senses, and convert them into a wave pattern utilisable by the physical body. (This is analogous to how mobile phones and televisions work.) This energy is then carried to each cell along the threadlike paths of subtle energy known as the nadis. Anatomically each chakra is associated with a major nerve plexus and endocrine gland and whatever organs are under their influence.

THE SEVEN MAJOR CHAKRAS

Ultimately the chakras, the energy field and the realms that lie beyond, are inseparable from and interwoven with the mind-body-spirit organism. These are all different aspects of the same life force. The degree of harmony between them dictates our physical, emotional, and mental state. Such balance can depend on the degree of openness or closure at any given moment of an individual chakra or all of them. Chakra imbalance frequently begins within a context of a setback. This can happen following a range of life difficulties such as childhood traumas, physical pain, social conditioning, deprived and oppressive environments, mental and emotional shocks, prolonged stress and anything that oppresses our unique personal consciousness and our full expression.

The *first chakra* is located at the base of the spine. The verbs that best describes it are 'I have' and 'I exist'. Its primary psychological role deals with survival and physical identity. My first chakra will tell me how much sleep I need, how much food to eat, how to find a place to live, a means of independent income, how to behave in the face of danger and provides me with the means to be grounded in all aspects of this physical reality. It can be compromised in the face of survival issues and threats to existence.

In depression our connection to the life-force is diminished, resulting in low energy and drive, sleep disturbances, loss of appetite, and a slowing down of bodily movement.

The *second chakra* is located below the navel and its verb is 'I feel'. The centre of feeling and emotional intelligence, it influences my ability to experience pleasure and to avoid pain, to respond to change, and to express my sexuality and deal with intimacy, parenting and all relationships.

In depression this chakra bears the brunt of the painful negative feelings associated with setback or difficulty, and in a state of overwhelm, closes. In this state the individual is unable to access joy, pleasure, desire and sexuality, and may feel numb and separated from the world as though a pane of glass stands between them. Feel-

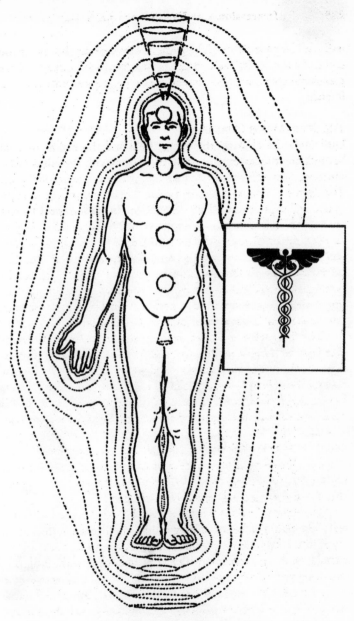

The Chakras and the Energy Field

Inset – The caduceus, the symbol of healing used by modern
medicine, is based on the chakra system

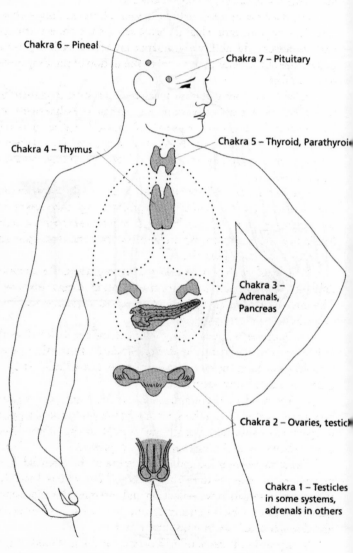

Chakra 6 – Pineal

Chakra 7 – Pituitary

Chakra 4 – Thymus

Chakra 5 – Thyroid, Parathyroid

Chakra 3 –
Adrenals,
Pancreas

Chakra 2 – Ovaries, testicles

Chakra 1 – Testicles
in some systems,
adrenals in others

*Common associations between the chakras and the glands of the
endocrine system*

ing little empathy or connection to others there is a sense of being an outsider, misunderstood and alienated.

The *third chakra* is located in the solar plexus and the verb is 'I can'. It deals with individual identity, self definition, ego strength and willpower – the ability to influence my life. Its issue is personal power, 'fire in the belly' and is vital to the notion of standing on our own two feet.

In depression our will is incapacitated, resulting in an inability to act, an absence of motivation, and a sense of helplessness and loss of control. Admonishments to 'pull yourself together' and to be more proactive go unheard. This is the centre which recommends rolling over in bed and going back to sleep, non-engagement now being its policy.

The *fourth chakra* is located in the middle of the chest, behind the breastbone and the verb is 'I love'. It is through this chakra that we feel acceptance of ourselves and others, compassion, hope, forgiveness, the ability to give and receive love, and that against all the odds anything is possible.

In depression, this chakra, once it has registered the trauma or difficulty, and is unable to accept the situation, closes defensively. The emotional tone now is one of cynicism, victim-hood, bitterness, self-loathing and despair.

The *fifth chakra* is located in the throat and the verb is 'I speak'. It helps me to speak my mind, be authentic, hear other people correctly, put form on my ideas, and think symbolically. It is the centre associated with creativity.

In depression, our communications centre, from which we sense how we are perceived by others, recoils. Fearing judgement, we cease to speak our truth, and feel the full weight of the stigma which exists relative to disclosing that you are depressed.

The *sixth chakra* is located in the centre of the forehead and is metaphorically referred to as 'the third eye'. The verb is 'I see'. It is the centre from which we reflect on and interpret the experiences which affect us, which helps us to develop insight and intuition, and through which we visualise and imagine.

In depression it becomes imbalanced, making it hard to continue seeing clearly, and to map out the future. It becomes skewed in favour of policies such as 'what's the point, nothing you do will make any difference'. Viewpoints err on the dark side of black and

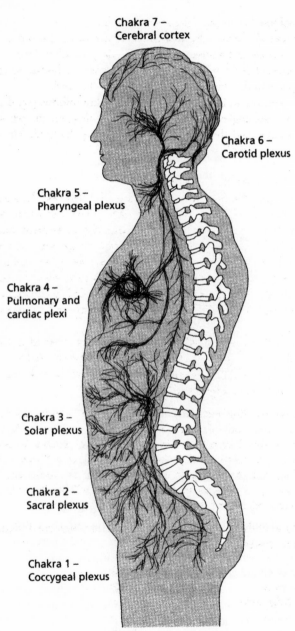

Chakra 7 –
Cerebral cortex

Chakra 6 –
Carotid plexus

Chakra 5 –
Pharyngeal plexus

Chakra 4 –
Pulmonary and
cardiac plexi

Chakra 3 –
Solar plexus

Chakra 2 –
Sacral plexus

Chakra 1 –
Coccygeal plexus

Chakras and nerve ganglia

white thinking, becoming rigid and inflexible.

The *seventh chakra* is located in the crown of the head and is where our beliefs and wisdom are housed, our spiritual understanding, our sense of divinity within, our connection to a higher power and our place in the grand design. The verb is 'I know'.

In depression an imbalanced seventh chakra informs you that your life is meaningless, there's no point in going on, the whole thing is a farce, and that you've been abandoned by God, left to drift alone in an indifferent universe.

REVERSING THE EFFECTS OF DEPRESSION

Revitalising the chakra system can be done through very ordinary everyday means, many of which we have already touched on throughout the book. Notwithstanding that the motivation may not be strong, the very act of taking exercise, engaging in pleasurable pursuits, sharing your feelings with those you trust, seeking psychotherapy, etc., all combine to have an opening effect on the chakra system. In the chapter on suicide we included an emergency drill involving exercise, breath-work, visualisations and the use of sound.

In depression in general the primary chakra affected is the heart, and it is our experience that if the heart can be healed to the point of opening again, this entrains the others to follow. The following is an exercise which will encourage this.

> Visualise inhaling and exhaling a gold spiral of light in and out through the front of your chest with each breath. Gradually lengthen your breath to a count of eight as you breathe in and eight as you breathe out again. When you have achieved this rhythm, add the following affirmation with the in-breath. 'I acknowledge the infinite nature of the heart. I will live beyond my expectations'. Repeat this until you feel ready to stop.

The qualities of the open heart are the qualities which are difficult to access in depression. These are:

Acceptance	Healing
Forgiveness	Peace
Non-judgement	Love
Compassion	Hope
Balance	Spirit

Further Reading

Barlow, David H., *Anxiety and its Disorders*, New York: Guildford Press, 1988. (*A scientific look at panic and anxiety.*)

Bourne, Edmund J., *The Anxiety and Phobia Workbook*, California: New Harbinger Publications Inc, 1990. (*An excellent practical DIY for stress and anxiety.*)

Bailey, Dr Philip, *Homeopathic Psychology*, California: North Atlantic Books, 1995. (*Portraits of the common constitutional remedies.*)

Brennan, Barbara Ann, *Hands of Light*, New York: Bantam Books, 1987. (*The most comprehensive study of hands-on healing.*)

Chopra, Deepak, *The Seven Spiritual Laws of Success*, New York: Bantam Press, 1996. (*A masterpiece of spiritual writing. Seven simple steps to mind-body-spirit living.*)

Cope, Stephen, *Yoga and the Quest for True Self*, New York: Bantam Books, 1999. (*How unifying mind, body and spirit through yoga can relieve depression.*)

Corry, Dr Michael & Tubridy, Dr Áine, *Going Mad?*, Dublin: Newleaf, 2001. (*A book for those seeking to understand what madness is – or is not, and which looks at alternative ways of treating it.*)

Gerber, Dr Richard, *Vibrational Medicine*, New Mexico: Bear and Co, 1998. (*A cutting edge tome on the emerging role of energy in medicine.*)

Grof, Christina & Gro, Dr Stanislaus, *The Stormy Search for the Self*, Thorsons, 1990. (*A view of mental distress as a spiritual emergency.*)

Holford, Patrick, *Optimum Nutrition for the Mind*, Piatkus, 2003. (*Nutrition guru's guide to getting the building blocks right for a healthy mind.*)

Judith, Anodea, *Eastern Body Western Mind*, California: Celestial Arts, 1996. (*The bible on the chakras and energy fields and how they are expressed.*)

Kabat-Zinn, Jon, *Full Catastrophy Living*, Delacorte Press, 1990. (*An accessible read on bringing meditation into everyday life which comes with a set of CDs.*)

Lynch, Dr Terry, *Beyond Prozac*, Dublin: Marino Books, 2001. (*The case for psychotherapy instead of pharmaco-therapy.*)

Matsakis, Aphrodite, *Post Traumatic Stress Disorder*, California: New Harbinger Publications, 1994. (*An academic look at post-traumatic stress.*)

Miller, Alice, *The Drama of Being a Child*, Virago 1983. (*This little gem looks at the childhood as a conditioning process.)*

Myss, Caroline, *Anatomy of the Spirit*, New York: Bantam Books, 1997. *(Examines the spiritual symbolism of the chakra system.)*

Nelson, Dr E. & Nelson, Andrea, Psy.D, *Sacred Sorrows*, G. P. Putnam's Sons, 1995. *(Collection of essays on striving to find spiritual growth in depression.)*

Nelson, Dr E., *Healing the Split*, New York: State University of New York Press, 1994. *(Transpersonal psychiatrist integrates spirit and mental conditions.)*

Pert, Candace, *The Molecules of Emotion*, London: Simon and Schuster, 1997. *(A scientific explanation of how our feelings are chemically created.)*

Pfeiffer, Dr Carl, & Holford, Patrick, *Mental Health & Illness*, London: ION Press, 1987. *(Nutritional avenues to managing mental symptoms.)*

Podvoll, Dr Edward, *The Seduction of Madness*, New York: Harper Collins, 1990. *(Chronicles of the journey into mania.)*

Rolf, Dr Ida P., *Rolfing: Re-establishing the Natural Alignment and Structural Integration of the Human Body for Vitality and Health*, Healing Arts Press, 1989.

Rowe, Dorothy, *Depression: The Way Out of Your Prison*, 3rd edition, Brunner-Routledge, 2003. *(It takes a liberation approach and pulls no punches).*

Schwartz, Dr Jeffrey M., *Brain Lock*, Regan Books, 1996. *(Self-help book for obsessive-compulsive disorder.)*

Seligman, Martin E. P., *Helplessness*, W. H. Freeman & Co., 1975. *(Documents the psychological basis to how helplessness can be learned.)*

Servan-Schreiber, Dr David, *Healing Without Freud or Prozac*, Rodale, 2004. *(Natural drug-free approaches to managing anxiety and depression.)*

Tubridy, Dr Áine, *When Panic Attacks*, Dublin: Newleaf, 2003. *(Comprehensive book on every aspect of panic, Includes a CD of relevant exercises.)*

Weintraub, Amy, *Yoga for Depression: A Compassionate Guide to Relieve Suffering Through Yoga*, New York: Broadway Books, 2004. *(Help for depression through yoga.)*

Youssef, H. A. & Youssef, F. A., 'Time to Abandon Electroconvulsion as a Treatment in Modern Psychiatry' in *Advances in Therapy*, Volume 16, No. 1, January/February 1999.

The authors may be contacted at:

The Institute of Psychosocial Medicine,
2 Eden Park,
Dun Laoghaire,
Co. Dublin,
Ireland.
Email: ipmed@eircom.net

Visit their website: www.depressiondialogues.ie